Ports in the Medieval European Atlantic

Ports in the Medieval European Atlantic

Shipping, Transport and Labour

Edited by
Ana María Rivera Medina

THE BOYDELL PRESS

First published 2021
The Boydell Press, Woodbridge

ISBN 978 1 78327 615 8

The Boydell Press is an imprint of Boydell & Brewer Ltd
PO Box 9, Woodbridge, Suffolk IP12 3DF, UK
and of Boydell & Brewer Inc.
668 Mt Hope Avenue, Rochester, NY 14620–2731, USA
website: www.boydellandbrewer.com

A CIP catalogue record for this book is available
from the British Library

This publication is printed on acid-free paper

Contents

Illustrations

The editor, contributors and publishers are grateful to all the institutions and persons listed for permission to reproduce the materials in which they hold copyright. Every effort has been made to trace the copyright holders; apologies are offered for any omission, and the publishers will be pleased to add any necessary acknowledgement in subsequent editions.

Contributors

María Álvarez Fernández is Associate Professor of Medieval History at the University of Oviedo (UNIOVI) (Asturias, Spain)

Eduardo Aznar Vallejo is Full Professor of Medieval History and Director of the 'Castile and Sea in the Late Middle Ages Research Group', University of La Laguna (ULL) (Canary Islands, Spain)

Amândio J. M. Barros is Professor of Medieval and Early Modern History at the Polytechnic of Porto / School of Education – CITCEM, University of Porto (Portugal)

Roberto J. González Zalacain is a lecturer in Medieval History at the University of La Laguna (ULL) (Canary Islands, Spain)

Sara Pinto holds a PhD in History and is a post-doctoral fellow at CITCEM, University of Porto (Portugal)

Ana María Rivera Medina is Senior Lecturer of Medieval History at the National University of Distance Education (UNED) (Madrid, Spain)

Enrique José Ruiz Pilares is a lecturer in Medieval History at the University of Cádiz (UCA) (Andalusia, Spain)

Jesús A. Solórzano Telechea is Full Professor in Medieval History and Director of the 'GOBPORT Research Group', University of Cantabria (UNICAN) (Santander, Spain)

Mathias Tranchant is Full Professor of Medieval and Maritime History, University of Bretagne Sud (UBS) (Lorient, France)

Preface

The last decade has witnessed the growth in number, quality and scope of Maritime History studies centred on historical dynamics of port spaces from Antiquity to current times. This has occurred to such a degree that case studies and general studies on the economic, social, political and cultural aspects of port spaces have granted the discipline a separate identity. There are several excellent overviews of the subject, such as the publications of the GIS d'Histoire Maritime which provide an account of the current historiography on medieval maritime studies; or the work coordinated by Amélia Polónia and myself, centred on *longue durée* case studies; or the recent publications of Michel Balard and Christian Buchet, or that of Wim Blockmans, Mikhail Krom and Justina Wubs-Mrozewicz, who explore port realities and 'their circumstances', in the words of José Ortega y Gasset. This is what a port and its connections with the city and mercantile dynamics represent. Within this context, Atlantic History emerged as a subdiscipline which, albeit centred mainly on the modern age, delves into the exploration of the port realities of medieval times.

Thus, Maritime History, Atlantic History, and Port History gravitate towards the analysis of large port spaces associated with the *new worlds*. This leaves a narrow margin for the treatment of minor and/or peripheral ports. However, a growing interest in the smaller enclaves is surfacing. Those enclaves Michael N. Pearson defines as central to or protagonists of any analysis of the maritime landscape, being the point of contact between the land and the sea; Alain Cabantous, Maryanne Kowaleski, Gérard Le Bouëdec or Frédérique Laget identify them as originators of civilisation on the waterfront; André Vigarie, Amélia Aguiar Andrade, Michel Bochaca, or Jesús Solórzano Telechea define them as a *koiné* between the salty sea and the port town, the interface between the foreland and the hinterland. Here the territorialisation of port activities evolved hand in hand with local communities to create a form of coastline civilisation as well as a maritime boundary. The *koiné* is also identified and described in work by Emmanuel Le Roy Ladurie, Josef Konvitz, Jan de Vries, Peter Rieterbergen and Michael N. Pearson as breathing life into Coastal History, which deals with the maritime dimension and the littoral society. Land and sea interlace in complex and diverse ways, forming integral parts of a whole, and the blending of maritime and terrestrial elements fashions the study of coastal societies to become a paradigm for maritime history in general.

In this sense, the littoral constitutes a separate and enclosed boundary which nonetheless expresses its purpose through its porosity. An effective frontier, fostering free exchange in the hands of the communities themselves, with the scant political intervention diluting the concept of governance *stricto sensu*. Thus, there we see the interplay of opposition and complementarity between the interior and the littoral.

This places littoral or coastal societies between the sea, the beach and some indeterminate boundary on land, with their interactions articulated through small boats as posited by Eduardo Aznar Vallejo; a space where coastal peasants supplemented farming activities with maritime activities that were characterised by expressions of mutualist sociability and pluriactivity, as described by Mathias Tranchant. Given the dynamics of commercial expansion of the time, these communities played a leading role in the construction of maritime or fluvio-maritime port spaces and services by becoming, according to Patrick O'Flanagan and Amélia Polónia, nodes in the local, regional, national and international development of economies and societies.

In sum, these littoral communities grew and developed in tune with the available opportunities. Some were to become mercantile centres, controlling the Atlantic port system; others, smaller in size or capacity and providing for local and regional economies, were confined to a secondary role as ports of call or intermediaries. Hence, the small port became a subsidiary unit of activity dependent on major ports, and the underpinning of early coastal civilisations.

Small ports attracted diverse occupational groups associated with industries or services. This has been studied by historians although, as explained by Maryanne Kowaleski:

> maritime historians have spent more time studying those who labored at sea than those who worked on shore, even though port laborers played an essential role in the smooth functioning of maritime trade and enterprise and probably outnumbered those who went to sea. Medievalists have had especially little to say about port laborers, in contrast to the fuller scholarship on late modern quayside workers such as stevedores and porters, among others.[1]

The main difficulty arises due to the paucity of sources in general, particularly when analysing small or peripheral ports of the European Atlantic.

1 Maryanne Kowaleski, 'Port Labor in Medieval England', in *The Sea in History – The Medieval World*, ed. Christian Buchet and Michel Balard (Woodbridge, 2017), pp. 619–628, at p. 619.

It is true that a port is determined by its infrastructure and its ability to adapt to the traffic it sustains, leading to the creation of a services sector to cater for the needs of vessels, men and cargo which was concentrated in specific areas within the port space. Further, as occurred in the cities, guilds, merchant associations and trade confraternities served the needs which authorities were unable or unwilling to satisfy.

Among these were, first, the maintenance of the accessibility of ports in an attempt to modernise enclaves by removing hindrances to navigation and articulating health and upkeep policies; second, the creation of logistic services with smaller boats and barges for vessel inspection or the transhipment and transfer of cargo; third, the establishment of mooring systems by order of arrival and type of cargo; fourth – transitioning into the urban mesh over this indeterminate boundary between the natural and the artificial – the establishment of a series of storage cellars and warehouses. The 'sea' is more than water and beaches; it permeates all surrounding activities, whether on the waterfront, riverbanks or even the interior.

This process of 'urbanisation' and modernisation of coastal communities by 'making a virtue of necessity' created infrastructures and incorporated new cargo handling techniques; it established loading and unloading systems for merchandise, performed by the communities themselves, and the presence – although not necessarily the intervention – of officials, overseers, guarantors, factors, etc. To complete and complement this port landscape, and as an assistance and solidarity network of sorts, the process stimulated the emergence of lodgings and hospitals, taverns and inns to cater for the 'people of the sea' on land.

Following this historical and methodological framework, a group of researchers specialising in medieval Maritime History and Urban History decided to delve into the available sources with the aim of reconstructing occupational landscapes in French, Spanish and Portuguese ports, where the topography had generated, in the resemblance of a garland, a string of minor maritime and fluvio-maritime enclaves. Establishing comparisons, complementarities and differences, we centred our attention on the conditions involved in port infrastructures and the movement of cargo; the mechanisms established in the enclaves for the reception, loading and unloading of merchandise; storage; the technical elements employed; the logistics of commercial transactions; the administrative and community strategies implemented in these activities; the capacity and entity of the labour market; and the modes of occupational association.

This edited collection is the final result of the collaboration between two of the most active Spanish research groups in the study the maritime world in late medieval Castile: *Castilla y el Mar en la Baja Edad Media*, of the University of La Laguna, and the Research Group *La gobernanza de los puertos atlánticos en la Edad Media* (*GOBPORT*), from the University of Cantabria.

For over fifteen years, the former has conducted continued research projects funded by the Spanish Government centred on multiple aspects of the maritime reality of late medieval Castile. This was precisely the object of the group's latest projects (*De mar a mar. Los puertos castellanos en la Baja Edad Media* [HAR2010-17693]; *Solidaridad y/o exclusión en las fronteras marítimas. Castilla en la Baja Edad Media* [HAR2013-48433-C2-2-P]; and, more recently, *El mar como frontera. Transgresiones legales en el Atlántico bajomedieval* [PGC2018-095719-B-I00]), focusing on organisational and social aspects of life in ports, in line with the work proposed in this collection.

The research group *La gobernanza de los puertos atlánticos en la Edad Media* (*GOBPORT*) has invested its efforts over the last decade in analysing the actuality of port towns in the northern kingdom of Castile through various projects funded by the Government of Spain (*Ciudades y villas portuarias en la articulación del litoral atlántico en la Edad Media* [HAR2009-08474]; *Las sociedades urbanas de las ciudades y villas portuarias de la Europa atlántica en la baja Edad Media* [HAR2012-31801]; and, more recently, *Política, instituciones y gobernanza de las villas y ciudades portuarias de la Europa atlántica en la baja Edad Media: análisis comparativo transnacional* [HAR2017-83801-P]).

The synergies generated between the two groups resulted in their integration within international research groups such as *The Governance of Atlantic Ports: XIVth–XXIth Centuries*; the participation in the Spanish State programme for scientific and technical excellence, Dynamization Actions 'Research Excellence Networks' [HAR2016-81812-REDT]; and the organisation of a dedicated session for the study of infrastructures and cargo handling in the ports of late medieval Atlantic Castile within the framework of the *European Social Science History Conference 2018*. The success of this session stimulated the widening of the scope of research to produce the present volume.

Ana María Rivera Medina
Senior Lecturer of Medieval History, National University of Distance Education (UNED) (Madrid, Spain)

Acknowledgements

As editor and coordinator, I wish to acknowledge the support of the research projects funded by the Government of Spain, research groups and networks and institutions already mentioned. Also, my gratitude to the historians who have generously commented on our contributions, offering opinions and suggestions that have enriched our work. I would also like to thank the authors who have contributed this collection for fulfilling our requests with enthusiasm. I convey my sincere thanks to Professors Dr Eduardo Aznar Vallejo and Dr Jesús A. Solórzano Telechea for warmly welcoming my request.

I also want to especially acknowledge and thank Professor Roberto José González Zalacain for his help and dedication in revising the manuscript, and Prisca Toftegaard for her silent and dedicated work in translating and revising the final version. Finally, I must express my gratitude to Peter Sowden, editor at Boydell & Brewer, for his patience, guidance and efficiency throughout the editorial process.

Abbreviations

AD 17	La Rochelle, Archives Départementales de Charente-Maritime
AD 76	Rouen, Archives Départementales de Seine-Maritime
ADP	Porto, Arquivo Distrital do Porto
AGS	Valladolid, Archivo General de Simancas
AHMP	Porto, Arquivo Histórico
AHN	Toledo, Archivo Histórico de la Nobleza
AHPV	Archivo Histórico Provincial de Vizcaya
AMB	Bayonne, Archives Municipales
AMJF	Jerez de la Frontera, Archivo Municipal
AMSP	Oviedo, Archivo del Monasterio de San Pelayo
AN	Paris, Archives Nationales de France
ANTT	Arquivo Nacional da Torre do Tombo
BFA/AFB	Bilbao, Archivo de la Diputación Foral de Bizcaya
BnF	Paris, Bibliothèque Nationale de France
DRAE	Diccionario de la Real Academia Española
FDM	Fuentes Documentales Medievales del País Vasco
FSV	Oviedo, Fondos del Monasterio de San Vicente
RGS	Valladolid, Registro General del Sello. Archivo General de Simancas
UCBG	Biblioteca Geral Da Universidade De Coimbra

Introduction

EDUARDO AZNAR VALLEJO

University of La Laguna (ULL) (Canary Islands, Spain)

Atlantic maritime life experienced a continued process of growth during the Middle Ages.[1] The outset can be found in the increasing colonisation of the littoral from the twelfth and thirteenth centuries onward. This process led to increased human activities in coastal areas, whether through fishing, salt production or commercial endeavours. The growing population fostered a process of urbanisation, with the transformation of pre-existing settlements or the creation of new ones. However, the occupation of the coastline did not entail the abandonment of inland territories. Quite the contrary, rivers and interior routes ensured the connections between these complementary economic spaces.

Development during the late Middle Ages was amplified as a result of two closely related phenomena: a shift in activities from the Mediterranean to the Atlantic, and European expansion in the Atlantic space. Both phenomena aroused the interest of nascent political powers, the national monarchies, to recognise the ocean as a means to profit from commercial policies and expand their spheres of sovereignty. Their subjects benefitted from royal protection when imposing themselves over the nationals of Mediterranean republics, adopting some of their commercial techniques, to gain dominion of commercial routes.

1 This chapter is the result of the project 'El mar como frontera. Transgresiones legales en el Atlántico bajomedieval' [PGC2018-095719-B-I00], Government of Spain-FEDER, and the project 'The Governance of Atlantic Ports: XIVth–XXIth Centuries', within the framework of the Dynamization Actions 'Networks of Scientific Excellence' State program of scientific and technical research of excellence, state subprogramme for the generation of knowledge [HAR2016-81812-REDT]. Government of Spain.

The end of this process brought about the birth of what has been defined as the 'Atlantic Civilisation', characterised by the emergence of a new world order. Even though the driving force lay in Europe, its field of action spread beyond: first onto the African coast and later to the Indies, both Eastern and Western.

The centuries of development brought improvements in all aspects. Among these are those related to technical matters, the subject of this work. These are little-known facets, on account of the traditional focus of Atlantic scholarship on analysing commercial movements of large ports with their rich archival resources. Such analyses have primarily brought to light the role of large companies and of their main products.

Recent research in maritime history has gradually inserted these ports within their respective territories, in line with the definition of the 'paramaritime' world. This work sets off by analysing the features and configuration of urban areas. For this, port facilities are identified, making a distinction between docks, berths and loading spots. Further, for each of these sites, the devices employed in handling cargo are described, distinguishing between lifting devices and small vessels. References to ports do not always imply artificial protective elements, since these sites could be located at the mouth of ravines and rivers, or on beaches protected by reefs or islets.

Port spaces usually had facilities for cargo handling, ship repair or customs control, some of substantial dimensions, as in the case of the Ribera das Naus in Lisbon. The 'marina' was also the backdrop for other activities, such as selling fish or stocking merchandise. The latter function had a twofold purpose: to facilitate inspection by appointed customs officials, and to effect the connection with transporters serving these areas. Finally, port spaces facilitated the development of occupations related to cargo handling, for example the coopers or basket-makers, who were exempt from the general regulations governing craftsmen located within the town walls.

Few ports were located within the city; these were usually separated by city walls acting as customs facilities, especially in larger urban spaces. City walls and other specific elements (towers, fortified extensions, chains, etc.) also served for the protection of port spaces. Both spaces were connected through city gates, by roads where carting and porterage services were offered.

Maritime transport was not limited to ports, since it usually extended inland, thus creating a larger traffic segment. The connection between maritime and land transport was guaranteed by a variety of transporters. The most numerous were muleteers and boatmen, who would ply their trade either as autonomous agents or as members of associations. River transport offered better prices, while land transport had the advantage of being more accessible. Smaller boats were not limited to inland waterways, but also catered for the connection between the coastline and rivers as well as between different spots along the coastline. Carts were used to cover short distances, especially within cities or between these and their ports. The circuits created by these reception and distribution activities, on occasion stretching over hundreds of kilometres, allow us to map the economic hinterland of port towns.

Ports attracted many craftsmen. In some cases, these were dedicated trades, such as shipwrights or caulkers participating in the building or repair of vessels, either at the service of royal shipyards or in the private practice of their craft. This was also the case of occupations related to maritime activities, such as cordmakers for nets and rigging. In addition, porters were employed in the loading and unloading of merchandise, and their activity was complemented by stowers who packed barrels with cork dunnage and built greenwood cargo cribs. In other cases, these port trades involved crafts practised in both sea and land activities. Among these were the coopers, potters, nailers, canvas weavers, tar makers and many others. Others developed their craft in a commercial capacity, as suppliers purveying bread, salt, wine, fish, etc., or acting as brokers by connecting merchants, transporters and buyers.

The presence or absence of these services determined the ranking of the enclaves within port hierarchies. Some ports combined their role as business and financial hubs with international commercial activities. Others offered a smaller portfolio of services, with local fishing and cabotage predominating. The latter were not necessarily limited to a restricted territory, since both small and large fleets displayed a great mobility. In most cases these sea lanes were not bound to pre-established routes but were the result of punctual contracts, as defined in freight charters, stipulating the type of vessels, berths and freight conditions. The mobility of seamen and the buying and selling of vessels contributed to the transfer of technology and the implementation of legal instruments to align differing regulations and norms.

The attributes of ports were further determined by social aspects. In larger port cities, the 'men of the sea' represented a small proportion of the overall population and municipal governments displayed clear aristocratic traits. In smaller ports, the members of professional seamen confraternities represented the majority of the population, thus granting them greater influence over government policies, including those related to infrastructures and craft regulation. Additionally, larger port cities usually had distinct 'mariner neighbourhoods', generally located by the sea or river port, while smaller settlements displayed a more homogeneous configuration.

These matters are analysed in the following chapters by historians from five universities in three Atlantic countries. The geographic scope of this collection spans from the French Atlantic coast to the first overseas territories with the purpose of providing a panoramic view of early Atlantic civilisations. This will complement predominant historiographic trends which limit the concept to the modern and contemporary eras and have frequently overlooked medieval precedents. The medieval precedent is indispensable for the definition of the concept of frontiers, of the link between private and state initiatives, and the analysis of technical and human resources. Furthermore, historical scholarship has to date focused almost exclusively on the northern Atlantic, largely ignoring the role played by the southern Atlantic in the construction of this space and the tricontinental nature of the new Mare Nostrum.

In these chapters, the geographic element is broached from several perspectives. First, the spatial influences on port development are considered, demonstrating the difference between ports born to serve a wide territory and those designed to cater for smaller areas. Second, the different port typologies are discussed by examining natural conditions (winds, tides, building materials, etc.). Third, we analyse the proliferation of intermediary establishments for the loading and unloading of cargo. Last, the relationship between physical and political geography is investigated, since natural features (rivers, valleys, etc.) served to establish jurisdictional frameworks both locally and nationally.

Human issues are also examined. We consider the actors involved, both the owners of businesses and their workers. The activities of both groups were channelled either through political institutions, mainly in cities, or by means of associations such as confraternities, consulates or universities (merchant guilds). These groups established work regulations (setting standards on places, conditions and so on) and contributed to conflict resolution. Economic collaboration between the different communities required this cooperation to be articulated in agreements, with the potential to create bonds of solidarity. The same concurrence could be found among specialists in different sectors (fishing, transport, towing), whose activities were not always clearly defined and delimited. Of course, we must not forget the legal status of the workers, given their great variety: self-employed, members of monopolistic services, agents, occasional workers, etc.

Finally, technical aspects are analysed – the utensils and facilities deployed in each port depending on the products marketed at any given time. Vessels, infrastructures and even the workforce varied in accordance with the type of business pursued. These characteristics assist us in establishing a wide catalogue of ports and their different modalities.

I

Defining Jurisdictional Frameworks for Maritime and Coastal Activities: The Example of the Atlantic Ports of the Kingdom of France in the Second Half of the Middle Ages

MATHIAS TRANCHANT

University of Bretagne Sud (UBS) TEMOS (Temps, Mondes et Sociétés) (UMR 9016)

ABSTRACT. Like all territories, ports must be legally defined, in one way or another. In the Middle Ages, as the sites of multiple human activities, port spaces were governed and supervised by public authorities. The safety of port users and their property, the soundness of the economic activities that took place there, the tax revenue they generated, and respect for the authority of their owners were at stake. Most of the time, and in a very ordinary way, seigneurial, municipal, princely or royal officers were supposed to resolve issues of harbour policing, taxation and security. This raises the question of what fell under the jurisdictions these actors were responsible for, how they overlapped, and the extent to which they covered the port territory.

What did the concept of a port territory cover in the Middle Ages? The etymologies of the terms most commonly used at the time to describe a port territory – namely, 'port' and 'harbour' – allude to the two main purposes that these facilities were expected to fulfil: allowing for the transport of men and their goods, and harbouring fishing vessels and merchant ships. In other words, a port territory could serve as a refuge and a berth space, a hub for the circulation of people and goods, a boarding point for passengers, a shipbuilding and ship repair area, an enclosed space housing naval weaponry workshops, and a tax collecting site. This variety of purposes led to a great disparity in port layouts and amenities: from simple beaching areas to 'port-channels' and rudimentarily equipped ports, to complex harbours with multiple basins, stone docks, defence systems, jetties, lighthouses, locks, cranes, etc., and corresponding regulations.

Both materially and spatially, port territories seem to have been rather poorly circumscribed. Ports were territories quite distinct from cities, and the latter sought to protect themselves from the former, since ports constituted entry points for invasion threats. Most often, a port included both a sea basin and a fringe of land of varying width, but sometimes it was merely a body of water, a section of river, or an anchorage near shore. Apart from enclosed ports, which were the exception at the time, ports were only roughly demarcated, most likely by means of a few natural or man-made landmarks. This lack of clear demarcation is particularly apparent when trying to determine the jurisdictional and fiscal scope and nature of the rights enjoyed by the authorities who supervised them.

And yet, like any territory, in one way or another, ports had to be defined in legal terms. As the sites of multiple human activities, ports were spaces governed and supervised by public authorities, for private ports did not exist at the time. The safety of users and their property, the soundness of the economic activities that took place there, the tax revenue ports generated, and respect for the authority of their owners were at stake. Most of the time, and in a very ordinary way, seigneurial, municipal, princely, or royal officers were supposed to resolve issues of harbour policing, taxation and security. This raises the question of what fell under the jurisdictions these various actors were responsible for, how they overlapped, and the extent to which they covered the port territory. To answer this question, I will base my analysis on the 612 sites that made up the port network of Atlantic France between the eleventh and fifteenth centuries, which I have compiled in a recently published geohistorical chart.[1]

First of all, in order to define the jurisdictional framework of ports, it is necessary to highlight the particularities of the territory that they occupied. Both then and now, this territory consists of three distinct spatial components: the supralittoral zone, which corresponds to the stretch of land that the tide never reaches; the intertidal zone, that is, the area within the tidal range; and the infralittoral zone. Given the imbroglio of jurisdictions that resulted from five centuries of feudal rule, it is very difficult to determine the scope of the jurisdictions under which each of these components fell, as well as the titles of their holders. If a detailed map of holdings and rights relating to coastlines were to be drawn, it would be incredibly complex. In the late fifteenth century, it would show – with subtle variations from one region to another – a tangle of prerogatives and privileges involving lay and ecclesiastical seigneurs and princes, as well as urban communities – sometimes for the same space. Within the scope of this chapter, I cannot undertake such an extensive work of reconstruction, as it constitutes a subject of research in its own right: namely the

1 Mathias Tranchant, *Les ports maritimes de la France atlantique (XIe–XVe siècles)*, vol. 1: *Tableau géohistorique* (Rennes, 2017).

birth and evolution of *seigneurie rivagière* [shoreline seigneury] in France.[2] This expression, which is preferable to the unsuitable '*seigneurie maritime*' [maritime seigneury], refers to estates and banalities located along the seashore. I will therefore limit myself to examining the most essential aspects of the issue.

Like its inland counterparts, *seigneurie rivagière* emerged in the eleventh century from the dismantling and more or less extensive dispersion of the sovereign rights normally vested in the king. In Flanders, however, it seems that comital authorities retained a certain pre-eminence over coastal life, supervising the improvement of the coastal plain and the defence of the shoreline and stimulating and taking part in the creation and development of urban and merchant communities, to which they granted various liberties. The Picardy coast fell into the hands of the Counts of Boulogne and of Ponthieu, with the latter sharing some of their rights with the abbeys of Saint-Riquier, Saint-Josse and Saint-Valery, as well as with some urban governments such as Étaples, Montreuil and Abbeville. In Normandy, the duke-king was seemingly able to maintain a certain pre-eminence over the entire coastline, thanks in particular to his own *dominium*. Before 1204, of the twenty or so ports whose status is fairly well known (not counting those in the lower Seine Valley), a dozen were part of the ducal domain. Yet the duke-king often shared his authority with bishoprics (Rouen, Bayeux), monasteries (abbeys of Fécamp, Boscherville, Montivilliers, Grestain, Saint-Wandrille, Jumièges, Valasse, Caen, Mont-Saint-Michel, etc.), high-ranking nobles (Counts of Eu, Counts of Tancarville, Viscounts of Bessin), low-ranking local seigneurs (Lion, Bernières, Courseulles, for instance), and cities (Dieppe, Rouen, Caen, etc.).[3] In Brittany, at first, the shore likely fell under the responsibility of waterside seigneurs, who belonged to networks of alliances controlled by great feudal vassals such as the Counts of Nantes and of Cornouaille, the Viscounts of Rohan, of Léon, of Daoulas and of Penthièvre, the barony of Rays, as well as the Bishops of Cornouaille, of Quimper, of

2 I have coined the phrase *seigneurie rivagière* from the adjective *rivage*, or *rivaige*, which was used in the Middle Ages to describe that which relates to the shore: Frédéric Godefroy, *Dictionnaire de l'ancienne langue française et de tous ses dialectes du IXe au XVe siècle* (Paris, 1881–1902). I distinguish it from *seigneurie bordière*, from the adjective *bordier*, which in the context of this article will refer to the part of the shore that remains dry.

3 Gilduin Davy, '*Consuetudines maris* et *maritimas consuetudines*: les coutumes maritimes en Normandie à la lumière des chartes ducales (fin Xe–milieu XIIe siècle)', *Les annales de droit*, 1 (2007), 91–110; Lucien Musset, 'Les ports en Normandie du XIe au XIIIe siècle: esquisse d'histoire institutionnelle', in *Autour du pouvoir ducal normand, Xe–XIIe siècles*, ed. Lucien Musset, Jean-Michel Bouvrin and Jean-Marie Maillefer Cahier des Annales de Normandie, XVII (Caen, 1985), pp. 113–128, at p. 120; Nicolas Leroux, 'L'anthropisation médiévale des rives de la Seine entre Rouen et le Havre et ses conséquences économiques' (PhD diss., Université de Rouen, 2012), annex 1, p. 56; Laurence Jean-Marie, 'Le prince, la Normandie et la mer (milieu du XIIe–1204)' (thesis for Accreditation to Direct Research, Université de Caen-Normandie, 2016), pp. 451–468.

Léon, of Saint-Brieuc and of Saint-Malo. To this must be added the community of inhabitants of Nantes, as well as a group of abbeys that received income based on naval activities. However, we may observe that ducal powers increased significantly from the thirteenth century on, as the central authorities sought to take advantage of the *droit de bris* [right of shipwreck] and revenues from port taxes. Under Pierre Mauclerc (1213–1237) and later Jean I, known as Jean le Roux (1221–1286), the viscountcy of Léon was dismantled, the barons had to give up their rights over the shore, and they lost most of their fiefs along the Channel.[4] It was perhaps between the Bas-Poitou[5] and Labourd regions that powers were most parcelled out. Other than in a few large maritime cities such as La Rochelle, Libourne, Bordeaux and Bayonne, power was in the hands of a multitude of *châtelains* and local ecclesiastical establishments, which the French and English Crowns strove to bring under their respective authorities – not without encountering resistance. Only the Mauléons and later the Viscounts of Thouars succeeded in building substantial estates between Loire and Gironde.[6]

The prerogatives of *seigneurie rivagière* – which, incidentally, were quite traditional – took on certain specificities when they related to goods and activities directly associated with the sea. Therefore, to define them clearly, both their geographic scope and the nature of their legal foundations must be clarified.

The General Principles of Shared Jurisdiction over Coastal Areas

Evidently, the jurisdictional territory of *seigneurie rivagière* was not defined everywhere and at all times in the same way and with the same level of precision. Special cases abound. Therefore, it will come as no surprise to find examples that qualify, and even contradict, the general principles that I am going to outline. The various documents I have gathered, most often

4 Jean Kerhervé, *L'État breton aux 14e et 15e siècles: les ducs, l'argent et les hommes* (Paris, 1987), pp. 674–676; Alain Gallicé and Laurence Moal, 'Les brefs de Bretagne: un exemple de réglementation publique en réponse aux risques maritimes dans le duché de Bretagne (XIIe–XVe siècles)', *Annales de Bretagne et des pays de l'Ouest*, 119.2 (2012), 81–108, at pp. 84–88; Brice Rabot, *Les structures seigneuriales rurales. Bretagne méridionale (XIVe–XVIe)* (Rennes, 2017).

5 Jean-Luc Sarrazin, 'Le littoral poitevin (XIe–XIIIe siècle): conquête et aménagement', *Annales de Bretagne et des Pays de l'Ouest* 99.2 (1992), 13–31 and 117–130, at pp. 24–25; Jean-Luc Sarrazin, 'La côte du Bas-Poitou au XIIIe siècle', in *Les Vendéens et la mer, de la grande pêche au Vendée Globe, Proceedings of the Conference Held at Les Sables d'Olonne on September 20, 21, 22, 2007* (La Roche-sur-Yon, 2008), pp. 33–54, at p. 50–53.

6 Robert Favreau, 'La côte du Bas-Poitou aux XIVe et XVe siècles', in *Les Vendéens et la mer, de la grande pêche au Vendée Globe*, Proceedings of the Conference held at Les Sables d'Olonne, 20–22 September 2007 (La Roche-sur-Yon, 2008), pp. 89–113, at pp. 96–99.

relating to jurisdictional disputes, seem to suggest that the physical scope of the powers exercised by a seigneur on the coastline depended on the power of justice he held. A low justiciar – called a '*bordier*' [dry-shore seigneur] in Normandy[7] – was not entitled to exercise his prerogatives beyond dry land (the supralittoral zone), which means that the intertidal zone was not in his remit. This is clear in particular in a dispute that arose in 1408 over enforcement of the right of shipwreck [*droit de naufrage*] between the Seigneur of Rays and Madame de la Suze, who had received her Bourgneuf land from him. As high justiciar of the barony of Rays, which he had obtained by means of an exchange made directly with the Duke of Brittany, he recalled that none other than he had '*justice ne congnoissance du fait de la mer*'.[8] As for the rights attached to the Bourgneuf property, they started from '*terre saiche*'[9] because, like any low justiciar, Madame de la Suze could '*avoir que fourches patibulaires à deux paux*'.[10]

Only those who held powers of high justice – an authority generally only obtained by those with the feudal rank of *châtelain* or above – could have rights over what we today call the intertidal zone [*estran*]. This area, called '*rivage*' in the centre-west of France and '*gravage*' in Normandy, had a hybrid status.[11] It was attached to the terrestrial domain; thus, as late as the seventeenth century, Estienne Cleirac defined it as follows in his *Us et coutumes de la mer*: '*faut entendre [...] le rivage, ou à l'étendue que peut faire un homme à cheval avec le bout de sa lance, qui est le varech de la Coûtume de Normandie, car s'il est trouvé plus avant en mer le seigneur n'y a nul droit*'.[12] But this area was also attached to the maritime domain. An inquiry from 1408 confirms this. It was specified there that '*la vase où vait chascun jour la mer est reputée pour mer*'.[13]

7 Joachim Darsel, 'Seigneuries maritimes de Bretagne', *Bulletin philologique et historique, année 1966* (1968), 35–59, at p. 35.

8 'powers of justice or cognizance over events taking place at sea'.

9 'dry land'

10 'only have two-column *fourches patibulaires*'. *Cartulaire des sires de Ray, 1160–1449*, t. XXX, ed. René Blanchard, 2 vols (Poitiers, 1898–1899), no. CCCXIV, pp. 457–474.

11 For instance, the Seigneurs of Fouras (AN, P 5551, no. 520), of Esnandes (AD 17, 7 J 7), of Marans, of Tonnay-Boutonne, and of Saintes declared their shore rights [*droits des rivage*]; Georges Musset, 'Les ports francs, étude historique', *Recueil de la commission des arts et monuments historiques de la Charente-Inférieure*, XVI (1902), 179–225, 235–275, 283–315, at pp. 235, 252, 259.

12 'the *rivage* must be understood [...] as the distance covered by a spear thrown by a man on horseback, which is called "*varech*" in the Customs of Normandy, and beyond this, at sea, the seigneur has no rights'. Estienne Cleirac, *Us et coustumes de la mer, divisées en trois parties. I. De la navigation. II. Du commerce naval, & contracts maritimes. III. De la juridiction de la marine. Avec un traicté des termes de Marine, & reglemens de la navigation des fleuves & rivieres* (Bordeaux, 1671), p. 114.

13 'the silt that the sea covers every day is said to be the sea'. *Cartulaire des sires de Rays*, ed. Blanchard, no. CCCXIV, pp. 457–474.

Although of a later date and thus marred by monarchical legal concepts quite different from those prevailing under seigneurial rule, the synthesis provided by René-Josué Valin in the eighteenth century seems to describe fairly accurately a reality already dominant in the Middle Ages. Relying on various statements of cases and rulings from the sixteenth and seventeenth centuries, Valin concludes that '*sera réputé bord & rivage de la mer tout ce qu'elle couvre & découvre pendant les nouvelles & pleines lunes, & jusqu'où le grand flot de Mars se peut étendre sur les grèves*'.[14] According to Valin, this intertidal zone is easy to '*reconnoitre par le gravier qui y est déposé, & nullement l'espace où parvient quelquefois l'eau de la mer, par les coups de vents forcés, caufes & fuites tout à la fois, des ouragans & des tempêtes*'.[15] He continues: '*c'est donc sur ce rivage ainsi désigné [...] que les officiers de l'Amirauté [la plus haute juridiction], privativement à tous autres juges, sont fondés à exercer leur jurisdiction, tant civile que criminelle & de police*'.[16] In confirmation of this statement, it so happens that the high justiciars of the coast were called '*gravagers*' in Normandy.[17] And in Brittany, according to Joachim Darsel, certain old Welsh laws stated that the owner of waterfront land owned the stretch of shore corresponding to the entire width of his land.[18] If this rule was indeed applied – and there is no reason to think otherwise – it did not survive the ducal stranglehold that began in the thirteenth century.

Then there is the question of the area that extends from the water column covering the intertidal zone to the infralittoral zone – that is, into maritime space itself: how was this area attached to *seigneurie rivagière*? It is here that legal concepts are the vaguest, and even contradictory. If general principles alone were taken into account, one would have to go by to the Roman doctrine, which considered the sea to be one of the '*chofes déclarées communes & à l'usage de tous [...], fondées, à cet égard, sur les principes du droit naturel, la mer & ses abords tenant le premier rang*'.[19] As part of the ducal *dominium*, the waters of the Garonne, the Dordogne and the Gironde rivers were public,

14 'shall be considered as the edge and shore of the sea all that the sea covers and uncovers during the new and full moons, up to where the great flood of March may spread onto the shores'.

15 'recognise by the gravel deposited on it, and [does not include] the area sometimes reached by the sea owing to strong winds, hurricanes, or storms'.

16 'it is therefore on the shore thus designated [...] that the officers of the Admiralty [the highest court], to the exclusion of all other judges, are entitled to exercise their jurisdiction, whether civil, criminal, or police'. René-Josué Valin, *Nouveau commentaire sur l'ordonnance de la marine du mois d'août 1681* (La Rochelle, 1760, 1766), t. I, pp. 571–572.

17 Darsel, 'Seigneuries maritimes de Bretagne', p. 35.

18 *Ibid.*, pp. 36, 41–42.

19 'things declared to be common and for the use of all [...], which, in this respect, are based on the principles of natural law, the sea and its surroundings being pre-eminent'. Valin, *Nouveau commentaire sur l'ordonnance de la marine*, t. II, p. 571.

and the inhabitants of the Bordeaux diocese enjoyed rights of use. In 1274, the residents of Bordeaux were granted the right to fish and to navigate freely.[20] This view could also be found in the arguments invoked in certain disputes. In a trial between the city of Montreuil and that of Étaples in 1424, the former, supported by the King's Prosecutor, argued that '*est la mer commune aussi est le havre et y puet chacun peschier et marchander franchement et par les ordonnances royaux et ancienes*'.[21] In the end, the parties agreed on the fact that '*la mer et les portz sont communs et y puet chacun peschier, mais selon les lieux et les coustumes et necessités des lieux et pais on puet moderer le droit commun*'.[22] This statement reminds us that, in reality, the holders of the *ban* fought for the rights exercised over this public and shared space.

However, in this area, the rule of feudal suzerainty still held great sway. It was first and foremost the king, as the custodian of the public domain, and by delegation the great princes of the kingdom, who were responsible for ensuring security and justice over the maritime space frequented by their subjects. They long dominated this shared space – theoretically at least – with no real limit but the shore, which was difficult to define in legal terms. In 1595, in his *Traicté des droictz royaux de bris et de brefs*, the jurist Christophe de Boisgelin explained that the Duke of Brittany's jurisdiction included a large oceanic zone that stretched 30 leagues from the coast.[23] Are we to believe him? As Marcel Gouron has pointed out, 'the distinction between the territorial sea and the high seas was practically non-existent; the legal boundary of the sea was the extreme limit of navigation'.[24] The measures taken by Henry II Plantagenet[25] (1174) and Philip Augustus[26] (1187) to restrict the *droit de bris*,[27] the gradual implementation of ducal *brefs* beginning in the late twelfth century, the expansion of the

20 Michel Bochaca, 'Typologie et fonctions des ports du Bordelais (fin XVe–début XVIe siècle)', *Historia, Instituciones, Documentos*, 35 (2008), 63–83, at p. 68.

21 'like the sea, the harbour is a common space, and everyone can fish and trade there freely, according to royal and ancient ordinances'.

22 'the sea and the ports are common spaces, and everyone can fish there, but depending on the location, customs, and needs of the site and region, the common law may be modified'. AN, X1A 4793, fols 405–405v; X1A 4794, fols 131v–132, 138–138v.

23 BnF, Ms. fr. 16735, Admiraut, vol. 1, fol. 94; Darsel, 'Seigneuries maritimes de Bretagne', pp. 36, 41–42.

24 Marcel Gouron, *L'Amirauté de Guienne, depuis le premier Amiral anglais en Guienne jusqu'à la Révolution* (Paris, 1938), p. 31.

25 *Foedera, conventions, literae, and cujuscunque generis acta publica, inter reges Angliae, and alios quosvis imperatores, reges, pontifices, principles, vel communitates, ab ineunte saeculo duodecimo, viz. ab anno 1101, ad nostra usque tempora, habita aut tractata, ex autographis, infra secretiores archivorum regiorum thesaurarias, per multa saecula reconditis, fideliter exscripta*, ed. Thomas Rymer, t. 1 (The Hague, 1740), p. 36.

26 *Recueil des actes de Philippe-Auguste, roi de France*, ed. Henri-François Delaborde, t. I (Paris, 1916), p. 254, no. 209.

27 Gallicé and Moal, 'Les brefs de Bretagne', pp. 84–86.

concept of *stroom* in Flanders beginning in the fourteenth century to designate the territorial waters of the coastal sea, which extended 20 kilometres from the coast in 1454,[28] as well as the birth and development of admiralties at the instigation of the king and his great feudatories, are all tangible illustrations of these suzerains' natural pre-eminence at sea. Moreover, as royal authority spread and the great principalities became part of it in the second half of the fifteenth century, the exercise of this power was concentrated. So much so that the jurisdiction of the Admiral of France began to replace those of his counterparts. The pleading made by his barrister in a dispute that occurred in 1497 clearly demonstrated this: he based his argument on the claim that '*le roy seul a la juridicion en mer depuis l'Escluse jusques à Saint Jaques en Galice*'.[29]

The Insertion of the Admiralties in the Allocation of Jurisdictional Prerogatives

It was in part this idea that legitimised the powers granted to the Admiral of France in the fourteenth and fifteenth centuries. From the creation of the position under Louis IX to the ordinances of 1342, 1351, 1373 and 1377, which established the office and defined its remit, the Admiral of France was first entrusted with missions exclusively aimed at protection, law enforcement and military action at sea.[30] This seems to have been fairly well accepted by those who held *seigneuries rivagières*, especially since in practice, these measures applied only to the royal domain (Picardy, Normandy, Aunis and Saintonge) and therefore did not affect the principalities of Flanders, Brittany and Guyenne.[31] However, some early concerns were raised in complaints that were filed as part of a 1377 dispute over jurisdiction involving, on the one hand, Jean de Vienne, Admiral of France and, on the other hand, the Count of Eu and his wife. The spouses argued that '*à cause de leur haute, moyenne et basse justice qu'ils ont en leurditte terre de Saint-Valery et d'Oeu*',[32] they were entitled to all the wrecks

28 Jacques Paviot, *La politique navale des ducs de Bourgogne, 1384/1482* (Lille, 1995), p. 31.

29 'the king alone has jurisdiction at sea, from L'Écluse to Saint-Jacques in Galicia'. AN, X^{1A} 4838, fols 345v–347.

30 *Les édicts et ordonnances des Roys de France depuis Louys VI dit le Gros, jusques à présent*, ed. Antoine Fontanon, t. III (Paris, 1611), p. 13; *Ordonnances des rois de France de la troisième race*, vol. 2, ed. Eusèbe-Jacob de Laurière (Paris, 1729), pp. 408–409, and vol. 8, ed. Denis François Secousse (Paris, 1750), pp. 640–644.

31 Mathias Tranchant and Sébastien Hamel, 'Le déploiement de l'Amirauté de France à La Rochelle à la fin du Moyen Âge', 'Les Amirautés en France et outre-mer du Moyen Âge au début du XIXe siècle, special issue, *Revue d'Histoire Maritime*, 19 (2014), 33–49, at pp. 34–35, 39.

32 'because of the powers of high, middle, and low justice that they have on their land known as Saint-Valery and Eu'.

'*qui viennent de la mer ou ayent esté apportez ou gettez hors de la mer*',[33] and that they had cognizance over all acts '*soyent commis, ou perpetrez en mer ou ailleurs*'.[34] Quite clearly, the spouses claimed that the powers of justice that went along with their comital power also applied to the sea.

The consensus was weakened when the king, in a later document supplementing the terms of the 1373 ordinance, expanded his admiral's jurisdiction by further specifying his rights:

> [1] Quiconques est admiral de France il a le droit de son office, la congnoissance, juridiction et diffinicion de tous fais, delitz et contraulx comme pour la guerre, marchandise, pecherie ou aultres choses quelconques advenus par la mer et par les greves d'icelle soubz le grant flo de mars, et par sa justice en doit estre disposé comme lieutenant general pour le roy seul et pour le tout es lieux dessusdits et non d'aultre.
>
> [12] Item, tout ce qui est prins en et dedens la mer a flo guerpy le tiers est a qui le trouve et a peu sauver, et les pars audit admiral.
>
> [13] Item, de tout ce qui est gecté de la mer a la terre, tant espaves, veresques que vabares et hors du flo, la tierce partie seulement en appartient audit admiral pour la recognoissance droit et dignité de son office, et le sourplus est au roy et aux seigneurs a qui le roy a donné telz droiz en leurs terres pareillement de tous navires et aultres marchandises perilz et peschies en la mer.
>
> [14] Item, tout ce qui seroit allé au fons de la mer et que par engins ou a force se pourroit peschier et tirer hors, les deux pars en appartiennent audit admiral et la tierce partie a cellui ou ceulx qui l'auront peu peschier en la mer ou sauver.[35]

33 'that come from the sea or were brought and thrown ashore'.

34 'committed or perpetrated at sea or elsewhere'. AN, X^{1A} 24, fols 47v, 77–77v, 272–274; X^{1A} 25, fols 33–33v; V^{7} 75, Saint-Valéry-sur-Somme file.

35 '[1] According to the rights of his office, whoever is Admiral of France has powers of cognizance, jurisdiction, and definition of all acts, offenses, and contracts, in war, trade, fishing, or any other events occurring at sea or on shore, under the great flood of March; and, by his justice, he acts alone as the King's Lieutenant General, in all the aforesaid places and not elsewhere.

[12] Item, for all is seized at sea, where the tide returns, one third goes to whoever finds and salvages it, and the rest goes to the admiral.

[13] Item, for all that washes ashore, out of the water, whether wrecks or *varech*, only one third goes to the admiral in recognition of the right and dignity of his office, whereas the rest goes to the King and the seigneurs to whom the King has granted these rights on their lands, whether this be ships, merchandise, or goods lost at sea when fishing.

[14] Item, for all that has sunk to the bottom of the sea and that, with the help of machinery or by force of arms, has been fished and dragged out of the water, two thirds go to the admiral, and one third goes to whoever was able to fish it out or salvage it.'

From then on, in addition to military and security operations, the admiral was charged duties relating to fishing and trade on behalf of the king. He had jurisdiction over not only the surface of the sea, but also the seabed, and especially '*les greves d'icelle soubz le grant flo de mars*'[36] – that is, the intertidal zone. He also received several fees in addition to fines and, in particular, was entitled to one tenth of the seizures that usually contributed to his budget. Several of these fees concerned ships: 5 *sous* for the launching of a new vessel; 1 silver *denarius* for ships with large tillers; 12 silver *denarii* for warships or merchant vessels.[37] He also received one third of wreckages[38] and one twentieth of the goods transported in convoy under the supervision of his fleet.[39] Thenceforth, his new prerogatives, in terms of both their nature and the littoral zone to which they applied, came into direct competition with the old rights high justiciars had inherited.

Most of the lawsuits between *châtelains* and admirals in the fifteenth century relate to unclaimed goods found on shore. Feudal laws commonly granted ownership of these goods to the holder of public power. According to this principle and depending on the reasons why the goods remained unclaimed, the seigneurial or royal authorities involved could claim various rights: the *droit d'aubaine*, the right of wreckage [*droit d'épave* or *droit de galois* – also called '*droit de varech*' in Normandy] – and the right of shipwreck [*droit de naufrage* – known as '*droit de bris*' in Brittany and '*droit de lagan*' in Flanders]. The first, also called '*droit d'aubenage*', allowed local agents to seize the property of a foreigner who died in their jurisdiction. The other two rights, sometimes attached to shore rights [*droits de rivage*],[40] concerned anything that washed ashore. If the recovery of goods did not require the assistance of salvors, and if the owners of the property did not come forward, the justiciar seigneur, depending on the extent of his authority, could assert his right of wreckage and reserve for himself full ownership of the goods.[41] Otherwise, the right of shipwreck applied, and the proceeds from the salvaged property were shared among the various parties involved.[42] Outside any economic considerations,

London, British Library, Ms. Sloane, 2423, fols 10–16v; BnF, NAF 10251, fols 7v–10; *The Black Book of the Admiralty*, ed. Travers Twiss (London, 1871–1876), vol. I, pp. 443–452; Heinrich Ludwig Zeller, *Die Rechte des Admirals von Frankreich nach der Handschrift Paris, National Library, New French Acquisitions no. 10251* (Heidelberg, 1914).

36 'its shores under the great flood of March'.

37 BnF, NAF 10251, fol. 8, 8.

38 *Ibid.*, fol. 8, 13–14.

39 *Ibid.*, fol. 9, 18.

40 AN, H^4 3036^2, no. 800, pp. 2–5.

41 *Le vieux coustumier de Poictou*, ed. René Filhol (Bourges, 1956), p. 249. Éric Barré, 'Le droit d'épave une aubaine', *Chronique d'histoire maritime*, 67 (December 2009), 109–126.

42 Robert Favreau, 'Les ports de la côte poitevine au XVe siècle', *Bulletin philologique et historique, année 1962* (1965), 13–61, at pp. 28–36; Jean-Luc Sarrazin, 'L'État et la seigneurie: le contrôle du littoral poitevin à la fin du Moyen Âge', in *Pouvoirs et littoraux du XVe au*

the mere exercise of these prerogatives symbolised the pre-eminence of the *seigneurie rivagière* over the intertidal zone.

Additional royal provisions enacted after 1373 had an immediate and lasting impact on high justiciars who owned coastal estates. This can be observed in Normandy. An initial disagreement occurred in 1346, and several other disputes between lieutenants of the admiral and local authorities arose in the fifteenth century. The Admiralty clashed with the Exchequer's decisions whenever shores were involved. Some, like the Count of Eu in 1375, even claimed the one-tenth share of seizures that was normally reserved for the grand officer.[43] In their pleadings during a 1401 trial involving the Bishop of Saint-Malo, the King's Prosecutor and the Admiral of France stated '*que le gouvernement de la mer en temps de guerre et des treves lui appartiennent*'.[44] In a 1403 case between the Admiralty and the Sire des Bordes, Seigneur of Cayeux, the latter argued that he fully held the power of justice there and that, as such, he was entitled to take cognizance of '*aubeyne et espaives trouvez illec [...] comme à haut justicier*'[45] and to receive a fee of 12 *denarii* on the vessels that '*illec ancrés y doivent siege*'.[46] Regarding the rights claimed by the admiral, he added '*qu'ils ne sont pas telz qu'il dit, car plusieurs haut justiciers ont juridiction en la mer, comme en Breteigne, aussy a il au dit lieu dont il a molte d'exploiz*'.[47] In 1411, the dispute was not settled, for the King's Prosecutor and the admiral maintained the contrary. The former stated '*qu'il a toute justice en la fosse de Cayeu à cause de sa chastellenie du Crotoy, [et que] puet estre que le seigneur de Cayeu pour petit baisteaulx qu'il y brievement querir de l'eau doulce dois pour chascun XII d*'.[48] As for the admiral, he said that he had '*la cognoissance des cas avenant sur la mer comme d'espaves et naufrages*'.[49] Their opponent corrected them by saying that this seigneury was attached to Saint-Valery, thus falling under the jurisdiction of the bailiwick of Amiens – not of Ponthieu. He continued to claim '*qu'il est seigneur de Cayeu, où a chastellenie ansienne, où a toute justice et aussy en la Fosse de Cayeu qui lui appartient avec autres drois*

XXe siècle, Proceedings of the International Conference of Lorient (September 24, 25, 26, 1998) (Rennes, 2000), pp. 29–40, at p. 32–33.

43 Éric Barré, 'Notes sur l'amirauté de France en Normandie au Moyen Âge', 'Les Amirautés en France et outre-mer du Moyen Âge au début du XIXe siècle', special issue, *Revue d'Histoire Maritime*, 19 (2014), 21–31, at pp. 22–25, 30.

44 'that government of the sea in times of war and truces belong[ed] to him'. AN, X[1A] 4785, fol. 263.

45 '*aubaines* and wrecks found there [...] like any high justiciar'.

46 'anchored there owe a beaching fee'.

47 'that they are not as he claims they are, for several high justiciars have jurisdiction at sea, as in Brittany; and, he makes a great deal of profit from these places'.

48 'that he has full powers of justice over the Fosse de Cayeux because of his *châtellenie* of Crotoy, [and that] perhaps the Seigneur of Cayeux owes 12 *denarii* for each small boat that briefly comes to fetch fresh water there'.

49 'cognizance of events occurring at sea such as wreckages or shipwrecks'.

appartiens à haut justicier et ainsy en a usez'.[50] In 1405, in another dispute, this time between the admiral and the Archbishop of Rouen, the admiral stated '*qu'il a jurisdiction non limitee ou determinee à certain lieu, maiz l'a tout au tour le royaume, environnant la mer et en la mer, telle comme les autres admiraux d'Angleterre et d'ailleurs*'.[51]

The introduction of the Admiralty into the judicial systems already in existence was therefore not immediate, and it encountered many obstacles. Some coastal regions even seem to have been spared the deployments of the Admiralty for a long time. In 1402, in his *aveu et dénombrement* for the barony of Châtelaillon, Jean Larchevêque detailed, without opposition, his right of shipwreck, as did the Seigneur of Voutron in 1488.[52] However, royal power was becoming stronger along the coasts, owing to generalised oversight of the sea. And more rules in favour of the Admiralty were enacted after 1373. Thus, the admiral would soon no longer tolerate any infringement on his jurisdiction. In an ordinance dated 2 October 1480, Louis XI stated that his grand officer was '*lieutenant general par la mer et greves d'icelle*',[53] and that, as such, he had cognizance of acts '*[commis] tant criminellement que civilement, soit faicts de guerre, marchandises, pescheries ou autrement*'.[54] After learning that, in Picardy, the authorities of Saint-Valery, Le Crotoy, Étaples and Boulogne were resisting the exercise of his rights, he firmly demanded that they all respect them from then on.[55] At the same time, the Viscount of Thouars' right of wreckage was challenged at Noirmoutier.[56]

Yet these cases aimed only at preserving the strict legal perimeter of the intertidal zone, something that local actors were more or less successful in doing. In the exceptional case of the Viscounts of Thouars, a much broader conception of *seigneurie rivagière* was invoked and defended. During an inquiry carried out in 1498 in order to verify the nature and extent of the possessions of Louis de La Trémoïlle, whose right of shipwreck had been challenged by the offices of the Admiralty of Guyenne, Louis de La Trémoïlle specified the scope

50 'that he is Seigneur of Cayeux, where there is an old *châtellenie* with full powers of justice, and the Fosse de Cayeux also belongs to him with other rights attached to a high justiciar, and that he thus has enjoyed these rights'. AN, X^{1A} 4786, fols 38–38v, 39–40, 125, 127v; X^{1A} 4789, fols 75–76.

51 'that he has jurisdiction that is not limited to or determined by any particular site, but extends to the whole kingdom, at the edges of the sea and at sea, as the other admirals, from England or elsewhere, have'. AN, X^{1A} 4787, fol. 117v.

52 AN, P 553^1, no. 329; P 554^3, no. 386.

53 'lieutenant general over the sea and its shores'.

54 'both criminal and civil, whether relating to warfare, trade, fishing, or otherwise'.

55 *Recueil général des anciennes lois françaises depuis l'an 420 jusqu'à la Révolution de 1789*, ed. François-André Isambert, Athanase-Jean-Léger Jourdan and Decrusy, t. X: *1461–1483* (Paris, 1825), pp. 825–828.

56 AN, 1 AP 1973, Letters of 28 July 1481.

of the jurisdiction attached to his seigneury of the island of Ré. He stated that, as a high justiciar, it included a vast territory, '*tant à ladite terre de ladite ysle, ports et rivages d'icelle que à la mer qui fiert, joinct et passe tout autour de ladite ysle, et jusques a l'isle d'Oleron en venant, et jusques au Chief de Boys et au long de la terre de Laleu, et jusques a la terre de la Tranche, le temps de la coustume sur ce introduict et passé*'.[57] Four of the witnesses called to testify confirmed this claim.[58] Clearly, the claim here was that seigneurial jurisdiction covered true maritime space. Thus, the disputes established a perimeter so large that the surface area of the waters it included was about ten times greater than the island itself. We should also note that only the eastern maritime boundaries of this fief were specified – that is, only the area adjoining the mainland; its western limits, bordering on the ocean, were apparently impossible to define.

This inquiry followed an earlier one brought before the Parliament of Paris in 1497 that had to do, more broadly, with the Viscount of Thouars' admiralty rights [*droits d'amirautés*], which the Admiral of France challenged. On this occasion, regarding military powers, the Viscount's barrister argued that it is '*le seigneur de Isles qui les ont et dont ilz joissent et non seulement de ce mais des naufrages qui sont droiz qui se peuvent prescripre quant ores il ne seroit fondé de les avoir par coustume ou privileige*'.[59] In response, the admiral's barrister refuted in particular '*le droit commun de prandre en sa terre les naufrages et autres choses etc., [parce que] le roy seul a la juridicion en mer depuis l'Escluse jusques à Saint Jaques en Galice*'.[60]

What about the other princely admiralties? In Flanders, the first mention of an admiral dates back to 1378. But that office seems to have included only some of the missions entrusted to the Admiral of France by the ordinance of 1373, without any particular authority over the shores.[61] In Brittany, the powers of the admiral, whose office was created under Duke Jean IV (1364–1399), were essentially military duties.[62] He had the right to examine *brefs* to find out about

57 'the land of said island, its ports and shores, as well as the wild sea that joins and surrounds said island, as far as the Island of Oléron, and until Chef-de-Baie and along the land of Laleu, and as far as the land of Tranche, since the past and as established by custom'.

58 AN, 1 AP 2001, no. 95, 22 March 1498.

59 'the seigneur of the islands that have them and enjoy them – and not only that, but also shipwrecks, which are rights that can only be prescribed when they are not based on custom or privilege'.

60 'the common right to take the shipwrecks and other things, etc., that are on his land, [because] the king alone has jurisdiction over the sea from L'Écluse to Saint-Jacques in Galicia'. AN, X^{1A} 4838, fols 345v–347.

61 Paviot, *La politique navale des ducs de Bourgogne*, pp. 19–27.

62 Michael Jones, 'L'amirauté et la défense des côtes de Bretagne à la fin du Moyen Âge', in *Défense des côtes et cartographie historique*, ed. Jean-Pierre Bois (Paris, 2002), pp. 17–32, at p. 20.

the routes taken by those who paid them.[63] But the handling of these documents and judicial treatment of the *droit de bris* was left to the ordinary officers of the duke. The latter reserved for himself full jurisdiction over both the sea and the intertidal zone.[64] The Admiralty of Guyenne was formally created in 1469, but, since the late twelfth century, admiralty offices had been established in Bayonne and Bordeaux for overseeing naval operations. Over time, the services that the English sovereigns expected of their admirals expanded, while still remaining limited to ensuring security and fighting against enemies.[65] Ultimately, the development of these provincial admiralties had little impact on the jurisdictional contours of *seigneurie rivagière*, since their duties were essentially naval and defensive in nature.

The Spatial Characteristics of *seigneurie rivagière*

After having examined the history of *seigneurie rivagière*, what can we say about its spatial characteristics? In its traditional form, as it appeared beginning in the eleventh century, it was based on the powers of high justice a *châtelain* obtained, and included the lands comprising the supralittoral zone as well as the intertidal area (figure 1.1). Here, in this very unique zone, in spite of invasive tides, a strong connection persisted between property rights – terrestrial rights, so to speak – and the exercise of the power of the *ban*. Further out, it seems that marine waters – in particular, those close to the coasts and regularly frequented by seafarers – constituted an imprecisely defined field that gave rise to shared rights, until the Duke of Brittany and then the Admiral of France began to interfere, inserting their own prerogatives.

This is what emerges from the difficult process of documenting eleventh- and twelfth-century Normand and Breton seigneuries.[66] The holders of these positions enjoyed most of the jurisdictional attributes of ducal power.[67] On the shores of the Bas-Poitou region, each seigneury included territorial waters, which were more like zones where rights applied rather than perfectly circumscribed spaces.[68] In Aunis, Saintonge and Guyenne, documents dealing with lay and ecclesiastical property seem to present a similar mode of operation. Thus, the seigneurs of Maremne, of Audenge, of Buch, of Lège, of Soulac, of Blaye, of Cônac, of Mortagne, of Talmont, of Royan, of

63 Gallicé and Moal, 'Les brefs de Bretagne', p. 93.

64 *L'Amirauté en Bretagne, des origines à la fin du XVIIIe siècle. Présentation de la thèse de Joachim Darsel*, ed. Gérard Le Bouëdec (Rennes, 2012), pp. 89–91, 123.

65 Gouron, *L'Amirauté de Guienne*, pp. 92–93.

66 Jean-Marie, 'Le prince, la Normandie et la mer', pp. 429–438.

67 Musset, 'Les ports en Normandie', p. 117.

68 Sarrazin, 'L'État et la seigneurie', p. 30.

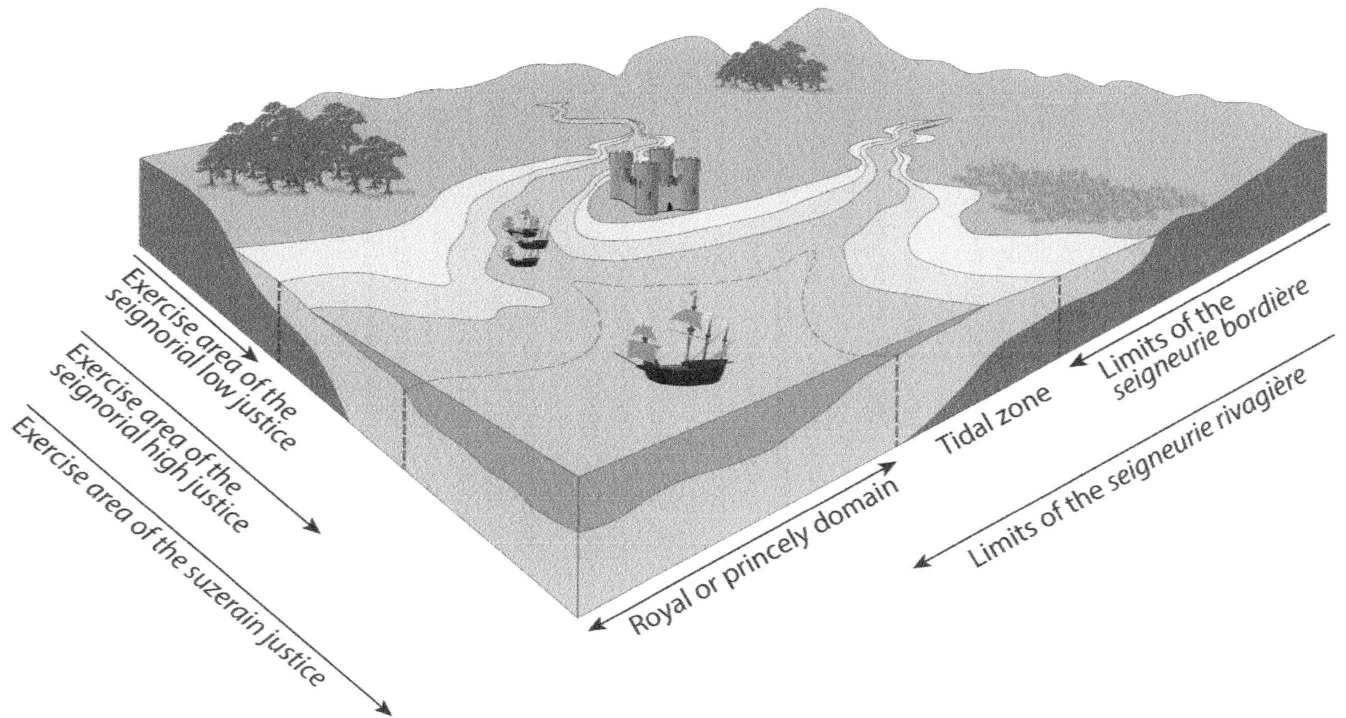

Figure 1.1. The *seigneurie rivagière* in the Middle Ages

Oléron, and so on enjoyed rights of wreckage and shipwreck, sometimes even claiming to have jurisdiction '*in mari de Vasconia*'.[69] Others arrogated the right to set up nets and fisheries, maintaining that their authority included navigable waters, *cum adjacenti aqua*, as well as the land.[70]

In other words, apart from some particular cases to which I will return, for a long time the power attached to *seigneurie rivagière* extended into seawaters, which were seen as a common space where high justiciars shared certain prerogatives. There is even reason to think that the vertical organisation of feudal-vassal relations was expressed geographically in the scopes of power exercised over maritime outskirts. The owner of a simple fief located along a shore could claim authority only over dry land that was never submerged under water. The holder of a *seigneurie rivagière* had broader rights, which included tidal zones as well as the waters that covered them. Further out was the public space, which only princely or royal high authorities could claim to rule. As I have said, we nevertheless find exceptions to these general fundamental principles. By reserving for himself the *droit de bris* [right of wreck] along the shorelines of Brittany beginning in the thirteenth century, the duke divested shore-dwelling seigneurs of the bulk of their jurisdiction over the intertidal zone, thus in a sense turning *seigneurie rivagière* into *seigneurie bordière* [dry-shore seigneury]. Other examples show, to the contrary, that the power *seigneurs rivagiers* exercised over the sea sometimes exceeded the usual framework. Thus, on the left bank of the Gironde river, the owners of the seigneury of Lasparre maintained that this part of the coast and the ocean that runs along it had been given to them by Jean sans Terre, and thus claimed ownership over any seizures made there. In so doing, they emphasised the original legal status of the shore, which initially did not give so many liberties to its owner.[71] The understanding of maritime domain connected to islands that the Viscount of Thouars defended in 1497–1498 must also be examined. Does it correspond to a more general reality in France during the Middle Ages? If so, owners of these island territories – located 'in the maritime outskirts' – enjoyed greater freedom of action over the sea than their mainland counterparts.[72] This echoes the position of English kings who used their properties in Jersey, Guernsey and Oléron to justify their claim to sovereignty over the English Channel.[73]

69 'In the sea of Gascony'. Sébastien Périsse, 'Les campagnes littorales saintongeaises à la fin du Moyen Âge (XIe–milieu XVIe siècle)' (PhD diss., Université de La Rochelle, 2011), pp. 91–97; Gouron, *L'Amirauté de Guienne*, p. 62.

70 Jacques Bernard, *Navires et gens de mer à Bordeaux (vers 1400–vers 1550)* (Paris, 1968), p. 188.

71 Gouron, *L'Amirauté de Guienne*, p. 62.

72 The work of Dominique Guillemet (*Les îles de l'Ouest, de Bréhat à Oléron, du Moyen Âge à la Révolution* [La Crèche, 2000]) does not echo this.

73 Gouron, *L'Amirauté de Guienne*, p. 33.

The Authorities of *seigneurs rivagiers*

On the grounds of their jurisdiction over banks and intertidal zones, *rivagiers*, whether they were *châtelains*, ecclesiastics, or *bourgmestres*, exercised numerous prerogatives relating to port activities. I will provide a brief overview of these here.

At the very end of the fifteenth century, the Archbishop of Rouen, arguing against the Admiral of France, who was encroaching upon the archbishop's authorities in '*la ville et seigneurie de Dieppe*',[74] stated the following facts:[75]

> [I] Y a haulte justice, basse et moïenne, seneschal et bailli, lesquelz ou leurs lieuxtenans, ont la court, jurisdiction et congnoissance de toutes les questions, debatz et proces qui y meuvent.
>
> [II] Et n'y a juge ne aultre qui y ait jurisdiction ne congnoissance de quelque matiere, excepté mond. Sr l'Admiral, lequel ou son lieutenant congnoist seullement des questions, debatz et proces qui se meuvent entre les gens de guerre et aultres, touchans et deppendans du fait de l'escumerie et gains de guerre, advenus en la mer.
>
> [III] Et de toutes les aultres matieres, questions et debatz meuz en lad. ville, touchans fait de marchandise par la mer et de pescherie, tant de frait de navire marchant, raport de marchandise, contratz fais par les marineaux pour aller en la mer en pescherie de harens, masquereaux et aultrement, iceulx contratz nommez vulgaument Associages, et aussi des debatz pour le paiement ou partaige de leur pescherie, et de tous les descordz et proces d'entre lesd. marineaulx, advenus en la mer dedens leurs navires et dedens le hable dud. lieu de Dieppe, tant pour perdicion ou rompture de rez et navires que pour baterie entr'eulx et aultrement, mond. seigneur le cardinal et ses predecesseurs archevesques en ont eu la jurisdiction, et en ont congneu leurs officiers aud. lieu de Dieppe, sans contredit de toute ancienneté.
>
> [IV] Item. Et aussi ont eu le raport, congnoissance, garde et entremise des biens et derrées trouvées vagans et flottans en la mer, qui ont esté apportées aud. lieu de Dieppe, tout ainsi comme des choses gectées à terres par la mer, nommées Varesc.
>
> [V] Et semblablement, ont eu le paiement de l'acquict ou coustume des biens et denrées prinses en guerre ou escumerie sur la mer apportées et deschargées

74 'The city and seigneury of Dieppe'.

75 Ernest de Fréville, *Mémoire sur le commerce maritime de Rouen depuis les temps les plus reculés jusqu'à la fin du XVIe siècle* (Rouen, 1857), t. II, no. XCVIII, pp. 404–407; AD 76, 1 B, registre 5, fol. 87.

> au hable dud. lieu de Dieppe, ainsi comme des aultres denrées qui y sont apportées marchandaument ou aultrement.[76]

The Archbishop of Rouen's claims are significant because they give us insight not into the taxation traditionally applied to revenues from his domain, but rather into the nature of his rights as a high justiciar exercising his power over a *seigneurie rivagière*. In this capacity, he of course held the right of *varech*. He also judged all cases having to do with maritime activities other than those having to do with war and piracy. These included everything that might have to do with commerce, shipping and fishing, from contracts and damages to fights, whether events took place at sea or in the port. What the document does not mention is that in delivering his decisions, the archbishop could also base himself on the *Rôles d'Oléron* as well as on the customary law of Normandy. He could also supplement the regulations with certain specific measures found in the *coustumier de Dieppe*.[77]

It is not clear that beyond their zone of jurisdiction over the intertidal area, all *seigneurs rivagiers* had jurisdiction over cases that arose at sea. Yet their rights were still fairly broad. We observe their exercise of this judicial power everywhere: in the bailiwick of l'Eau de L'Écluse, among the Viscounts of Thouars or the Seigneur of Lesparre, in the authorities of the bailiffs and provosts of Eu and

76 '[I] The *sénéchal* and the *bailli* have powers of high, low, and middle justice there, and they or their lieutenants have powers of court, jurisdiction, and cognizance over all questions, debates, and trials that take place there.

[II] And no other judge has powers of either jurisdiction or cognizance over any matter there, except Seigneur the Admiral; he or his lieutenant have exclusive cognizance of the questions, debates, and trials that arise between men of war regarding piracy and spoils of war, and which arise at sea.

[III] And with regard to all other matters, questions, and debates arising in the aforementioned city and having to do with sea trade and fishing, as for example the freight of merchant ships, profits from commerce, the contracts drawn up by sailors to go to sea to fish for herring, mackerel, and so on – contracts usually called "Associations" – as well as disputes over payment, or division of their catch, and all disagreements and trials between these sailors that arise at sea, on their ships, and in the harbour of Dieppe, whether over the loss or breakage of nets or ships or over altercations between them or in other circumstances, Seigneur the Cardinal and his archbishop predecessors have had jurisdiction over all these, as have their officers in Dieppe, without contradiction and since time immemorial.

[IV] Item. And they also have had the right to report, take cognizance of, guard, and arbitrate goods and merchandise found floating at sea that have been brought back to Dieppe, as well as objects thrown up on shore by the sea, which are called "varech".

[V] And similarly, they have had the right to receive "acquittance" or custom payment on goods and merchandise taken at sea in war or by piracy and brought to and unloaded in Dieppe, as they do for other merchandise that has been brought there commercially or otherwise'.

77 Guillaume Tieullier, *Le coustumier de la vicomté de Dieppe*, ed. Emmanuel Coppinger (Dieppe, 1884).

Harfleur, as well as in the urban communities of La Rochelle and Bordeaux. It was only in Brittany that this power, which had not been delegated, remained in the hands of the duke and was exercised by his own agents.

In addition to the capacity to deliver and enforce judgements, seigneurs had the right to manage shores and, at a minimum, the waters that covered or bordered them. Indeed, if *rivagium* systematically took the form of the right to collect monetary fees – called 'anchoring' or 'beaching' fees, depending on whether ships remained in the water or were brought onto shore – it also gave its holder the opportunity to intervene in the commercial activities that took place on or traversed the intertidal zone. It was on these legal bases that seigneurial authorities intervened in fishing matters, in particular when it was a matter of spreading nets along a shoreline or building fishponds. This was also what justified the establishment of port police. Shore right [*droit de rivage*] was thus essential to a port territory, for it was the basis of the regulations necessary for that territory to operate.

The political authority of some figures may have led them to transgress, at least for some time, the limits of the privileges usually attached to *seigneurie rivagière*. Here we may look again at the claims of Louis de La Trémoïlle, who also held the titles of Seigneur of Talmont and of Olonne. He claimed the right to deploy his own admiralty on the waters along his properties, with all that this usually entailed: warships, rights to seizures, judicial prerogatives, etc. It is quite difficult to identify the beginnings of this usurpation. Defending his supposed rights of *amiraudage*, he maintained they were long established: '*dit est aussi a il privilege et est en possession dudit droit de tel temps qu'il n'est memoire du contraire*'.[78] These claims are not unlike those made by the Count of Eu, first in 1374 and then again in 1482.[79] It is possible that, as a result of the difficulties of the Hundred Years War and the weak presence of the Admiral of France in this area, the *châtelains* of Talmont had long been taking liberties in this regard. Nevertheless, beginning in the last quarter of the fifteenth century, conflicts regarding this inherited admiralty appear clearly in the source material: first under Philippe de Commynes and then under the rule of the powerful Louis II de La Trémoïlle.[80] The latter claimed to be no less than

78 'it is also said that he has had the privilege and possession of this right for so long that there is no memory of the contrary'. AN, X^{1A} 4838, fols 345v–347.

79 Jean Du Tillet, *Recueil des Roys de France, leurs couronne et maison* (Paris, 1580), p. 285.

80 Favreau, 'Les ports de la côte poitevine', pp. 36–40; Louis-Charles de La Trémoïlle, *Les La Trémoïlle pendant cinq siècles*, t. II: *1431–1525* (Nantes, 1892), p. 126; Laurent Vissière, 'La *Gabrielle*, navire des La Trémoïlle (1489–1496)', *Revue d'histoire maritime*, 2–3 (2001), 5–99, at pp. 8–12; Charles Mourain de Sourdeval, 'L'amirauté patrimoniale de Talmont', *Annuaire départemental de la Société d'émulation de la Vendée*, 2nd ser. 4 (1874), 49–69, at pp. 55–56.

'*admiral en ses terres maritimes*'.[81] The trial he faced between 1496 and 1499 to respond to the admiral's challenges did not call into question his jurisdiction or his rights of *amiraudage*, which had been granted to him by Charles VIII.[82] Only his status at the time can explain the exception that was made for him.

An even less common form of *seigneurie rivagière* emerged in the Seudre river basin. From Le Gua to Chapus, the entire intertidal zone along the length of the river's course, '*tant en long qu'en large, et que les ondes de la mer couvrent et découvrent*'[83] belonged to a particular seigneury, which was doubled by a provostry, and was named *la Rivière de Seudre*. Initially, it was divided into two parts, one held by the Count of Poitou and the other by the King of France. In 1076 and 1141, they each gave their share to the Sainte-Gemme Priory, granting the monks there certain rights over this sector on the basis of their jurisdiction, including rights of shipwreck, fishing rights and the right to charge unballasting and anchoring fees. In exchange, the monks were required to guarantee '*la conservation d'icelle [rivière] et des canaux et ruissons en dependant, pour les vaisseaux qui viennent charger du sel ou autres marchandises*'.[84] What is unique about this seigneury is that its land base was defined not by dry banks but solely by the river's two shores and the seawater that flooded and separated them. Such a configuration raises questions when it comes to understanding how rights to the Seudre's ports were shared between the monks of Saint-Gemme and the proprietors of riverside seigneuries. The imposition of anchorage fees suggests that large merchant vessels anchored in the river under the monks' jurisdiction, whereas salt traders' ships berthed in the small ports at the end of the *achenal* [canal].

The *rivagière* Jurisdictions of Large Commercial Cities

In the case of large commercial cities, it is no easier to establish port jurisdictions, which here too depended on the power relations between municipal governments and the regulatory authorities above them. Beginning in the twelfth century, the Count of Poitou and his successors, the Kings of England and France, conceded land from their estate to allow for the creation and development of the city of La Rochelle. In doing so, they were careful to maintain

81 'admiral in his maritime lands'. Du Tillet, *Recueil des Roys de France*, p. 285.

82 AN, 1 AP 193, letters from 30 July 1496; 1 AP 1983, accounts from Olonne from the year 1494.

83 'both its width and breadth, and which the waves of the sea cover and uncover'.

84 'the preservation of this river and the canals and streams that depend on it, for the vessels that arrive to load salt and other merchandise'. AN, V^7 73, admiralty of Marennes, unnumbered. Their rights were confirmed and consolidated in 1278, 1312, 1313, 1315, 1364, 1393, 1433, 1460, 1479 and 1486.

their natural prerogatives over the waters and shore where the port was established. According to an inquiry in 1268, in La Rochelle, the enclosed harbour was part of the *costumau*, a provostial jurisdiction that extended beyond its ramparts and clearly included the waters of the neighbouring site of Port-Neuf – but no more detail is given.[85] It was on the basis of this power that successive sovereigns refrained from applying the right of shipwreck that they held in this area to victims of *bris* [wrecks]. Decisions to this effect were rendered and confirmed in 1174, 1191, 1331, 1360 and 1461.[86] It was also for this reason that several of the king's sergeants supervised various operations of unballasting, sea marking and so on, that were carried out in the waters of the *costumau*. As for the port's slipways, they long remained the responsibility of the provostry.[87] In other words, legally, the commune had the right to exercise only *bordière* authorities – for example, building and repairing ramparts – not *rivagière* authorities.

This, however, did not take into account the pugnacity of the *échevinage*, which, beginning in the thirteenth century, constantly sought to expand its field of action across all domains, patiently enlarging its jurisdiction. In 1317 and then again in 1319, Philippe V recognised that, as the first instance, within the limits of its walls, the commune held all high, middle and low civil and criminal judiciary powers over the *bourgeois*, their entourages and their property. He also granted them criminal judiciary powers '*sur les forains et estrangers*'.[88] These measures were renewed on multiple occasions, through the end of the fifteenth century. In 1343, they even expanded to include the *faubourgs*.[89] At the same time, the *corps de ville* [township] succeeded in obtaining the creation of a *banlieue* [suburb] over which it had broad authority.[90] The next step was to expand into the maritime domain. This was a long-term project. The commune

85 *Comptes et enquêtes d'Alfonse comte de Poitou, 1253–1269* (Poitiers, 1879), pp. 133–158.

86 Mathias Tranchant, 'Au risque de l'étranger: un sujet majeur de gouvernance à La Rochelle à la fin du Moyen Âge', in 'Au risque de l'étranger: le protéger et s'en protéger dans les sociétés littorales de l'Europe atlantique au Moyen Âge et à l'époque moderne', special issue ed. Mathias Tranchant, *Annales de Bretagne et des pays de l'Ouest*, 117 (2010), 91–108, at pp. 95–97.

87 Mathias Tranchant, 'La sécurisation du port de La Rochelle et de son accès: actions épisodiques ou véritable politique?', 'Risque, sécurité et sécurisation maritimes depuis le Moyen Âge', special issue ed. Mathias Tranchant and Jean-Pierre Poussou, *Revue d'Histoire Maritime*, 9 (2008), 67–86, at p. 84.

88 'over outsiders and foreigners'.

89 BnF, Ms. fr. 18970, fols 26v–27, 52–52v; NAF 7285, fol. 2; Amos Barbot, *Histoire de La Rochelle* (Paris, 1886), pp. 129–131, 145, 337, 387.

90 Mathias Tranchant, 'La constitution de la banlieue rochelaise à la fin du Moyen Âge', *Histoire Urbaine*, 8 (2003), 23–40, at pp. 25–28.

obtained unballasting rights beginning in the 1460s.[91] The slipways and docks were gradually brought under the sole authority of the commune thanks to a patient effort begun in 1384 to purchase and appropriate shore lands.[92] And, beginning in 1451, sea marking rights were also granted to the city.[93] Thus, by the end of the fifteenth century, the city had jurisdiction over the bulk of the port's activities.

Like their competitors from La Rochelle, the Bordelais also constantly sought to wrest prerogatives over the river and its shores from the sovereign authorities. Originally, the commune's jurisdiction was limited to the perimeter defined by its ramparts. Logically, it was the Provost of L'Ombrière, the representative of the king-duke, who held power over the space of the river.[94] Only a few concessions – use rights – had been granted over the public lands of the port, known as *padouens*. And then, according to a document dated 20 March 1274, the municipality acknowledged that it had received from the king-duke rights to '*pêcher, naviguer et toutes choses nécesssaires et utiles*'.[95] Not content with this, in a 1294 charter the commune claimed jurisdiction over the waterways situated in the *banlieue* that at the same time it claimed existed – which implies that it had gained authority over the section of the river within the strait, to the detriment of the Anglo-Gascon authorities. In reality, the commune did not immediately exercise this authority, which was jealously guarded by the ducal administration. It was the official creation of the *banlieue* in 1342 that constituted a decisive turn in favour of the Bordelais. The following year, they received confirmation of their jurisdiction over the waters of the harbour; this privilege was renewed in 1462 and even expanded by Louis XI in 1473, when the king effectively ceded police powers over the port to them. In 1342, the *maires* and *jurats* also obtained power of high, middle and low justice over the city and *banlieue*, although some jurisdictional enclaves remained out of their reach: the Provost of L'Ombrière, for example, retained rights over foreigners. This gave them regulatory power over the *padouens*; they originally shared this power with the king-duke's

91 BnF, Ms. fr. 16906, fols 105, 122v–123; Ms. fr. 18970, fol. 57; Barbot, *Histoire de La Rochelle*, pp. 356, 388–389, 420–421, 441. *La Rochelle au fil des ans avec Nicolas Baudouin*, t. II: *XVe siècle*, ed. Mathias Tranchant (Saintes, 2008), pp. 90–91, 101, 140, 142.

92 Mathias Tranchant, *Le commerce maritime de La Rochelle à la fin du Moyen Âge* (Rennes, 2003), pp. 138–139.

93 Barbot, *Histoire de La Rochelle*, pp. 317–318, 389; *La Rochelle au fil des ans*, ed. Tranchant, pp. 90–91.

94 Michel Bochaca, *La Banlieue de Bordeaux. Formation d'une juridiction municipale suburbaine (vers 1250–vers 1550)* (Paris, 1997), p. 20.

95 'to fish, sail, and all other necessary and useful things'. *Livre des Bouillons, Archives Municipales de Bordeaux*, t. 1 (Bordeaux, 1867), no. CXVII, pp. 365–373; *Livre des coutumes, publié avec des variantes et des notes, Archives Municipales de Bordeaux*, t. 5 (Bordeaux, 1890), no. V, pp. 186–196.

representatives, but the commune obtained full authority over them in Henri IV's concession of 21 April 1401. From then on, it had control over '*tous les padouens de la ville et sa banlieue [...] à perpétuité*',[96] including the power to authorise or forbid building there. The process was completed during the second half of the fifteenth century. Once the difficulties of reconquest had been overcome, in May 1473, Louis XI granted the Bordelais power over the entirety of the fluvial space where port activities were carried out:[97]

> avons donné et octroyé, donnons et octroyons, par ces presentes, de nostre certaine science, grâce especial, plaine puissance et auctorité royal, la police, regard, court, juridicion et cognoissance sur tous lesdicts navires, soit en last, ancrage, grevage ou autrement, en quelque maniere que ce soit, qui, d'ores en avant, viendront et seront menez et conduitz au port et havre de nostredicte ville et banlieue d'icelle, de quelque pays, contrée ou nación qu'ils soient.[98]

The example of Bayonne is perhaps even more significant. Its leaders were very early on convinced that it was crucial to their commerce and safety that they expand their jurisdiction over the Nive and Adour rivers. On 27 October 1296, on the basis of nothing more than unilateral will, the *corps de ville* took the liberty of drawing up a property title according to which the *boucau de La Pointe*, near Capbreton and the original mouth of the river, became the northern border of the jurisdiction of Bayonne. In spite of the contestable nature of this decision, it does not seem to have bothered the higher authorities, who never challenged its validity. Consequently, the Bayonnais later used it as a legitimate foundation on which to base the expansion of their domain; this is how they justified their claim to rule over the stretch of dunes separating the Adour from the sea. In 1174, King Henri II had already ceded to them, for an annuity of 1 *marc* of silver, the right to beached whales.[99] They also received his

96 'the free-use lands of the city and its *banlieue* [...] in perpetuity'.

97 *Livre des Privilèges, Archives Municipales de Bordeaux* (Bordeaux, 1878), no. 5, p. 258; Bochaca, *La Banlieue de Bordeaux*, pp. 136–144; Michel Bochaca, 'El control del puerto de Burdeos y de su tráfico mercantil del siglo XIII al XV: jurisdicciones y estructuración del espacio', in *Ciudades y villas portuarias del Atlántico en la Edad Media*, ed. Beatriz Arízaga Bolumburu and Jesús Ángel Solórzano Telechea (Logroño, 2005), pp. 91–113, at pp. 95–104.

98 'we hereby have given and granted and do give and grant, in virtue of our science, special grace, full power and royal authority, powers of police, surveillance, court, jurisdiction, and cognizance over all the aforementioned ships, whether in ballast, anchored, berthed on the shore, or other, in any manner whatsoever, which henceforth shall arrive and be brought or steered to the port and harbour of our aforementioned city and its *banlieue*, from any and all countries, regions, and nations'.

99 Arthur Giry, *Les établissements de Rouen: études sur l'histoire des institutions municipales de Rouen, Falaise, Pont-Audemer, Verneuil, La Rochelle, Saintes, Oleron, Bayonne, Tours, Niort, Cognac, Saint-Jean d'Angély, Angoulême, Poitiers, etc.* (Paris, 1883–1885), t. I, p. 105.

droits de marque et de représailles [right to seize goods or their equivalent from a foreigner when reparations cannot be obtained through the justice system] as well as his rights of wreckage [*wrecum*] and shipwreck.[100] In so doing, the mayor of the city took on the qualities of an admiral.[101] Furthermore, the Bayonnais claimed jurisdiction over the *bourg* of Saint-Esprit in order to ensure their control over the right bank of the Adour, at the head of the bridge they had built in the twelfth century and regularly maintained thereafter. That jurisdiction was recognised on 11 October 1294 by Raymond de Durfort, governor and *maire* for Philippe le Bel. For a time, jurisdiction was taken back by the *Sénéchal* of Gascony; Edward III restored it to them until a new challenge – from the Sieur of Albret – obliged them to pay a fee in exchange for recognition of their right.[102] For many urban authorities, gaining the capacity to rule a river's lower valley, to which a port was connected, seems to have been a major priority. On the Zwin river, the cities of Bruges, Damme, Mude and L'Écluse each had their own rights and zones of intervention.[103] Saint-Omer had ownership, jurisdiction and maintenance responsibilities over the *Grande Rivière* that channelled the Aa river to Gravelines.[104] Ryckaert even maintains that in Flemish areas, 'the port was considered an integral part of the city'.[105] That was the situation in Labourd and in maritime Flanders; it was similar on other coastlines.

All these initiatives by urban communities to take control over the shores and waters where port activities were carried out did not mean that challenges died out – in particular challenges from the admiralty. We find evidence of this in royal letters from 1490, which affirmed the precedence of the Admiral

100 AMB, AA 13, fol. 3; Jules Balasque and Ernest Dulaurens, *Études historiques sur la ville de Bayonne* (Bayonne, 1862), t. III, p. 474; Eugène Goyheneche, *Bayonne et la région bayonnaise du XIIe au XVe siècle. Études d'histoire économique et sociale* (Leioa, 1990), pp. 234, 326; Gouron, *L'Amirauté de Guienne*, p. 54.

101 Goyheneche, *Bayonne et la région bayonnaise*, p. 96.

102 Beatriz Arízaga Bolumburu, 'Bayona y el control del curso inferior del Adour del siglo XV al principio del siglo XVI', in *Musulmanes y Cristianos frente al agua en las ciudades medievales*, ed. Isabel del Val Valdivieso and Olatz Villanueva Zubizarreta (Santander, 2008), pp. 215–229, at pp. 215–229; Goyheneche, *Bayonne et la région bayonnaise*, pp. 51–53, 83–84.

103 *Cartulaire de l'ancienne estaple de Bruges. Recueil de documents concernant le commerce intérieur et maritime, les relations internationales et l'histoire économique de cette ville*, ed. Louis Gilliodts van Severen, 6 vols (Bruges, 1904–1909), t. I, no. 201, p. 142.

104 Alain Derville, *Saint-Omer: des origines au début du XIVe siècle* (Lille, 1995), pp. 62–72; *Histoire de Saint-Omer*, ed. Alain Derville (Lille, 1981), pp. 36–37; Alain Derville, 'Le marais de Saint-Omer', in *Le paysage rural: réalités et représentations*, actes du 10e congrès de la Société des historiens médiévistes de l'enseignement supérieur public (Lille, 1979), *Revue du Nord*, 62 (1980), 73–93, at pp. 81–85; Alain Derville, 'Les origines de Gravelines et de calais', *Revue du Nord*, LXVI (October–December 1984), 1051–1096, at pp. 1053–1054.

105 Marc Ryckaert, 'La gestion des ports flamands au Moyen Âge', in *I porti come impresa economica*, ed. Simonetta Cavaciocchi (Florence, 1988), pp. 347–368, at p. 367.

of France's jurisdiction over La Rochelle, Bordeaux and Bayonne, as well as Rouen, Dieppe and Honfleur. The municipalities of La Rochelle and Bordeaux were particularly targeted, as they were suspected of having taken advantage of the admiralty's hesitation in order to attempt to claim its prerogatives as their own privileges.[106] This affirmation clearly did not have an immediate effect – and then a case arose between the viscountcy of la Mer de Fécamp and the Admiral of France. The representatives of the latter were obliged to face the facts: they had only theoretical, and very relative, authority over the ports of this coastal area. A decision by the Parliament of Rouen on 27 October 1509, rendered on appeal of the Lieutenant General of the Admiralty's earlier *Table de Marbre* decision, describes the confiscation of goods carried out on a ship in the harbour of Fécamp. The royal judges of the admiralty wished to preside over the matter, but, given the rights of the monks of the Abbey of Fécamp, the case was sent before the viscountcy, thus confirming the latter's jurisdiction in the area of maritime law. Two years later, on 12 November 1511, the Abbey received letters of commission, '*par lesquelles il apparaît notamment qu'ils ne répondent de leurs causes ailleurs qu'au Parlement, avec défense aux juges royaux de connaître des différends qui touchent les droits de pêcherie et vendage du poisson*'.[107]

Conclusion: Did Port Jurisdictions Exist in France in the Middle Ages?

In conclusion, understanding the significance of the territorial characteristics of a jurisdiction attached to *seigneurie rivagière* is essential to understanding the regulations that applied to the three spaces that comprise every port: the bank, the shore and the water, for the intertidal zone of contact between land and water is crucial here. Indeed, it is in this zone that, in one way or another, all maritime economic activities took place, whether fishing, salt harvesting, commercial traffic, or naval manoeuvres. The authorities of *seigneurs rivagiers* could give them the right to revenues as well as the right to exercise regulatory and judicial powers. In addition, it seems that oversight and policing of ports was primarily the initiative and responsibility of local actors. It is thus not surprising that, in contrast to certain universal measures relating to trade, taxation, security, or military action promulgated by sovereign authorities

106 *Ordonnances des rois de France de la troisième race*, vol. 21, ed. Jean-Marie Pardessus (Paris, 1849), pp. 370–371.

107 'by which it appears, notably, that they [the monks] are not to bring their cases anywhere else than to Parliament, and that the royal judges are forbidden from taking cognizance of disputes having to do with fishing rights and the sale of fish'. Joachim Darsel, 'L'Amirauté en Normandie. III. – Amirauté de Fécamp', *Annales de Normandie*, 20.2 (1970), 85–117, at p. 98.

themselves, no wide-reaching law applied to French ports or their operation during the Middle Ages.

In light of the rules that usually governed the division of powers in the coastal context, how should we understand the place of ports within these systems of jurisdiction? In fact, the documentation rarely mentions this question which, given what we have just described, could be rapidly settled.

In their *aveux et dénombrements*, owners of fiefs usually limited themselves to general formulations when it came to citing their rights of *rivage*, *ancrage*, *naufrage*, etc. – including rights that concerned only port activities – without providing specifications that would make it possible to correctly delimit the exercise of these rights. One of the particular features of ports is that they were legally conflated with the rest of the coastal continuum, without any real distinctive marking – in contrast to the sites of castle, monastic, or urban life, or spaces such as *sauvetés* and *banlieues*, or agricultural plots or salt marshes, all of which were scrupulously and laboriously circumscribed during this same period. The specific site where port rights could be exercised was often overshadowed by the claim to and maintenance of the right itself. This observation holds true for the vast majority of port sites, which, let us recall, were no more than rudimentary facilities chosen to harbour and berth ships and allow for loading and unloading operations, and which saw only modest levels of activity. And let us also recall what we have just seen in the cases of Bayonne and Bordeaux: their respective hard-won jurisdictions largely exceeded the areas dedicated to port activities and covered a larger space, allowing them to control the river. Thus, in principle, legally, ports were not distinct territories.

And yet several exceptions demonstrate that in certain situations, the spaces where port regulations applied could be distinguished from the rest of a *rivagier* jurisdiction. Several interior ports, whose configuration in a way excluded them from the common maritime domain, ended up, rather logically, being defined by a proper legal perimeter. The example of La Rochelle proves this. The ramparts and chain that surrounded the basin and docks separated urban waters from the public sea. They protected the port from the sea as well as from the potential dangers that threatened its surrounding areas. At the same time, they made concrete the boundaries of specific rights and duties having to do with taxation, armament, unballasting, naval traffic and berthing, the construction of buildings on banks, public health, etc. And staff from the administrations of the provostry and the *échevinage* were specifically dedicated to them.

2

Basque Stevedoring and Cargo Handling Infrastructures (14th–16th Centuries)

ANA MARÍA RIVERA MEDINA

National University of Distance Education (UNED)

ABSTRACT. This chapter will analyse the legal support granted to the task of stevedoring, the organisation of port spaces (loading and unloading areas), and the workforce (men and women), by establishing a hierarchy in these orders. These activities were firmly controlled by confraternities, guilds and consulates, both in ports of origin and in ports of destination. Accordingly, and given the importance of loading and unloading tasks, I shall also present a comparative analysis with other primary Atlantic spaces, with a particular focus on technical and logistical transferences, the evolution and strategies of 'mutualisation' processes in port labour and the settlement of conflicts generated by a trade that required precision and legal protection, practised as it was on the maritime frontier, a sphere of intersections or a living membrane leading to both positive and negative manifestations. And this, with an emphasis on the correlations between the different realities involved.

From the thirteenth century, maritime commerce crossed borders and inaugurated a network of routes, from Scandinavian port towns to Castile and Mediterranean markets; a network of seaways giving rise to the consolidation of an increasingly prosperous and fluent mercantile traffic.[1] Medieval maritime commerce was governed by consuetudinary uses and customs of mariners,

1 This chapter is part of the research project funded by the Spanish Ministry of Education entitled 'The Sea as a Border: Legal Transgressions in the Late Medieval Atlantic' [PGC2018-095719-B-I00], in collaboration with the projects 'Politics, Institutions and Governance of the Port Towns and Cities of Atlantic Europe in the Late Middle Ages: Transnational Comparative Analysis' [HAR2017-83801-P] and 'The Governance of Atlantic Ports: XIVth–XXIth Centuries', within the framework of the Dynamization Actions 'Networks of Scientific Excellence' State program of scientific and technical research of excellence, state subprogramme for the generation of knowledge [HAR2016-81812-REDT].

transporters and carriers; it later became necessary to commit these norms to writing as a means of facilitating their dissemination and enforcement, providing security to mercantile traffic, offering assurance for merchants and seamen and expediting the resolution of conflicts.

Thus, a set of legal corpora – *ius privatista* – was developed and disseminated along the Atlantic waterfront, systematising maritime transport services, with the main aim of preserving the cargo, since 'the ship is its cargo'. Areas covered include the loading, type and form of stowage, protection during the voyage and the unloading, storage and, if necessary, the transhipment of merchandise.[2]

A task as complex as that of cargo handling drove the adaptation of port compounds through the building of infrastructures to facilitate tasks and incorporate specialised technology for the handling of cargo that on occasions was weighty and voluminous. Hence, a long chain of players participated in maritime transport, men of the sea and men of the land, the latter being the final actors in the loading and unloading of merchandise.

Medieval historiography has to a large extent focused on analysing the work performed by the 'people of the sea' and disregarded the men and women who, being on land, were in charge of tasks related to transport, the 'people of the port'.[3] They played an essential role in the undertaking of maritime commerce and, probably, outnumbered the individuals who took to sea. The lack of interest in this area of study is exacerbated by the scant medieval documentation regarding these individuals, who were generally disorganised, poorly paid and lacking in social recognition.[4]

The aim of this chapter is to identify the relationship between port infrastructures, maritime transport, and the organisation of stevedoring tasks in the ports of the Atlantic periphery from the late Middle Ages to the early modern times. I will analyse the conditions that gave rise to stevedoring work, the human workforce and the drivers mobilising the group of men and women involved in the activity, establishing a hierarchy in this order. For this, I have used

2 Betsabé Caunedo del Potro and Margarita Sánchez Martín, 'Exportación de lana: Diferentes manipulaciones en su transporte marítimo', in *Actas de las I Jornadas sobre minería y tecnología en la Edad Media peninsular* (Madrid, 1995), pp. 704–716; José Evaristo Casariego, *Historia del Derecho y de las instituciones marítimas del mundo hispano* (Madrid, 1947); Santos M. Coronas González, 'La jurisdicción mercantil de los Consulados del Mar en el Antiguo Régimen', in *Actas del V Centenario del Consulado de Burgo* (Burgos, 1995), pp. 251–279; José Martínez Gijón, 'La jurisdicción marítima de Castilla durante la Baja Edad Media', in *X Coloquio Internacional de Historia Marítima. Les grandes escales* (Brussels, 1974), vol. 1, pp. 347–363.

3 In maritime communities a distinction is made between the *gens du navire* and the *gens du port*. Éric Guerber and Gérard Le Bouëdec (eds), *Gens de mer. Ports et cités aux époques ancienne, médiévale et moderne* (Rennes, 2013), p. 7.

4 Maryanne Kowaleski, 'Port Labor in Medieval England', in *The Sea in History – The Medieval World*, ed. Christian Buchet and Michel Balard (Woodbridge, 2017), pp. 619–628.

manuscript and printed sources, digital, cartographic and iconographic collections and repositories, and a bibliography too extensive to cover in this chapter.

Port Space and Infrastructure

In the late Middle Ages, Atlantic ports were poorly endowed in infrastructures, buildings and devices for loading and unloading. Whether due to their location, size, shallow waters, the presence of sandbars or banks impeding access to the ports, or due to the rudimentary nature of the technology, the possibilities of manipulation and transhipment of goods were limited. Physical reality was a determinant, allowing few of these enclaves to develop solid port installations providing the necessary tools to perform a task as complex as cargo handling.

The port landscape of the Atlantic façade was transformed through the reclamation of land and marshes, containment of sandbanks and sandbars, building of bridges, sluices, docks and breakwaters, the installation of signalling systems, the demarcation of port compounds, the organisation of docking, loading and unloading areas, and the fitting of hoists, pulleys, cranes and other devices to facilitate the handling of cargo. This process was dependent on the location of the port, the status it occupied within the international commercial network, and the movement of merchandise, that is, the actual volume of business.[5]

The building of wharves (*cay*), breakwaters, groynes, jetties, canals and mooring areas occupied and preoccupied maritime towns, forcing them to turn to diverse means of funding (indirect taxation, levies, contributions, licenses and leasing contracts, etc.) to defray the cost involved in this venture – all for the 'common good', for it was a benefit for the community as a whole.[6] These

5 Simonetta Cavaciocchi (ed.), *I porti come impresa economica. Atti della XIX settimana di studi dell'Istituto Internazionale per gli Studi Economici 'F. Datini'* (Florence, 1988); Mathias Tranchant, 'Les ports maritimes en France au Moyen Âge', in *Ports maritimes et ports fluviaux au Moyen Âge* (La Rochelle, 2004), pp. 21–31. Philippe Contamine, 'Équipements et installations portuaires en France, de la fin du Moyen Âge aux temps modernes', in *I porti come impresa economica*, ed. Simonetta Cavaciocchi (Florence, 1988), pp. 7–20; Amândio Barros, 'A construção de um centro portuário atlântico: O Porto nos séculos XV e XVII', in *La gobernanza de los puertos atlánticos, siglos XIV–XX: políticas y estructuras portuarias*, ed. Amélia Polónia and Ana María Rivera Medina (Madrid, 2016), pp. 193–218.

6 Jesús Ángel Solórzano Telechea, 'Protestas del común y cambio político en las villas portuarias de la España atlántica a finales de la Edad Media', in *La comunidad medieval como esfera pública*, ed. Hipólito Rafael Oliva Herrer *et. al.* (Seville, 2014), pp. 45–72; David Igual Luis, 'Merchant Groups and Urban Oligarchies in Late Medieval Castile: Different Models of Interrelationship?' paper presented to European Social Science History Conference (Belfast, 4–7 April 2018), online version through Researchgate, DOI: 10.13140/RG.2.2.27423.87201.

investments continued throughout the fourteenth and fifteenth centuries as timber was replaced by stone and mortar for the building of wharves, docks, levées, piers and breakwaters.[7]

This was expressed by the stonemasons of the town of Bilbao:

> Yten los edifiçios e costa que se a de azer en rremediar los cais y muelles de la carga y descarga de las mercaderías y de otras cosas de la dicha villa y de su rribera porque sin ella ni el pueblo ny estranxeros no se podrían entretener por estar todo perdido o derraizado del centro en muchas partes.[8]

Thus, the early thirteenth century, from the north to the south of the Atlantic, witnessed the erection of signalling systems and beacons or seamarks such as fire baskets, light towers, watchtowers, luminaries, landmarks and buoys to warn of perils and aid in navigation; this technological evolution culminated in the early modern age with the development of lighthouses. The existence of these elements is paramount to understanding the significance of a port within the Atlantic network, as well as identifying the most illuminated areas, which coincide with the international hub of commerce in Bruges.

Simultaneously, and also from north to south, the increase in traffic would 'make a virtue of necessity', driving the transformation of these compounds by means of the incorporation of cargo hoisting and distribution mechanisms based on the devices used in architecture: pulleys, hoists powered by mechanisms, animals, or humans (*magna rota*), etc. These devices are documented for Utrecht in 1244, Antwerp in 1263, Bruges in 1288 and Hamburg in 1291, while in England these devices are not documented before 1331. In the Atlantic periphery of Iberian ports, these devices make a belated appearance in the late fifteenth and early sixteenth centuries,[9] we have evidence of the installation of

7 Ana María Rivera Medina, 'La construcción-reconstrucción de un espacio portuario. El canal y ría de Bilbao en los siglos XIV–XV', in *La gobernanza de los puertos atlánticos*, ed. Polónia and Rivera Medina, pp. 171–191.

8 'And the building and costs that must be done to repair the wharves and docks for the loading and unloading of merchandise and other things of the aforesaid town and its shore, for without this neither the town nor the foreigners will be able to remain there since all is damaged or uprooted at the base in many parts': BFA/AFB, Municipal, Bilbao, Antigua, 263/001/012, 'Cuentas de lo gastado por la villa de Bilbao en el pedido del año 1463, la construcción de muelles y otras cosas, elaboradas para girar los repartimientos necesarios'. See also FDM (San Sebastián, 1995), no. 55, doc. 2, 'Acuerdos tomados por la villa de Bilbao en 1463'. Bilbao, 13 de mayo de 1463; FDM, no. 71, 'Cuentas y repartimiento vecinal realizado en la villa de Bilbao para pagar el pedido de 1463 además de otras deudas. Edificios de los muelles y puentes'. The sum collected was 323.580 maravedis. Bilbao, 19 de enero de 1464. BFA/AFB, Municipal, Bilbao, Antigua, 0028/001/006; 0028/001/007; 0076/001/028; 0076/001/029; 0076/001/030;0076/001/037; 0076/001/043.

9 Tomas Doop, 'People, Ships, Harbours and Towns: Exploring the Impact of Maritime Commerce on Urban Topography in 12th to 14th Century Northern Europe', in *Sea Lines*

cranes in Lisbon, Oporto, Seville, Santander and Bilbao. In general, Iberian and Atlantic coasts had minor ports, which, according to J. Bernard, were a chain of small-scale hithes that faded into oblivion by the end of the Middle Ages.[10]

In the Iberian Peninsula, the Basque ports – belonging to the Crown of Castile[11] – were tributaries of their estuaries inasmuch as these locations hosted the services sectors and were chosen for the building of bridges. Indeed, as has already been ascertained in the English, French and Spanish cases, a substantial services sector developed at the 'feet' of the bridges.[12] Thus, from Fuenterrabía to Plencia a virtually identical scenery manifested mirroring the landscape displayed by other Portuguese, Galician, Cantabrian or Asturian ports.

During the later medieval centuries, these small enclaves united the interests of merchants, confraternities and town councils,[13] to embark in a campaign to modernise port infrastructures with the construction of docks, berths, dry docks, signalling and defence systems, as well as vast service and loading and unloading areas.[14] A similar situation was found in the ports of the province

---

of Communication Conference Proceeding, ed. Brena Gibson, Minke Jonk and Joel Found (Southampton, 2014), pp. 109–127. Rivera Medina, 'La construcción-reconstrucción de un espacio portuario'; Andrea L. Matthies, 'Medieval Treadwheels: Artists' Views of Building Construction', *Technology and Culture*, 33.3 (1992), 510–547.

10 Jacques Bernard, *Navires et gens de mer à Bordeaux (vers 1400–vers 1550)* (Paris, 1968), p. 53.

11 Castilian monarchs, after the conquest of Alava and Guipúzcoa in 1200, continued with the same policies of founding towns, favouring strategic locations by the sea or on crossroads connecting Castile with the ports of the Cantabrian Sea to safeguard wool exports. For the same reasons, throughout the thirteenth century and part of the fourteenth, Biscayan lords founded their towns.

12 On the development and function of bridges: Ana María Rivera Medina, 'Los espacios portuarios vizcaínos: mutaciones y adaptaciones de los puertos vizcaínos, Siglos XIV–XVI', *CEM. Cultura, Espaço & Memória*, 4 (2014), 56–59.

13 On the funding of port construction see: Ernesto García Fernández, 'Finanzas municipales y fiscalidad real en el País Vasco en el tránsito del Medievo a la Modernidad', in *Fiscalidad de Estado y fiscalidad municipal en los reinos hispánicos medievales* (Madrid, 2006), pp. 171–196; Ana María Rivera Medina, '"E tobimos por bien echar sisa". Los impuestos al consumo como medio de financiación concejil. Bilbao, 1300–1550', in *La gobernanza de la ciudad europea en la Edad Media* (Logroño, 2011), pp. 429–449; *eadem*, '"Por tanto reparo y adereço". Las infraestructuras portuarias y la red de intereses de las villas vizcaínas medievales en la ejecución de las obras', in *Gentes de mar en la ciudad atlántica medieval*, ed. Jesús Ángel Solórzano Telechea, Michel Bochaca and Amélia Aguiar Andrade (Logroño, 2012), pp. 345–357.

14 Ana María Rivera Medina, 'Los espacios portuarios vizcaínos', tables 1–3, pp. 64–66; *eadem*, 'Espacios urbano y portuario: las dinámicas de gestión del Canal y Ría de Bilbao, siglos XIV–XVI', in *De mar a mar. Los puertos castellanos en la Edad Media*, ed. Eduardo Aznar Vallejo and Roberto J. González Zalacain (San Cristóbal de La Laguna, 2015), pp. 93–122. Mariano Ciriquiáin Gaiztarro, *Los puertos marítimos vascongados* (San Sebastián, 1951). Mathias Tranchant *et. al.*, 'Géographie portuaire de la Galice à la Bretagne

of Guipúzcoa. Still, within the Basque port system, two ports wielded the necessary economic power and infrastructures and services to enter the modern age: Bilbao and San Sebastián.

By the end of the fifteenth century, the merchant representatives of Bilbao described the conditions of the ports from Laredo to Fuenterrabía:

> no había ningún puerto sin barra, y estas de muy poco agua, y en tanto grado que ninguna nao de dozientos toneles podía entrar ni salir en ninguno de los dos puertos ni barras eceto en el puerto de Pasajes e concha de Laredo sin esperar a las aguas bibas que acodian de quince en quince dias e que entonces con mucha dificultad e pocas agoa que ay en las dhas barras e porque si tiempo contrario les tomaban por necesidad corrian de mar adelante y esperaban la misericordia de Dios. Los barcos menores, por el contrario, entraban y salían fácilmente con aguas bibas e muertas.[15]

Despite its peripheral position within the Atlantic web, the area of the Bilbao estuary prior to 1300 was dotted with settlement clusters, each with its own infrastructures for navigation, including the town of Bilbao. However, in the canal and estuary of Bilbao, the existence of both a port on the river mouth and another fronting the ocean was insufficient: the estuary offered many advantages and as many problems due to the shifting sandbar on the river mouth, a sand and gravel bar, the sinuosity of the river and the influence of tidal bores reaching up to 14 kilometres inland. The river margins, wide and well endowed, became a port and industrial landscape hosting all manner of facilities, from wharves, shipyards and warehouses to naval industries and services.

But as with any estuary, this was a vulnerable space, partly due to the orography, but, particularly, due to climate conditions that incessantly battered infrastructures that had to be built and rebuilt repeatedly.[16] This was the fate of the Bilbao and Portugalete clusters. Thus, after each disaster, the reconstruction included: rechannelling and dredging of the estuary, construction of dykes and wharves in the town, mitigation of the sandbar, and refitting of docks in

méridionale à l'aube des Temps Modernes', in *Les ports du golfe de Gascogne de Concarneau à la Corogne (XVe–XXIe siècle)* (Paris, 2013), pp. 19–32.

15 'there was no port without sandbar, and they had very shallow waters, and to the extent that no twelve tun vessel could enter or leave any of the town ports or bars, except for the port of Pasajes and Concha of Laredo without waiting for high tides that arrived every fifteen days and even then, with much difficulty and the shallow water of the harbour. Should they for lack of time venture into sea they would be at the mercy of God. Smaller vessels, on the contrary, could easily enter and leave with high and low tides'. Teófilo Guiard y Larrauri, *Historia del Consulado y Casa de Contratación de Bilbao y del Comercio de la Villa* (Bilbao, 1972), pp. 23–24.

16 Rivera Medina, 'La construcción-reconstrucción de un espacio portuario'.

Portugalete. Renovations were carried out in masonry, with stone and mortar to build sturdier cargo handling areas.[17]

In the fourteenth century, a retaining wall was built in the town port next to the bridge, to provide for docking, loading and unloading spaces; additionally, bays and embankments were reconditioned. Furthermore, a compound of facilities evolved, setting the stage for the industrial and commercial profile the town was to achieve later. A significant factor was the increase of more or less illegal loading and unloading spots cropping up from the substantial increase in commercial traffic and the limited ability of the authorities to control the facilities spread over the 14 kilometres of the estuary.

In the province of Guipúzcoa, the most prominent port was that of San Sebastián, a port described as 'rough and dangerous in many ways where they had suffered great damage',[18] and so small in size that it could be used only by smaller vessels. The real port was in the town of Pasajes, where 'each day many ships and pinnaces [...] loaded with merchandise leave [...] the docks [...] of the port [...] which was not well-built nor repaired as it should and much merchandise is lost and damaged'.[19] San Sebastián also counted another port, known as Puerto Mayor, which grew in significance thanks to its deeper waterways and better conditions for storage and for the loading and unloading of vessels.[20]

From the mid-fourteenth century, in an attempt to attract merchants of the area, renovations were carried out in the towns, *villas*, throughout the Bay of Biscay. These were funded by direct and indirect taxes to repair the town wall, the wharves and quays and the loading and unloading areas. So, exactions for wharfage, anchorage and docking, among others, constituted the basis of the funding for this transformation of the port space. A wharf and a dock were built, following the petition to Juan II for the right to collect taxes to defray costs, which he granted with set amounts and for a limited period.[21]

17 *Ibid.*

18 Luis Suárez Fernández, *Navegación y comercio en el Golfo de Vizcaya. Un estudio sobre la política marinera de la Casa de Trastámara* (Madrid, 1959), p. 162. Ana María Rivera Medina, 'Construire des ports, ouvrir des routes: les villes biscayennes en bord de mer au Moyen Age', in *Ports nouveaux, Ports pionniers, XIVe–XXIe siècle*, ed. Martine Acerra and Bernard Michon (Rennes, 2019), pp. 377–394.

19 FDM, 1997, II, 72, p. 159.

20 María Soledad Tena García, 'Comercio y transporte marítimo en San Sebastián durante la Edad Media (1180–1474)', *Itsas Memoria. Revista de Historia Marítima del País Vasco*, 4 (2003), 137–138. María Rosa Ayerbe Iribar, 'Las ordenanzas de San Sebastián de 1489', *Boletín de estudios históricos sobre San Sebastián*, 40 (2006), 11–91.

21 José Damián González Arce and Joaquín Gil Sáez, 'El Puerto de San Sebastián y su Cofradía de Mareantes de Santa Catalina (1450–1550)', in *Tst: Transportes, Servicios y telecomunicaciones*, 21 (2011), 84–111, at p. 97.

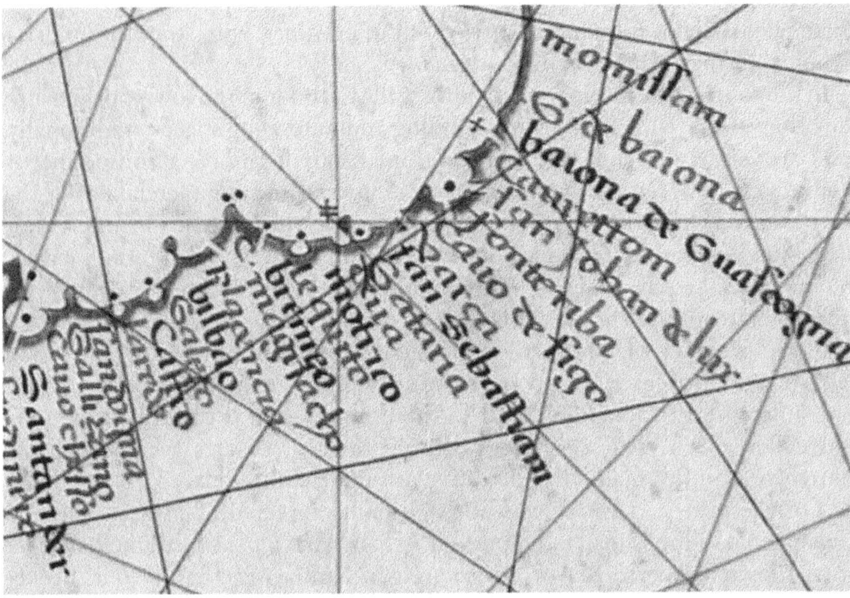

Figure 2.1. Grazioso Benincasa, nautical atlas of the northeast Atlantic Ocean, the Mediterranean Sea and the Black Sea. Ancona, Italy, 1467. Detail. BnF, GE DD-6269

In the fifteenth century, Basque ports were already known for their facilities for cargo handling tasks. Thus, the navigation chart of Grazioso Benincasa of Ancona (1467; figure 2.1) distinguishes international ports with the colour red, indicating their right to load and unload foreign merchandise. Among the Basque ports that were thus signalled, we find San Sebastián, Motrico, Bermeo or Bilbao. A different colour was used to signal secondary ports, such as Fuenterrabía, Varca (Pasajes), Guetaria, Deba, Lequeitio and Portugalete.

Port Services

It is well known that one of the most arduous tasks of maritime transport is the entry and landing of vessels in estuary ports, a task that on occasions required much experience and skill. The waters of the Bilbao estuary were perilous given the existence of cliffs, sandbars, sandbanks; but also due to the pollution caused by maritime traffic. Estuaries were full of refuse – discarded ballast, anchors, wood and equipment – that could seriously damage the vessels.[22]

22 Regulations of guilds and consulates include rules thereon. Equally, these are found in Municipal Ordinances of the coastal towns: '*Mandamos a vos los maestres de qualesquier*

The *Rôles d'Oléron* address these perils by regulating the beaconing of estuaries, a task to be carried out by the ship crews.[23] In the late fifteenth century, records document the presence of beacons on the estuary of Bilbao and Fuenterrabía,[24] as well as the hiring of an estuary warden, who would also control buoys and beacons 'of this shore, beaches and banks'.[25] A 1518 provision clearly describes the location of these signals: 'on the estuary canal are certain buoys and beacons and fires and other signals so those navigating by night and day can sail securely'.[26] Furthermore, from early on we find the use of fire beacons on protruding points at the entry of the Portugalete sandbar to signal wrecks and grounded vessels, following the custom of Flanders. Also, a guard hut was built in Las Arenas for the aid and rescue of ships in distress, and a warehouse was built in the tower of Luchana.[27]

In general, when entering or leaving a port, vessels were left in the hands of port pilots, known in the Cantabrian as '*lemanes*' or helmsmen, who would steer vessels along the estuary to their berth in the port compound or lead them to open sea.[28] These '*lemanes*' were specialists in the towing of vessels and assisted in crossing port bars, approach manoeuvres, berthing and cast off.

---

naos e navios e vaxeles de qualquier parte sean, que desde la punta gales fasta el cabo de suero (Lucero); fasta la villa y puerto de portogalete, non echeides ningún lastre de piedra, nin de arena, nin de çorra, nin de sables de Flandes nin de ningún otro lastre qualquira que sea [...] se recreciere gran dapno e perdida a las naos ye navegantes que entran e salen por la barra' ('We command that you, the masters of all ships and vessels and boats from wherever, from the Punta Galea, to Cabo de Suero, to the town and port of Portugalete, refrain from throwing any stone, sand, clay, or Flanders metal ballast nor any other type of ballast [...] which cause great damage and loss to vessels and sailors navigating the bar'.) FDM, 15, Portugalete, 21 de agosto de 1492. BFA/AFB, Municipal, Bilbao, Libro copiador: Bilbao, 3 de agosto de 1480; Bilbao, 3 de abril de 1495; Bilbao, 10 de enero de 1496; Bilbao, 1 de junio de 1514. FDM, no. 70, pp. 70–171. Bilbao, 3 de agosto de 1480. In 1517 Juan Ochoa de Bertendona reports to the *corregidor* on the condition of the canal and the bar, where '*ay muchas penas y otras vasuras que echa la mar, y que a causa della peligran muchos navios [...] y era necesario echar boyas e otros aparejos que fuesen neçesarios para que alimpiasen la entrada de la dicha varra*' ('there is much refuse and other litter washed unto shore and causing great peril to many ships [...] and it was necessary to throw buoys and other utensils necessary to clean the entrance of the said bar').

23 Margarita Serna Vallejo, *Los Rôles d'Oleron. El coutumier marítimo del Atlántico y del Báltico de época medieval y moderna* (Santander, 2004).

24 Guiard y Larrauri, *Historia del Consulado*, p. 438.

25 Rivera Medina, 'La construcción-reconstrucción de un espacio portuario'.

26 'Provisión real aprobando y confirmando las ordenanzas que incluye hechas por el Consulado de Bilbao en razón de las averías' ('Royal provision approving and confirming the ordinances that it includes made by the Bilbao Consulate due to average'). Bilbao, 28 de enero de 1528. FDM, 2007, no. 135, pp. 164–160.

27 Guiard y Larrauri, *Historia del Consulado*, pp. 102–103.

28 Timoteo O'Scanlan, *Diccionario Marítimo Español, que además de las definiciones de las voces con sus equivalentes en francés, inglés e italiano, contiene tres vocabularios de*

The ports of Portugalete and Pasajes offered a significant number of barges and personnel who habitually performed these tasks. In Bilbao and San Sebastián these tasks were controlled by the guilds and, later, by the consulates who would administer towage and steering work. In the sixteenth century, the confraternities of helmsmen were established in Santurce and Ciervana, under the patronage of the Consulate of Bilbao, creating a dedicated body of workers employed in pilotage, steering and towage operations.[29] With the advent of the modern age, the occupations of pilots and helmsmen were institutionalised through an exam where they had to demonstrate their competence and skills, achieving thus the professionalisation of this trade and the social and professional recognition of its members.

Later, the order of entry to port compounds was regulated to prevent incidents and accidents between the vessels. The Consulate of Bilbao and the Confraternity of Bermeo established that the priority in handling merchandise was to be determined by the order of entry to the bar, or, in other words, the order of arrival, regardless of the ship's cargo.[30] However, the ordinances of both Bermeo and San Sebastián ordered that, should the provisioning of the towns be necessary, the first vessels to enter port were to be those transporting wheat.[31]

Between the fourteenth and fifteenth centuries, port spaces witnessed the creation of warehouses, cellars, weigh houses[32] and port markets.[33] These could be sited adjacent to the unloading areas between the strand and the urban area, or close to the town walls for the safekeeping of merchandise to be loaded onto the vessels. This development included buildings devoted to

estos idiomas con las correspondencias castellanas, redactado por orden del Rey Nuesto Señor (Madrid, 1831), p. 434.

29 Guiard y Larrauri, *Historia del Consulado*, pp. 59 and 571. In the mid-sixteenth century, the salaries of helmsmen are established: 5 ducats for large vessels and 4 for smaller ships. In 1561 ordinances are promulgated on helmsmanship, regulating the certification of helmsmen by means of an exam. Later, in 1596, further ordinances are promulgated, 'Of what pilots and helmsmen are to charge for the entering and leaving of ports'. See also: Josu I. Erkoreka Gervasio, *Análisis político institucional de las Cofradías de Mareantes del País Vasco* (Vitoria, 1991), pp. 260–262.

30 Guiard y Larrauri, *Historia del Consulado*, p. 33; Erkoreka Gervasio, *Análisis político institucional*, p. 264.

31 Ayerbe Iribar, 'Las ordenanzas municipales', ch. 97 (p. 56): 'Que los navíos descarguen la mitad de las provisiones' (That the ships unload half of the provisions).

32 Called '*Casa de peso*', located in San Lazaro and San Nicolás. FDM, no. 56.

33 Located on the shores of the town, 'beyond the bridge' and in the suburbs, they were administered by means of a leasing system. Ordenanzas de la Villa de Bilbao. 25 de setiembre de 1495. FDM, no. 55, p. 44. FDM, no. 56: 'Hordenança de las lonjas de los revales'. Bilbao, 14 de noviembre de 1515; and 'Hordenança de las casas, lonjas, bodegas y tiendas alquiladas'. Bilbao, 8 de junio de 1513.

council tax and due collections, a fundamental revenue for both the Crown and the towns themselves.[34]

These warehouses and cellars custodied both merchandise or goods arriving from inland to be loaded onto vessels, and those arriving by sea to be transported to the hinterland. These wares were charged stockage, or storage dues. These dues were established in the Charter of San Sebastián in the same manner as the privilege of the host or warehouse owner to purchase half the merchandise from the merchant at a wholesale price as an exemption from lodging costs. Whether under the influence of French ports or the Charters of neighbouring towns, handling duties were also levied in Bilbao. Here the amount was calculated according to the nature and the volume of the merchandise.[35]

The price of depositing merchandise in the warehouses is documented in Bilbao in municipal ordinances of 1444.[36] At a later date, in the fifteenth century, the agreement signed between the Consulate of Burgos and the merchants of Portugalete established that:

> el alonjar y hostelaje de las mercaderias se entendiese en semejante manera como se entendiese en Bilbao, y habría de mantener en Portugalete acopio de posadas y mesones, alberques.[37]

Merchandise was to be custodied:

> a donde no se moje ni estrague e puestas muy bien retejadas y preparadas por lo alto y enmaderadas por los suelos e bajos [...] para evitar 'que si por falta o defeto de las lonjas las sacas e otras mercaderías rezibieren algún dano [...]. En caso de ser así, 'el daño sea imputado a los uéspedes o dueños de las lonjas [...] y sean obligados a pagar el tal daño a los dueños de tales las mercancías llanamente y sin pleito alguno.[38]

34 In Lequeitio, the existence of markets is documented from the end of the fifteenth century. FDM, no. 30.

35 Bonifacio de Echegaray Corta, *La vida civil y mercantil de los vascos a través de sus instituciones jurídicas* (San Sebastián, 1923), pp. 590–600.

36 FDM, no. 55. Acknowledgement of debt for iron bars and storage. In September 1495 in the rental contract in the Customs House, establishing the price of storing Castilian and foreign merchandise.

37 'storage and hosting of merchandise is to be administered in similar manner as in Bilbao, and Portugalete was to provide a supply of inns and taverns, lodgings'. Guiard y Larrauri, *Historia del Consulado*, p. 29. It is interesting to consider that maritime traffic generated spaces of sociability: inns, lodgings and taverns. Ana María Rivera Medina, 'Del mar a la taberna: el vino en Bilbao (ss. XV–XVII)', *Itsas Memoria. Revista de Estudios Marítimos del País Vasco*, 6 (2009), 615–662; *eadem*, 'Tavernes, vin et péchés publics dans le Bilbao du Moyen Âge (XIVe–XVIe siécles)', *Bulletin du Musée Basque*, 174 (2009), 5–22.

38 'where it be safe from water and damage and well covered and prepared on top and on wooden structures on the bottom [...] to prevent that by fault or default of the warehouses,

Labour Logistics of Stevedoring in Basque Ports

Port logistics determined the success of commercial ventures, given other types of difficulties that loomed within the port compound. Logistical considerations included the condition of the estuaries;[39] the availability of barges, lighters and batels should such be necessary to transfer the merchandise from the boat to the wharf;[40] the suitability of docking berths, since shipmasters preferred areas with platforms and loading docks to load livestock onto the ship; the presence of wooden pilings to secure the vessels; and the provision of breakwaters or walls to protect ships from the onslaught of waves, etc.[41] Loading and unloading work had to be carried out diligently[42] – in the presence of receivers or dispatchers,

---

that sacks and other merchandise should suffer damage [...]. Should this be the case, the damage is to be attributed to hosts or owners of the warehouses [...] and they will be liable to compensate the owners for the damage of said merchandise directly and without litigation'. Guiard y Larrauri, *Historia del Consulado*, p. 175.

39 Rivera Medina, 'Construire des ports, ouvrir des routes'; Ana María Rivera Medina, '"*Mengua y desonestidad*": La polución en la villa y puerto de Bilbao, Siglos XIV–XVI', *Fundación para la Historia de España*, 12 (2015), 438–449.

40 '*Otrosi, hemos de costumbre antigua y hordenamos que quando pareciere alguna vela que aquel que pussiere escamas y estropos assi como es acostumbrado que baia la tal pinaza a la tal vela y que diga al tal navio si quiere tomar pinaza para entrar en Portuondo o al Puerto Chico; y si no quisiere tomar pinaza para entrar en Portuondo, que la tal pinaza sea tenudo de no hir mas adelante de la peña nombrada Morgoña y dende venga al puerto, so pena de quinientos maravediz, la mitad para el servicio del altar de San Pedro y la otra mitad para los pobres del dicho Cavildo, y los dichos maiordomos sean obligados de lo egecutar so la misma pena.*' ('Also, as of ancient custom, we order that whenever a vessel arrives, the boatman with burlap and padding as is the custom, said pinnace approach the vessel and ask said vessel whether they wish to use the pinnace to enter Portuondo or Puerto Chico; and if the ship refuses to use the pinnace to enter Portuondo, that said pinnace refrain from going beyond the rock known as Morgoña and return to port, under penalty of five hundred maravedis, half for the altar service of San Pedro and the other half for the poor of said council, and that said stewards be required to execute the sanction under penalty of same fine.') 'Ordenanzas de la Cofradía de pescadores de Bermeo 1353'. Estanislao Labayru y Goicochea, *Historia general del Señorío de Bizcaya* (Bilbao, 1968), pp. 820–840.

41 Tena García, 'Comercio y transporte marítimo', p. 138.

42 '*Otrosi, hemos de costumbre antigua y hordenamos que cada y quando binieren algunos navios o caravelas con ropa, assi de Flandes como de otras partidas, que la pinaza que primeramente pussiere las escamas y estropos baia al tal navio; y si hubiere de hacer alguna descarga que antes y primero se cargue la tal pinaza y que entre tanto otro ninguno no le pertrue* [sic] *ni le haga embarazo ninguno, so pena de cincuenta maravediz. Y después de assi cargada la dicha pinaza y hecha iguala con maestre lo que le ha de pagar, despues de assi igualado, se haian de cargar las otras pinazas cada uno como fuere.*' ('Also, as of ancient custom, we order that whenever vessels or caravels arrive with cloth, from Flanders or other parts, that the first pinnace to place burlap and padding go to the said ship; and any unloading of merchandise be done first by said pinnace, that none interfere or bother it,

who supervised the process[43] – and the shipmaster had to control his subordinate crew members in case they disembarked without leave,[44] deserted or absconded with goods belonging to others. At the same time, they had to ensure that no unauthorised individuals approached the merchandise.

So, ports required berths – natural or artificial – protected from the winds and providing refuge to vessels during the frequent storms and gales of the Cantabrian Sea. In addition to this refuge, they required dry docks in the sand where ships could remain during low tides for loading and unloading, during the seasons when they did not venture out to sea or required repair. This inspired the building of wooden platforms and loading docks – structures that were subject to constant destruction by the sea – allowing easier access to the holds of grounded vessels, when during high tide these were set afloat anew. These areas had to be protected by walls and breakwaters to provide refuge to the vessels in those ports that fronted open seas and were subjected to the onslaught of the waves.[45]

Loading the merchandise was not a simple task. The scant service infrastructure, the weight and condition of the goods, and the additional complication of the shape and capacity of the vessels required the assistance of personnel with specific skills. In fact, Mediterranean legislation establishes that:

under the penalty of fifty maravedis. And once the said pinnace is loaded and the payment arranged with the shipmaster, let the other pinnaces load the merchandise as needed.') 'Ordenanzas de la Cofradía de pescadores de Bermeo 1353', ch. 43.

43 The receivers (*recibidores*) were representatives of the merchants, in charge of the supervision and negotiation of the different operations of reception, loading, unloading and delivery of the merchandise before these reached their final destination. Betsabé Caunedo del Potro, 'El desarrollo del comercio medieval y su repercusión en las técnicas mercantiles. Ejemplos castellanos', *Pecvnia*, 15 (2012), 201–220, at p. 218.

44 '*Otrosi, hemos de costumbre antigua y hordenamos que ningun marinero de nuestra Cofradia no sea osado de descender al puerto quando alguna pinaza quiera hir a alguna vela, antes y primeramente que el dueño de la tal pinaza llamare a su gente y marineros haciendo tiempo; y si le llamare el dueño de la tal pinaza que pueda hir libremente sin pena alguna, y no de otra manera, so pena de zincuenta maravediz.*' ('Also, as of ancient custom, we order that no mariner of our Confraternity go of his own accord to the port when a pinnace sets out toward an incoming vessel, before the owner of said pinnace calls on his men and mariners; and if the owner of said pinnace calls on him he may go freely without penalty, and not in any other manner, under penalty of fifty maravedis.') 'Ordenanzas de la Cofradía de pescadores de Bermeo 1353', ch. 44.

45 María Soledad Tena García, 'Composición social y articulación interna de las cofradías de pescadores y mareantes (Un análisis de la explotación de los recursos marítimos en la Marina de Castilla durante la Baja Edad Media)', *Espacio, tiempo y forma. Serie Historia medieval*, 8 (1995), 111–134, at pp. 117–118. Rivera Medina, 'La construcción-reconstrucción de un espacio portuario'. Ana María Rivera Medina, *Estudio Histórico del puerto de Bermeo* (Vitoria, 1997); *eadem*, *Estudio Histórico del puerto de Lekeitio* (Vitoria, 2008).

> los marineros están obligados a recibir los géneros en la escotilla, y no a estibarlos, si el patrón no lo prometió a los mercaderes; y si lo prometió, tendrá entonces que ponerse de acuerdo con los marineros, si acceden éstos a ello; pero si se halla en lugar despoblado y no se encuentran faquines ni hombres que lo hagan por dinero, están los marineros obligados a cargar y a descargar. Y se les debe retribuir de acuerdo con lo que el maestre entienda que deberían cobrar los que efectuaran la carga o la descarga.[46]

Additionally, charterers had to pay the expenses of stevedoring tasks, though when no skilled workers were available, the shipmaster and his crew were the ones to load or unload the ship at the charterer's expense.[47]

In Atlantic legislation, more specifically, in the *Rôles d'Oléron*, two provisions are included on stevedoring. Law 10 concerns the form or manner in which tuns were to be secured, and law 11 the method of stowing the tuns in the hold. They also deal with any damage during unloading in law 26: '*Si durante la desestiba dejan abierto o mal arrumado un tonel [...] de modo que se cae, pierde o golpea, el maestre y los marineros deben pagar el daño*'.[48] Similarly to Mediterranean codes, the *Rôles* imply that the crew was allowed to carry out stevedoring tasks, and so it seems to have been, since, in later periods, the shipmaster was in charge of enlisting individuals to carry out this task.[49]

Charter contracts specified the procedure for loading and unloading and the time allowed to complete the process. The shipmaster was responsible for the vessel, its fitting, and the loading and unloading of merchandise until it was delivered to the owner or his representative, with the obligation to comply with all the terms of the charter contract. This involved bringing the cargo to

46 'mariners are required to receive the merchandise on deck, but not to stow it, unless the master has agreed to do so with merchants; if this has been agreed, then the master must negotiate with the mariners, to confirm whether they agree to do this; but if they land in an isolated place and no lads or men are to be hired for money, the mariners will be constrained to load and unload the merchandise. And they must be rewarded with what the master considers the wages to be paid to hired workmen'. Antonio Capmany Surís y de Montpalau, *Codigo de las costumbres marítimas de Barcelona, hasta aqui vulgarmente llamado Libro del Consulado. Nuevamente traducido al castellano con el texto lemosin restituido á su original integridad y pureza; é ilustrado con varios apéndices, glosarios, y observaciones históricas* (Madrid, 1791), online at <https://archive.org/details/CodigoDeLasCostumbresMaritimas/page/n8Costumes>, Title V, 'On loading, stowage and unloading and the damage caused therein' (El título V 'De la carga, estiba y descarga y de los daños causados en ello').

47 *Ibid.*, chs 189 and 199.

48 'If during the unloading a tun is left open or poorly stowed [...] causing it to fall, be lost or damaged, the shipmaster and the crew must pay for the damage', in Margarita Serna Vallejo, *Textos jurídicos marítimos medievales* (Madrid, 2018), transcription of the *Rôles d'Oléron*, pp. 940–944.

49 José Martínez Gijón, 'La práctica del fletamento de mercancías con las Indias (siglo XVI)', *Historia. Instituciones. Documentos*, 10 (1983), 119–155, at p. 129.

land and the use of barges in the discharge.[50] Additionally, these contracts established the conditions of the vessel before setting sail, which was to be:

> puesta e aparejada e bien e completamente fornecida y bastecida de todos los bastimentos e mantenimientos necesarios [...] q.semejante nao e biaje requiere y bien proveyda [...] de manera que no haia falta nynguna sopena que el dho.maestre les aya de pagar la falta que por su parte fuere e por su culpa e causa de no prober y bastecer de todo lo necesario [...] e asi puesta e aparejada probeyda e bastecida con la buena ventura aian de partir e partan.[51]

As a rule, the merchant would pay the wages of helmsmen and fund the leasing of cranes, a cost that could vary from one port to another.

An important aspect in this process is related to the selection of the crew. In some ports it was preferable to recruit them among local townsmen and members of the port's confraternity. In Fuenterrabía ordinances stipulated that '*todo navío de la rivera [...] quando quiere ir fuera del bocal [...] que el maestre sea tenido de equiparse de confrades*'.[52] This was because mariners were responsible for the handling of the cargo and on occasions answerable for the cargo itself.[53] In this sense, the ordinance dwells on the concept of mutuality, without neglecting the authority and hierarchy on board, and protects members of the confraternity by allowing them to participate in all maritime activities.

For stevedoring tasks, some confraternities developed calendars for loading and/or unloading, as occurred in the *Cofradía de los comerciantes y marineros de Santa Catalina* of San Sebastián, where local and foreign vessels anchored in local ports were banned from loading and unloading during holidays without special authorisation from the vicars of the churches of Santa María and Santa Catalina, the two seats of the confraternities. Contravening this prohibition involved a penalty of 200 maravedis, which were used to fund renovation work

50 *Ibid.*

51 'set and fitted and well and properly furnished and victualled with all necessary apparel and rigging [...] required by such ship and journey and well furnished [...] such that nothing is lacking, and if there should be lack of anything, the shipmaster is to pay for it as it will be his fault for not providing all necessary apparel [...] and thus fitted and furnished may they leave', AHPV, Notarial, Sebastián de Ceballos, 3288. Año 1519. We have gathered approximately forty charter contracts for the period 1480–1519. See also Juan José de Mugartegui, 'Cómo se reclutaba en el siglo XVI, en nuestras costas, una tripulación para la pesca del bacalao en Terra-Nova', *Revista Internacional de los Estudios Vascos, RIEV*, 19:4 (1928), 632–636, at p. 632.

52 'for all local ships [...] when intending to travel beyond the mouth of the estuary [...] the shipmaster must hire members of the confraternity', in Victoriano José Herrero Liceaga, 'Ordenanzas de la Cofradía de San Pedro de mareantes de la villa de Fuenterrabía (1361–1551)', *Vasconia: Cuadernos de historia – geografía*, 10 (1988), 315–334.

53 FDM, no. 30, pp. 3–5.

on the docks. Equally, the council of Lequeitio banned loading and unloading iron, steel '*nin ninguna otra nin en dia que ouiere proçesion*'.[54] The council of Bilbao ordered a similar ban, so on holidays no '*ayan de cargar nin descargar mercaderías nin otras cosas ningunas de los bateles e pynaças a la tierra nin de tierra a ellos*'.[55] In Cádiz in southern Castile there is mention of an ancient custom of the port and region limiting the loading and unloading to the ships owned by the locals.[56]

The size of the vessels also became a matter of consideration, particularly for voyages to Flemish and English ports. Apparently, until the late fifteenth century, local vessels did not exceed 100 tuns, which the authorities deemed insufficient. Justified by the need to increase shipping capacities, Queen Doña Juana in 1521 confirmed the ordinances of the Consulate of Burgos to alleviate the scarcity of large-tonnage vessels. These ordinances established that ports from Fuenterrabía to La Coruña were to:

> llebaren naos de porte que sean de 200 toneles y dende arriba [...] porque las grandes naos se puedan mejor e mas presto aviar e cargar [...] y que estas cargaçones se hagan en el puerto o en los puertos que dispongan los priores y cónsules del Consulado de Burgo.[57]

However, time and experience proved that these large vessels were inconvenient, since vessels exceeding 60 tuns were unable to navigate shallow waters, such as the estuaries of Nantes and Rouen.[58]

54 'or any other merchandise or on any other holiday'. FDM, no. 38, p. 99. Lequeitio 25 de octubre de 1486. Los mayordomos de la Cofradía de San Pedro piden copia de las Ordenanzas Municipales de la villa ('The members of the Confraternity of San Pedro request a copy of the Municipal Ordinances of the town').

55 'loading nor unloading of merchandise nor other things from barges and pinnaces were to land or be loaded onto ships', FDM, no. 56, 'Hordenanças que el dicho concejo mando a plegonar'.

56 AGS, RGS, 22 de diciembre 1497, fol. 124.

57 'use ships with a capacity of 200 tuns and more [...] because large ships are more convenient to prepare and load [...] and that these loadings must be made in the port or ports determined by the heads and leaders of the Consulate of Burgos', FDM, no. 39, doc. 213. Burgos, 22 de noviembre de 1511. 'Juana I confirma las ordenanzas elaboradas por el prior y cónsules de la universidad de Burgos para paliar la falta de navíos de gran tonelaje que había en los puertos.' ('Juana I confirms the ordinances drawn up by the prior and consuls of the Guild of Burgos to make up for the lack of large tonnage ships that were in the ports').

58 '*porque se ha visto que por la experiencia*' ('because it has been proven by experience'); '*para subir las riberas [...] por ser estas secas y de poca agua*' ('to navigate upriver on waters [...] that are dry and shallow'). Guiard y Larrauri, *Historia del Consulado*, p. 33.

The ships were loaded with merchandise belonging to different merchants, marked accordingly, and after going through port dispatch procedures[59] these were distributed in their assigned locations on board. Perhaps, as has already been mentioned, the most arduous task was that of loading the goods, as these were packed in different types of containers, depending on their content: liquid, solid, etc.[60] Hence, all merchandise was stowed in a specific container and each had a specific location, some stacked, others fitted in a sort of wooden checkerboard or mesh to protect the container itself.

Loading methods varied according to the material of the containers: wood, ceramic, cloth, or vegetable fibres. The cargo was stowed on three levels depending on size and volume. The most abundant were wooden containers, used to transport products such as wine, oil, flour, fish, vinegar, etc. Among these, the largest and most frequent were the casks, used as the base of the stowage. On a second level, boxes and barrels were stowed. A third level consisted of sacks and canvas bags used for flour and grain. Palm sacks were used for tallow. Finally came ceramic containers, specifically jars, usually waxed

59 *Ibid.*, p. 335. 'Las mercaderías burgalesas estaban bajo el control del despachador y las vizcaínas eran controladas por los diputados de la universidad, más tarde consulado.' ('The goods from Burgos were under the control of the dispatcher and the Biscayan women were controlled by the deputies of the guild, later the consulate.')

60 In his articles, Ricardo Córdoba de la Llave makes an extensive analysis of the tools used in navigation: textile containers, leather receptacles, earth and wood containers, allowing us to confirm the investment involved in their protection and transport. Thus, we see the importance of bags, sacks, pouches, bales, barrels, tuns, pipes, casks, steel pans, chests, trunks, carafes, baskets, hampers, etc. Ricardo Córdoba de la Llave and Pilar Hernández Iñigo, 'El utillaje de los transportes en la Andalucía del descubrimiento', *Historia. Instituciones. Documentos*, 30 (2003), 159–180. Ricardo Córdoba de la Llave, 'Los instrumentos de la relación comercial: Medios, técnicas y útiles de transporte en la España bajomedieval', in *El comercio en la Edad Media: XVI Semana de Estudios Medievales* (Logroño, 2006), pp. 237–249. See also: Raymond Fagel, 'Los hombres de la lana y del hierro: mercaderes vascos en los Países Bajos siglo XVI', in *El licenciado Poza en Flandes, dos conferencias* (Bilbao, 1996), p. 57. José Damián González Arce, 'Los flujos comerciales en el puerto de Bilbao con la Europa Atlántica (1481–1501)', *Cuadernos Medievales*, 19 (2015), 82–110. Also, the capacity of pipes, barrels and tuns is variable. However, studies carried out by M. Bochaca, Y. Renouard and K. Porcher in the French sphere, as well as those carried out by Eduardo Aznar and Ana María Rivera Medina for the Iberian littoral, demonstrate a certain similarity as well as the possibility of establishing equivalences. Michel Bochaca, 'Un témoignage des relations maritimes et commerciales entre Bordeaux et la Bretagne le plus ancien contrat d'affrètement conservé dans le fonds de la Garde-Note de Bordeaux (27 décembre 1445)', *Anales de historia medieval de la Europa atlántica: AMEA*, 2 (2015), 65–79, at p. 74; Yves Renouard, 'La capacité du tonneau bordelais au Moyen Âge', *Annales du Midi*, 65 (1953), 395–403; Ana María Rivera Medina, *La civilización del viñedo en el primer Bilbao (1300–1650)* (Madrid, 2011).

and used to transport oil, vinegar, pitch, soap and similar products. Rarely, carafes, pitchers and jugs were used.[61]

Part of the cargo travelled in the hold, stowed within wooden structures and held in place, or '*arrumadas*' (accommodated), with cork barks to prevent it from moving or being damaged. Other elements of the cargo were placed on the deck in packets of light wood and cloth.[62] The latter method was forbidden, unless the merchant had given permission to employ it, in which case the shipmaster was not liable for loss or damage to cargo travelling thus. This situation is detailed even further with merchandise transported in a *leño* (a type of lembus), this type of transport being exempt of the damage that is known today as 'deck cargo exclusion', but not of those damages attributable to the shipmaster or the vessel.[63] In this regard, the Guild of Merchants of Bilbao mandated that all sacks of wool for Nantes and Flanders be stowed in the stern hold.[64]

This meant the placement and organisation of the cargo was vital to prevent it from moving, breaking or being lost. Moreover, the safety of the vessel depended on the appropriate loading of the cargo in terms of the vessel capacity, the distribution of vertical weight and the position of ballast, armament and cargo.[65] Hence it is an exercise of skill, practice and some luck. So merchant ships needed a workforce dedicated to the vigilant custody of the cargo and trained in a new specialty: that of ensuring the correct stowage while loading the goods. This workforce included those in charge of the safety and those in charge of day- and night-watches, both in the port and during the voyage.[66]

In the port of destination, except in cases of *force majeure*, the cargo was unloaded at the sites established by the municipality, confraternities or guilds of merchants. In other cases, and more specifically in the Mediterranean areas, it is established that:

> llegadas estas galeras con esta lana al puerto de Génova, llevaros y descargaros dicha lana de la forma como se descarga según vuestra voluntad [...] y deben cargar y estibar dicha lana en las galeras hasta los dos hierros y uno

61 Eduardo Aznar Vallejo, 'Marinos y pescadores', *Medievalismo: Boletín de la Sociedad Española de Estudios Medievales*, 13/14 (2004), pp. 234–235. Eduardo Aznar Vallejo, 'El mar fuente de conflictos y exigencia de paz', *Edad Media. Revista de Historia*, 11 (2010), 63–89, at p. 74.

62 Capmany Surís y de Montpalau, *Codigo de las costumbres marítimas de Barcelona*, ch. 74.

63 *Ibid.*, chs 189 and 249.

64 Contrafuerte. DRAE.

65 Jacques Bernard, *Navires et gens de mer á Bordeaux (vers 1400–vers 1550)* (Paris, 1968), t. I, pp. 379–380.

66 Ana María Rivera Medina, 'Vivir a bordo: necesidades y vicisitudes de los navegantes medievales' (forthcoming).

en el centro del casco, y no más. Y si hicieran mayor estiba, deben descontar 15 sueldos de flete por cada cantaría.[67]

Additionally, when unloading, the shipmaster could weigh or measure the merchandise if it had not been done at the time of loading, to charge the corresponding freight dues according to the real weight or volume.[68] Biscayan ports followed the order of arrival scrupulously when conducting the unloading tasks:

> Otrosi, hemos de costumbre antigua y hordenamos que cada y quando binieren algunos navios o caravelas con ropa, assi de Flandes como de otras partidas, que la pinaza que primeramente pussiere las escamas y estropos baia al tal navio; y si hubiere de hacer alguna descarga que antes y primero se cargue el tal pinaza y que entre tanto otro ninguno no le perturue (sic) ni le haga embarazo ninguno, so pena de cincuenta maravediz. Y después de assi cargada la dicha pinaza y hecha iguala con maestre lo que le ha de pagar, despues de assi igualado, se haian de cargar las otras pinazas cada uno como fuere.[69]

The ordinances of the town of Bilbao privileged the unloading of foreign vessels, establishing that:

> que todos los mercaderes estranjeros e maestres de los nabios en que traxieren las tales mercaderias sean tenidos de manifestar e manifiesten las dichas tales mercaderias al tienpo de descargar e non sean tenidos de las descargar syn que sean manifestados antes que los descarguen al fiel e deputados de los mercaderes desta dicha villa...e den rason e quenta en que retorno lo sacan

67 'when these galleys arrive in the port of Genoa with the wool, unload said wool according to the fashion of unloading of your choice [...] and they must load and stow said wool to a height of two beams and one in the centre of the hull and not more. Should it be stowed higher, they must discount 15 sols for each sack.' René Doehaerd, 'Les Galères génoises dans la Manche et la Mer du Nord à la fin du XIII et au début du XIVs', in *Bulletin de l'Institut Historique Belge de Rome*, 19 (1938), 5–76. Quoted in Antonio Ortega Villoslada, 'Las relaciones marítimo-comerciales entre el Mediterráneo y el Atlántico. El papel de Mallorca en el comercio entre Oriente y Occidente Siglos XIV y XV', *Memòries de l'Acadèmia Mallorquina d'Estudis Genealògics*, 20 (2010), 61–80.

68 Antonio Capmany Surís y de Montpalau, *Codigo de las costumbres marítimas de Barcelona*, ch. 269.

69 'Also, as of ancient custom, we order that whenever vessels or caravels arrive with cloth, from Flanders or other parts, that the first pinnace to prepare the burlap and padding should go to the aforesaid ship; and any unloading of merchandise be done first by aforesaid pinnace, that none interfere or hinder it, under the penalty of fifty maravedis. And once the aforesaid pinnace is loaded and the payment arranged with the shipmaster, let the other pinnaces load the merchandise as needed.' 'Ordenanzas de la Cofradía de pescadores de Bermeo 1353', ch. 43.

> e la cantidad de las mercaderias...e aver liçençia del fiel e deputados non sean hozados de partir los tales mercaderos e maestres.[70]

This part of the process was not simple, especially during the transhipment of merchandise, the most common method of bringing cargo to land given the small size and shallow depth of most ports and the likely conditions of the port compound: sandbanks, underwater rocks and branches, shallow waters, sandbars, etc. This is where the barges came into play, known by different names in local sources: *batel*, *barca*, *charrúa*, *barcaza*, *gabarra*, *bote*. These boatmen were often investigated as possible participants in fraudulent activities during transhipment and transport tasks.

Regarding the system and organisation of merchandise transhipment, we can identify diverse procedures along the Atlantic coast. In general, most ports offered a boatman service, dedicated to the transfer of merchandise from the ships to the boats to then be carried to the port compound. This service was administered by the municipalities, using a leasing system, by the guilds and merchant confraternities, *ad hoc* guilds or free workers. The status of the port was attested by the availability of this service, and boatmen services were increasingly included in the legal texts on maritime commerce. Among the functions of the boatmen we find: transporting merchandise in the boats – from ships moored in the port roadstead, near the coast – to land, and vice versa; and loading and unloading cargo, victuals and fittings.

In the northern Baltic, English and Scottish seas we find effective and regulated services. In Bruges, Antwerp and Basque and Cantabrian ports, the tasks of shippers included leasing larger vessels and smaller barges.[71] In Bordeaux, La Rochelle, Bilbao and Portugalete we find the '*bateleros*' or '*gabarreros*', boatmen or bargemen, an occupation practised on a freelance basis. Finally, one of the more developed and best-studied boatmen services was that of the port of Seville, organised around a leasing system that involved numerous workers and rendering important services for the Sevillian fleet.[72] This service constituted one the assets 'owned' by the municipal council.

70 'that all foreign merchants and shipmasters of the ships carrying aforesaid merchandise are constrained to declare said merchandises when unloading them, and refrain from unloading them without declaring the goods to the bailiff and merchant agents of this town [...] and declare the amount they obtain and the amount of merchandise [...] and aforesaid merchants and shipmaster must obtain a license from the bailiff and agents before leaving the port.' FDM, no. 55. Ordenanzas de Bilbao 1477, p. 22.

71 Hilario Casado Alonso, 'Los agentes castellanos en los puertos Atlánticos: Los ejemplos de Burdeos y los Países Bajos (Siglos XV y XVI)', in *Navegación y puertos en la época Medieval y Moderna*, ed. Adela Fábregas García (Granada, 2012), pp. 163–194, at p. 182.

72 Boats employed for the transhipment of cargo of larger vessels had a high participation in the Sevillian fleet, as shown in the statistics by Otte for the period 1472–1515, where nineteen trips correspond to *naos*, eight to caravels, thirty-seven to 'ships', thirty-five to

The intense commercial activity in Basque ports and the towns of Bruges and Antwerp is well known. In the Sluys, known as *La Esclusa*, Castilians and Basques were able to load and unload their merchandise freely. At this enclave all handling tasks for Spanish vessels was thoroughly regulated, with the consulates of Castile and Biscay being the institutions in charge of designating a person to supervise the discharge and collect mutualist contributions. Once these vessels reached the Sluys, merchandise was transferred to smaller vessels piloted by boatmen known as '*charrueros*'. These created their own guild in the custom of northern ports. Later, merchandise arriving in barges to Bruges and Antwerp was discharged by the so-called '*bruteros*', who also belonged to a guild.[73]

In Basque ports, conversely, neither boatmen nor individuals engaged in cargo handling created a confraternity or guild. Individuals – frequently unskilled workers – were hired for the tasks of loading and unloading. In these ports, as in Bordeaux, the transhipment of merchandise was carried out by means of a plank crossing from the boat to the shore. Porters carried bales on their shoulders, stones were transported in carts, and barrels and casks were rolled off the ships. In 1499, the Consulate of Burgos and the Guild of Merchants of Bilbao established:

> Que por quanto se ha visto que estivando las sacas en las naos con drao74 que de ello se sigue gran daño de la mercaderia que se mande e defienda que ningún maestre no estive ni faga estivar con drao salvo como ancianamente se ha fecho con tablas.[75]

Despite this ordinance, derricks and levers were employed to move heavy items,[76] or even a pulley crane[77] as in Bilbao. In this sense, most Basque ports

boats and one to barges. These were usually leased for fixed periods or seasons from the owner, who probably owned a business with several boats. Eduardo Aznar Vallejo, 'Barcos y barqueros en Sevilla', *Historia. Instituciones y Documentos*, 21 (1994), 1–12, at p. 6.

73 Casado Alonso, 'Los agentes castellanos en los puertos Atlánticos', pp. 188–189.

74 Large piece of heavy wood hitting on a plane when pulled by cables, serving as a mallet to produce great force against bodies in order to move them. O'Scanlan, *Diccionario Marítimo Español*, p. 228.

75 'Having seen that unloading bales from the ships with a drao, great damage is done to the merchandise, it is ordered that no shipmaster unloads merchandise with a counterpoise lift, except as done from ancient times with planks.'

76 Michel Bochaca, 'El control del puerto de Burdeos y de su tráfico mercantil del siglo XIII al XV: jurisdicciones y estructuración del espacio', in *Ciudades y villas portuarias del Atlántico en la Edad Media*, ed. Beatriz Arízaga Bolumburu and Jesús Ángel Solórzano Telechea (Logroño, 2005), pp. 91–113, at p. 97.

77 A frame with two perpendicular beams placed vertically at its foot and on each side facing the fore by the main-mast, both held by a cantilevered beam placed as a scaffold, and

had to wait until the sixteenth century to equip their infrastructure with more sophisticated hoisting devices, notably cranes.[78]

The Organisation of the Human Workforce: The Impact of Female Workforce

Throughout the Atlantic façade cargo handling was organised in a similar manner, particularly in those cases where ships were hindered from directly berthing at the loading and unloading areas. Hence, we can identify three forms of occupational regulation: guild associations, leasing and free hiring. In the Zwin estuary and in Scottish ports, boatmen and stevedores were organised in guilds; however, in other ports, these workers never established mutualist organisations. Meanwhile, companies were created in London to negotiate the hiring of boatmen, that is, the individuals dependent on an employer who did not necessarily have any relation with the cargo or the ship. The activities they performed were strictly regulated by town authorities, making a distinction between specialised and occasional porters (skilled and unskilled). Mostly, it appears that this group was composed of men who not only worked in the loading and unloading of the vessels, but also undertook the storage tasks in warehouses and cellars: stowing and safeguarding the cargo until the moment of delivery. This group constituted what Maryanne Kowaleski calls an 'occupational identity' that is, they enjoyed a recognised social status for their professional specialisation. Conversely, occasional porters were not recognised, and their salaries were lower; they can be defined as temporary workers.

In contrast with what occurred in ports of the English Channel and the northern Atlantic, workers employed in loading and unloading tasks in Castilian ports never created associations or guilds and never offered their services by means of a leasing system. Basically, the shipmaster would find strong and able men and women to perform these tasks. This contrasts with the associations of other ports with larger business volumes, more potent institutionalisation and professionalisation of cargo handling, and more advanced technology consistent with their status within the international commercial network.

Hence, it is evident that in northern Peninsular ports, cargo handling was an occupation for temporary workers rather than skilled and specialised individuals. In these specific ports, women achieved a certain prominence since, to a great extent, this occupation was either a distinctly feminine

with a series of grooves and cables necessary to guide and exert force. O'Scanlan, *Diccionario Marítimo Español*, p. 310.

78 FDM, no. 70, p. 84.

occupation, or one in which their participation was significant. Known in texts as '*moças*' (wenches), their work was paid by piece or per day in the domestic sphere, civil construction work, quarries, smithies, loading and unloading of ships, ballasting vessels, in shipyards and dockyards, net and sail making, and any task they were able to perform dependent on their age and physical strength.[79] Bowles noted that in Bilbao women of the lowest classes worked harder than men:

> Ellas son ganapanes y mozas de cordel de la villa que cargan y descargan navíos [...] Van descalzas de pie y piernas, y desnudos los brazos; y por la robustez de los músculos se puede conjeturar las fuerzas que alcanzan. El cuello particularmente lo tiene semejante a los toros pues sostienen sobre la cabeza fardos tan pesados, que son menester dos hombres regulares para ponérselos encima [...] y bien bebidas y cargadas de peso, corren sueltas y firmes.[80]

So, their occupation was as precarious as it was varied, with two main areas of activity: port tasks and building work.[81]

In Guipúzcoa, women operated the boats connecting both margins of the port of Pasajes, a habitual task in towns where people, animals and merchandise had to be ferried from one bank to the other of the estuary. These boatwomen and bargewomen worked the route between Renteria and Pasajes. Barges were used during high tides to transport iron, stones, etc.[82]

79 The case of Mallorca is interesting, where young women worked in the shipyards moving earth and preparing the ramps to launch or beach the vessels, and sewing sails. Antonio Ortega Villoslada, 'El trabajo femenino en Mallorca: la labor de la mujer en la actividad marítima de la primera mitad del siglo XIV', in *Espacio, tiempo y forma. Serie III, Historia medieval*, 17 (2004), 461–470, at p. 466. Ana María Rivera Medina, 'Superando fronteras. Mujer y cultura laboral en los puertos del Norte Peninsular, siglos XIV–XVI', in *Fronteras de agua: las ciudades portuarias y su universo cultural (siglos XIV–XXI)*, ed. Manuel-Reyes García Hurtado and Ofelia Rey Castelao (Santiago de Compostela, 2016), pp. 17–42.

80 'The women are labourers and porters of the town who load and unload vessels [...] They are barefooted and barelegged, and do not cover their arms; and from the robustness of their muscles one can conjecture the strength they exert. Their necks, in particular, are similar to that of a bull since they carry on their heads bales so heavy, that it would take two regular men to carry these [...] and being given their wine ration and bearing the weight, they run light and firm'. Guiard y Larrauri, *Historia del Consulado*, t. V, p. 590.

81 María Álvarez Fernández, 'Abastecimiento y consumo de pescado en Oviedo a finales de la Edad Media', in *La pesca en la Edad Media* (Santiago de Compostela, 2009), pp. 71–86, at p. 83.

82 It is known that some women ran their own boating businesses, and were proprietrices of the barges they operated, at times carrying loads of 300 quintals (over 20 tons), and accepting even more complicated commissions, such as participating in moving newly built ships from Renteria, a task requiring their assistance and their barges. José Antonio Azpiazu

In Lequeitio women bore barrels of wine and fish on their heads,[83] a task they only could perform during the daytime since, in general, they were banned from wandering out at night due to their tendency towards petty theft, the practice of informal exchanges and transactions, and their 'predisposition' to stir up quarrels.[84] In Bilbao, where they were known as '*cargaderas*' or '*pasaderas*', they drove carts in the town and the docks for building sites,[85] they transported bales of wool from the weighing house, the *Casa del Peso*, to the shore, or they performed surveillance tasks on building sites.[86] They were also in charge of courier services and were known as '*andadoras*', walking to other towns to deliver messages.[87] Also, they performed work requiring strength and robustness, such as bringing vessels to dry docks, towing vessels back to sea from the shipyards, ballasting, loading and unloading vessels. Extant data describes the modes of hiring and their salaries; on average these women were paid between 12 and 16 maravedis per day, but they were also given lunch and supper.[88] These women represent around 25 per cent of port workforce: '*trujimos en la pynaça […] de Renteria a Ondarroa seis ombres y dos moças para cargar y descargar*'.[89]

In contrast, medieval documents of Peninsular ports do not provide sufficient information about the men involved in stevedoring tasks, limiting our ability to describe their work, salaries or social status. The reason for this silence is possibly due to three factors: the absence of sources, the scarcity of men for these tasks as most of them were embarked voluntarily or forcibly,[90] or their engagement in fishing activities. Further, in the towns and the ports, the information regarding women's work in transport and cargo handling was better documented. And, as has been explained, guild associations in Basque towns

Elorza, 'Las mujeres vascas y el mar', *Itsas Memoria. Revista de Estudios Marítimos del País Vasco*, 8 (2016), 811–829, at p. 818.

83 FDM, no. 38, doc. 215.

84 FDM, no. 44, doc. 1.

85 The owner of the grain had to hire six women for the weighing of the wheat. Guiard y Larrauri, *Historia del Consulado*, p. 180.

86 '*por quatro moças que estouieron a dar recaudo en el gelso e madera quando se desbarataba la pared, veynte e quatro maravedís*' ('for four lasses who worked mortar and wood when the wall collased, twenty-four maravedís'), FDM, no. 71, doc. 1.

87 FDM, no. 130, doc. 83.

88 In the late fifteenth century, the *moças* earned half of what a male labourer did. As a comparison we want to point out that an 8-ounce loaf of bread cost 10 maravedis. Guiard y Larrauri, *Historia del Consulado*, t. V, p. 392.

89 'we brought on the pinnace […] from Renteria to Ondarroa six men and two women to load and unload', FDM, no. 44.

90 Luis Suárez Fernández, *Navegación y comercio en el Golfo de Vizcaya*; Eduardo Aznar Vallejo, 'Marinos vascos en la guerra naval de Andalucía durante el siglo XV', *Itsas Memoria. Revista de Estudios Marítimos del País Vasco*, 5 (2006), 41–52.

occurred much later, limiting a full description of the various ways in which men participated in cargo handling tasks.

Final Considerations

With the increase in maritime traffic, the ports of coastal towns located in northern Castile exploited their geographic position within the Atlantic network, what some authors define as 'locational advantage', and became ports of critical significance, despite their peripheral location. Their early mercantile contact with Mediterranean ports and the northern European Atlantic, their position as points of redistribution towards the hinterland and with southern Castile, as a 'gateway' to the Mediterranean, allowed them to implement a process of modernisation and adaptation of their infrastructures within their port compounds, with the support of the guilds, merchant consulates and local oligarchs.

In this scenario, and building on the uses and customs of seafarers, a maritime law (*ius privatista*) evolved to cater for the complex system of transport, loading and handling of merchandise. The ports of northern Spain and some ports of the English Channel developed mutualist associations influencing all aspects of the ports, activities and operators. In the ports of the north of the Crown of Castile, this mutualist process involved only merchants, through the creation of guilds and consulates, in an attempt to regulate every aspect of transport and handling of merchandise in accord with the articulation of maritime transport ordinances. Local authorities and municipalities, on their part, also participated in this process through the administration of the matters regarding the 'urban' elements of the ports: port infrastructures.

As infrastructures developed – adapting port spaces with signalling systems, hoisting devices and port services – the systems of cargo handling also evolved, being a fundamental aspect of maritime transport where the interests of diverse operators converged: shipowners, charterers, owners of the merchandise and, not least, the cargo handlers themselves. Unlike the busy ports of northern Europe and the English Channel, these peripheral ports, holding a secondary position within the port hierarchy of the Atlantic façade, did not create guild associations during the late middle ages. Cargo handling logistics remained the business of charterers and was negotiated through charter contracts. This circumstance has obscured any evidence of mutualist characteristics of the activity. This way partly due to the *mare clausum* policies, by which sailing was allowed from March to September, with convoy navigation of fleets, hence impeding a continuity in the work of the cargo handling workforce and, consequently, the need for an association to protect their interests.

To a greater or lesser extent each port gradually regulated cargo handling activities, possibly contingent upon their operative capacity and the availability of a workforce for a tough and demanding task. Although port workers throughout the Middle Ages did not constitute guild corporations, we can posit the existence of an intentional strategy to control and regulate the activities proper to port compounds: the existence of signalling systems; controlled access and movements in the estuary; the adaptation of infrastructures for loading and unloading; the use of primary technology for the handling of merchandise; the organisation of berths; the implementation of a dedicated human workforce for the control of the activities, such as the dispatchers, helmsmen or port pilots; a system of boats or barges for the transhipment of merchandise; regulation of leasing of warehouses and cellars; regulations for lodgings; the creation of sociability structures; and, lastly, the regulation of human resources in charter contracts. All this denotes a clear awareness of the need to protect the business, controlling all aspects of the same and demonstrating a clear transition from medieval capitalist practices to modern times.

Finally, it is worth mentioning the participation of women in the tasks of loading and unloading, which is not an exclusive characteristic of Basque ports, but seems to have had a significant impact in this area. The role of women is obvious, as lead players, in the cargo handling of the maritime universe of the northern Peninsula. Young and strong women, 'light and firm', willing to earn their wages performing jobs considered to be masculine, who, by chance or necessity, are clearly visible in the port landscape, either loading or unloading ships, operating boats and barges, or performing other tasks in the port compound.

It is obvious that in Basque ports, the guilds of port operators, '*gente de puerto*' (people of the port) or '*gente de mar en tierra*' (people of the sea on land), created their own mutualist organisations in the sixteenth century. These were imbued with the spirit of ordinances on maritime insurances, granting the activity a professional status with the subsequent qualification and structuring of the different work categories. Over time, this monopolistic system became generalised thanks to several factors: the growth in traffic, the sophistication of infrastructures and facilities, the intervention of port administration, the need to organise and capitalise an activity requiring specific skills by establishing a professional hierarchy based on division of labour; the availability of workers for the loading and unloading of ships; work distribution dependent on qualifications; and, lastly, the priority of hiring guild members to prevent theft and misconduct. These motives have held since the Middle Ages to the present day, as defended by today's stevedore syndicates to protect their collective interests in an attempt to perpetuate their monopoly.

3

Port Structures and Cargo Handling in Asturias and Galicia (13th–16th Centuries)

MARÍA ÁLVAREZ FERNÁNDEZ

University of Oviedo

ABSTRACT. This chapter aims to describe the degree of development of the western Cantabrian ports (Galicia and Asturias) through their port activities (loading and unloading) and their infrastructures. Extant historical sources deliver a very modest image, with exceptions, of these small port 'cities' in the Cantabrian northwest coast, as a minor microcosm striving for survival through fishing activities. As a direct effect of these limitations, the ports had simple infrastructures more in keeping with small berths and fisheries than with the large and middling ports of the European Atlantic. This discreet economic activity was mirrored in the modest trade associations that the people of the sea established in their places of origin. At the same time, however, those 'harvesters of the sea' activated local economies through a common effort that even today upholds the very evident bonds of solidarity in Galician and Asturian maritime communities.

Asturias and Galicia in the Medieval Atlantic Koiné: The Organisation of the Northwestern Cantabrian Port Space

Historiography has long addressed the study of small port towns in the northern Peninsula and their impact on local economies on account of documentary evidence of their economic influence in the late Middle Ages.[1]

1 This chapter is part of the research carried out in the project 'Politics, Institutions and Governance of the European Atlantic Ports in the Late Middle Ages: A Transnational Comparative Analysis' (HAR2017-83801-P), funded by FEDER / Spanish Ministry of Science and Innovation / National Research Agency.

All evidence appears to verify the leading role of these minor northern ports in the maritime development of the Cantabrian façade from their foundation in the mid-thirteenth century. The foundational text, *Las polas asturianas en la Edad Media*, published in 1981, was the first serious methodological attempt to consider not just coastal communities but also the medieval Asturian urban phenomenon as a whole.[2] In the wake of this work, several revised analyses of the new coastal towns, both general and based on specific case studies, have endeavoured to gradually build a fuller historiographical survey; however, even today, rigorous research and comparative proposals for many Asturian towns is lacking, leaving a wide and untouched field of study.[3]

Hence, at least in the Asturian case, the present historiographical challenge involves the reinterpretation of an old historiographic theme in the light of new sources, the confirmation of hypotheses, the reconsideration of hitherto confirmed certainties, and the formulation of new inquiries, such as the type of contacts established between the different port towns, the economic consequences of such exchanges, the characteristic traits of the societies that generated them, the creation of regional networks, the hierarchy of ports and their possible function as ports of call on the Atlantic trade corridor.[4]

2 Juan Ignacio Ruiz de la Peña Solar, *Las polas asturianas en la Edad Media. Estudio y diplomatario* (Oviedo, 1981). The same author would, years later, establish the foundations of the studies of the commercial and fishing functions of these small urban nuclei of the Asturian coast. It is impossible to reproduce the long roster of publications on this subject, but among them are Juan Ignacio Ruiz de la Peña Solar, 'La atracción del mar: en los orígenes de la apertura de la fachada costera galaico-cantábrica al mundo atlántico (1157–1252)', in *Fernando III y su tiempo (1201–1252), VIII Congreso de Estudios Medievales* (Ávila, 2003), pp. 183–208; and *idem*, 'Comercio a escala interregional e internacional: el espacio comercial asturleonés y su proyección atlántica', in *El comercio en la Edad Media. XVI Semana de Estudios Medievales de Nájera* (Logroño, 2006), pp. 39–92.

3 The first steps towards a comprehensive and individualised knowledge of medieval Asturian coastal towns have already been taken for Llanes, Villaviciosa and Castropol. See the studies of Marta Álvarez Carballo, 'Arquitectura y ciudad. Urbanismo medieval en Asturias: Llanes' (PhD diss., Universidad de Oviedo, 2012) <http://digibuo.uniovi.es/dspace/handle/10651/13006> [accessed 30 April 2020]; Álvaro Solano Fernández-Sordo, *De Maliayo a Villaviciosa. Un territorio de la marina centro-oriental de Asturias en la Edad Media* (Oviedo, 2016); and Jesús Fernández Suárez, *'Entrambasauguas'. La marina occidental asturiana en la Plena Edad Media* (Oviedo, 2017).

4 Cf. with a general approach, the work in *The Sea in History / La mer dans la histoire: The Medieval World*, ed. Michel Balard and Christian Buchet (Woodbridge, 2017); Cátia Antunes and Louis Sicking, 'Ports on the Border of the State, 1200–1800: An Introduction', *International Journal of Maritime History*, 19 (2007), 273–286; Amélia Aguiar Andrade, 'A importancia da linha costeira na estruturaçao do Reino medieval portugués. Algumas reflexões', *Historia Instituciones, Documentos*, 35 (2008), 9–24; Gérard Le Bouëdec, 'Small Ports from the Sixteenth to the Early Twentieth Century and the Local Economy of the French Atlantic Coast', *International Journal of Maritime History*, 21.2 (2009), 103–126; *Gens de mer. Ports et cités aux époques ancienne, médiévale et moderne*, ed. Éric Guerber

Regarding these coastal centres, historiography has focused on their limited, albeit effective, mercantile traffic and their socio-professional frameworks, proving the success of these small coastal towns within the regional context of the territory they articulated. Indeed, they created a complex network of relationships within an urban system that was closely linked to the 'large' centres, and, in most cases, surrounded by small rural markets supplying nearby towns, with which they sustained strong relations of dependence.

Avilés and Ferrol, both early settlements within the ancient kingdom of León on the Cantabrian seaboard, consolidated their strategic position by benefitting from an excellent geographical location and direct access to the sea.[5] However, and despite their early foundation, the port system of the Galician coast remained practically disjointed until the mid-twelfth century, with Ferrol as the only urban nucleus with the ability to exploit the wealth of maritime resources offered by the Cantabrian sea. It was not until a second foundational

and Gérard Le Bouëdec (Rennes, 2013); Michel Bochaca and Beatriz Arízaga Bolumburu, 'Ports, havres et mouillages de Bayonne (Gascongne) à Bayona (Galice) d'après les routiers de la fin du Moyen Âge', in *Fronteras de agua: las ciudades portuarias y su universo cultural, siglos XIV–XXI*, ed. Manuel Reyes García-Hurtado and Ofelia Rey Castelao (Santiago de Compostela, 2016), pp. 47–58; Mathias Tranchant, *Les ports maritimes de la France atlantique (XIe–XVe siècles)*, vol. 1, *Tableau géohistorique* (Rennes, 2017); *idem*, 'La urbanización del litoral atlántico del reino de Francia en el siglo XII', in *Los fueros de Avilés y su época*, ed. Juan Ignacio Ruiz de la Peña Solar, María Josefa Sanz Fuentes and Miguel Calleja Puerta (Oviedo, 2012), pp. 97–117; Maryanne Kowaleski, 'The Maritime Trade Networks of Late Medieval London', in *The Routledge Handbook of Maritime Trade around Europe, 1300–1600* (Oxford, 2017), pp. 383–410; *eadem*, 'Peasants and the Sea in Medieval England', in *Peasants and Lords in the Medieval English Economy: Essays in Honour of Bruce M. S. Campbell*, ed. Maryanne Kowaleski, John Langdon and Phillipp Schofield (Turnhout, 2015), pp. 353–376; Beatriz Arízaga Bolumuru and Jesús Ángel Solórzano Telechea (eds), *Ciudades y villas portuarias del Atlántico en la Edad Media* (Logroño, 2005); Jesús Ángel Solórzano Telechea, 'Integración económica, competencia y jerarquización de los puertos atlánticos del Norte de España (siglos XIII–XV)', *Anuario de Estudios Medievales*, 48.1 (2018), 213–242; *idem*, 'La influencia del mar en la conformación de los puertos de "la Marisma e costera de España" en la Baja Edad Media', in *De mar a mar: los puertos castellanos en la Baja Edad Media*, ed. Eduardo Aznar Vallejo and Roberto J. González Zalacain (San Cristóbal de La Laguna, 2015), pp. 59–92; *idem*, 'Las Nereidas del Norte. Puertos de identidad urbana en la fachada cantábrica entre los siglos XII–XV', *Anales de la Universidad de Alicante: Historia Medieval*, 16 (2009–2010), 39–61; *idem*, 'Villas y redes portuarias en la fachada atlántica del Norte peninsular en la Edad Media', in *Castilla y el mundo feudal. Homenaje al profesor Julio Valdeón* (Valladolid, 2009), pp. 485–502; and *idem*, 'Los puertos del rey. Síntesis interpretativa del fenómeno urbano en el norte de España durante los siglos XII y XIII', *Temas medievales*, 17 (2009), 207–228.

5 Juan Ignacio Ruiz de la Peña Solar, 'Funciones y paisajes urbanos de las villas marítimas del norte de España: Avilés (siglos XII–XV)', in *Mercado inmobiliario y paisajes urbanos en el occidente europeo, siglos XI–XV* (Pamplona, 2007), pp. 691–736. Cf. with a general approach, *Los fueros de Avilés*, ed. Ruiz de la Peña Solar, Sanz Fuentes and Calleja Puerta.

impulse generated by the repopulation policies of Fernando II, responsible for the urban growth of centres such as La Coruña, Ribadeo or Noya, that this oceanfront became populated with minor port enclaves. Of the substantial roster of regal foundations, Pontevedra was to lead the way in the great Atlantic expansion of the westernmost corner of the Leonese kingdom, with a privileged charter (1169) encouraging urban growth and commercial and fishing industries in the town.[6]

Indeed, Pontevedra was destined to be the foremost Galician fishery under the auspices of the archbishopric of Santiago de Compostela, and experienced an impressive development of its primitive urban nucleus.[7] Again, prompted by the policies of Fernando II, the easternmost corner of Galicia witnessed the birth of the burgh of Ribadeo (1182), a direct competitor of the neighbouring Asturian town of Roboredo in the exploitation of the Eo estuary. Ribadeo was to be refounded years later under Alfonso IX of León.[8] To this Leonese monarch, possibly the greatest benefactor of urban Galicia, we also owe the foundations of Vivero (1200) and Bayona (1201), two clearly mercantile towns, very soon to benefit from privileges and fiscal exemptions to stimulate their economic growth.[9]

It is reasonable to affirm that the great Leonese creation on the Galician littoral was to be the foundation in 1208 of La Coruña. A minute coastal burgh located on a pre-existing settlement at the head of an estuary, La Coruña's exceptional location allowed it to intercept Atlantic traffic and encouraged thriving port activity that would soon give rise to large suburbs, such as the fish quarter, significantly expanding the primitive urban nucleus.[10] A clear commercial intention can also be gleaned from the foundation by Alfonso IX of Santa Marta de Ortigueira, a burgh that would come into its own as a

6 The monograph on this town remains an exception, despite the time gone by, José Armas Castro, *Pontevedra en los siglos XII a XV. Configuración y desarrollo de una villa marinera en la Galicia medieval* (Pontevedra, 1992).

7 The town experienced a fast multiplication of its population, forcing them to abandon the primitive walled town – *burgo pequeño* – to settle in fishing suburbs – *barrio de la moureria* – which finally became integrated with the urban centre. *Ibid.*, pp. 115–118.

8 It does not, in my opinion, surpass the excellent synthesis by Fernando López Alsina, *Introducción al fenómeno urbano medieval gallego a través de tres ejemplos: Mondoñedo, Vivero y Ribadeo* (Santiago de Compostela, 1976).

9 Álvaro Solano Fernández-Sordo, 'Historia urbana en la Galicia medieval. Balance y perspectivas', *Cuadernos de Estudios Gallegos*, LVII, no. 123 (2010), 55–90; and Elisa Ferreira Priegue, 'Galicia en la Marisma de Castilla. La dinámica de los intercambios mercantiles', in *Ciudades y villas portuarias*, ed. Arízaga Bolumburu and Solórzano Telechea, pp. 165–186.

10 He devotes a documented study to La Coruña from the perspective of trading volume. Amparo Rubio Martínez, *El reinado de los Reyes Católicos en Galicia: actividad económica y fiscalidad regia* (Santiago de Compostela, 2016), pp. 383–406.

result of the foundational charter of Fernando III, to be confirmed years later by Alfonso X.[11]

Present-day coastal Asturias remains, as it was in the Middle Ages, perfectly delineated by the two estuaries – Eo and Deba – which defined, from ancient times, the physical limits of the Asturian domain. With its vast littoral, Asturias was primarily a fishing territory, with many inlets and sheltered natural harbours offering safe havens for the local coastal communities. A maritime and port vocation is represented in the portolans of the time, which recorded with great detail and precision the tiered distribution of the various ports.[12] However, it was not until the late thirteenth century that this natural maritime projection would coalesce with a strong urban development policy, allowing Asturias to partake in Cantabrian commercial growth and leave behind the rural image that previously only the inland towns of Oviedo and Avilés had been able to shed.[13]

Despite this close connection with the sea, the natural obstacles of the shore meant that the Asturian coastline remained the least favourable enclave for commercial exchanges, leaving its central part – the stretch connecting the port of Gijón with the mouth of the river Nalón – as the area enjoying more intense maritime activity. The remaining examples – Llanes, Ribadesella, Villaviciosa, Luarca – manifested, in general, a far more modest maritime and mercantile activity.[14] Still, what criteria must be applied to judge the commercial success of a port town in the Middle Ages? Was the impact of port traffic on local economies the determining factor? Were Asturian coastal towns fishing towns, commercial towns, or 'simple' ports? Were there landing spots without towns?

Overall, Asturian ports, though active, never rivalled the role of Basque or Galician ports – or, naturally, that of other commercial nations on the Atlantic arc. Neither did they embark on the great seaways connecting first-order European centres. In Asturias, as Elisa Ferreira states for the Galician case,

11 See, among others, Juan Ignacio Ruiz de la Peña Solar, 'Le ville nuove del nord della Corona di Castiglia (secoli XII–XIV)', in *J. I. Ruiz de la Peña Solar. Estudios de Historia Medieval*, ed. María Soledad Beltrán Suárez and María Álvarez Fernández, vol. II (Oviedo, 2014), pp. 213–252.

12 'Existen en Asturias muchos e diversos puertos de mar y todos los más de los vecinos e moradores del Principado son personas que continuamente andan y tratan con la mar' ('there exist in Asturias many and diverse seaports and most of the neighbours and inhabitants of the Princedom are persons continually working and dealing with the sea'). AGS, RGS, 15-VIII-1500, no fol.

13 We have analysed it thus in María Álvarez Fernández, 'Alfonso X el Sabio, promotor del desarrollo urbano de la Asturias Medieval', in *El mundo urbano en la Castilla del siglo XIII*, ed. M. González Jiménez, vol. 2 (Seville, 2006), pp. 21–32.

14 With a general approach, Juan Ignacio Ruiz de la Peña Solar, 'El desarrollo urbano de Asturias en la Edad Media', in *El fenómeno urbano medieval entre el Cantábrico y el Duero: revisión historiográfica y propuestas de estudio*, ed. Jesús Ángel Solórzano Telechea and Beatriz Arízaga Bolumburu (Santander, 2002), pp. 349–366.

'we move within a domain of modest figures, there are no heavy investments, no risks are taken. Although the mercantile population is very large, there are no prominent businessmen.'[15]

Despite their limitations, Asturian ports did endow Asturias with an unparalleled economic vitality, enabling the creation of organised and relatively well-provisioned markets, with a resolute and autonomous performance. The artisanal Asturian fleet enjoyed a limited exterior projection – except for Avilés – but it was functional, catering for the provisioning of towns and the immediate hinterland. In addition to the ports of Gijón, Villaviciosa, Llanes and Castropol, we find documentary evidence of accounts, albeit dispersed and for very specific periods, of other havens where fishing activity was significant at a local level.

A good example of the enormous vitality of the minute havens in the Asturian coast is, undoubtedly, the whaling port. Extant documents indicate organised whale hunting on the Asturian coast from 1232, with a significant number of references to an expansive fishing sector that, even in modest settlements, counted slaughterhouses, whaling ports and whale processing facilities as points of commercial activity in the thirteenth century.[16] And with these, other Asturian fishing centres became active burghs, such as Puebla de Gozón (Luanco), where fishermen hailing from Santander and Castro Urdiales, or Ribadesella, would operate. These centres formed leagues with other towns on the seaboard, such as San Vicente de la Barquera, Santander, Laredo, Castro Urdiales and Llanes, to sail together to the coasts of Finisterre in search of salt and wine from the Galician ports of Noya and Muros.[17]

15 Ferreira Priegue, 'Galicia en la Marisma de Castilla', pp. 177–178. Preserved tax data regarding customs and maritime levies in Asturias, which are directly proportional to the volume of marketable goods, confirms the hypothesis of the author. Following a first overall analysis, we have endeavoured to articulate the Asturian port hierarchy by analysing the modest traffic and the result we obtain is that of Llanes in first place, outperforming Villaviciosa, Gijón and Avilés, in the year 1494. María Álvarez Fernández, 'De alcabalas y arrendadores. La contribución de concejos y parroquias asturianas a la hacienda regia en 1494', *Cuadernos de Estudios Gallegos*, 129 (2016), 205–242.

16 Juan Ignacio Ruiz de la Peña Solar, 'Noticia de Tazones y de otros puertos balleneros de la costa asturiana (siglos XIII–XIV)', in *J. I. Ruiz de la Peña Solar*, ed. Beltrán Suárez and Álvarez Fernández, pp. 131–144.

17 In 1255, fishermen of Santander and Castro Urdiales and *of other places* appeared in the waters of the Asturian fishery (AMSP, FSV, no. 1217). The fact that the powerful monastery of Saint Vincent in Oviedo held the rights of passage for the fish leaving Luanco and the ownership of several towns – Nembro, Salines, Lloreda, Bárcena – does not diminish the relevance of the ports. All edited and available documents for this monastery are in María Josefa Sanz Fuentes and Juan Ignacio Ruiz de la Peña Solar, *Colección diplomática del Monasterio de San Vicente de Oviedo, 1201–1230* (Oviedo, 1991); Celia Álvarez Arias, *Documentos orixinales del monasteriu de San Vicente d'Uvieu (1231–1238)* (Oviedo, 2008); Andrea María Miranda Duque and Celia Álvarez Arias, *Documentos orixinales del*

Ports and Fisheries: Characteristic Traits of Port Infrastructure

In 1634, Pedro Texeira, the Portuguese cartographer, was commissioned by King Felipe IV to draw the *Descripción de España y de las costas y puertos de sus reinos* (Description of Spain and the Coasts and Ports of Its Kingdoms), known as the *Atlas del rey Planeta*.[18] In spite of its purely military motivation, this depiction of seventeenth-century Spanish ports clearly reveals the condition of port infrastructures along the Asturian coast in those years and allows us to draw very valuable information for determining the image of these structures during medieval centuries.

Meanwhile, we have scant documentary evidence regarding port infrastructures prior to the second half of the fifteenth century, either for Asturian coastal towns or for any others on the Cantabrian Atlantic strip, and this prevents our ascertaining the physical characteristics of the sites where inbound goods were held and stored, regardless of their size. The devastating action of the sea must have caused frequent damage to these precarious structures, and the tasks of building and maintenance became a heavy burden for councils and confraternities, in both financial and human terms.[19]

Furnishing the berthing of vessels and streamlining the loading and unloading of goods drove local councils to insist on building structures that would be less vulnerable than timber quays, and to opt for consolidated structures, preferably in stone. In some cases the topography facilitated the work of the councils, providing freely what others had to invest heavily in building. In Galicia, for example, with a coast favoured by natural conditions, simple boats sufficed to fish along the beaches and estuaries and from simple bridges built at the mouth of the estuaries, as well as for transport and commerce. This is well proven by

monasteriu de San Vicente d'Uvieu (1239–1250) (Oviedo, 2012). All accounts regarding Ribadesella come from the AGS and allude to both the signing of agreements with other Cantabrian ports (AGS, RGS, enero 1491, fol. 498) and the traffic of illegal coinage to Ireland from Ribadesella (AGS, RGS, noviembre 1499, fol. 34; AGS, RGS, abril 1500, fol. 43; AGS, RGS, julio 1500, fol. 293, etc.).

18 *El atlas del Rey Planeta. La 'descripción de España y de las costas y puertos de sus reinos' de Pedro Texeira, 1634*, ed. Felipe Pereda and Fernando Marías (Hondarribia, 2002).

19 Of particular interest is the study by Beatriz Arízaga Bolumburu and Jesús Ángel Solórzano Telechea, 'La construction d'infrastructures portuaires dans les villes du nord de la Péninsule Ibérique à la fin du Moyen Âge', in *Ports et littoraux de l'Europe Atlantique. Transformations naturelles aménagements humains (XIVe–VIe siècles)*, ed. Michel Bochaca and Jean-Luc Sarrazin (Rennes, 2007), pp. 121–140; and Beatriz Arízaga Bolumburu and Michel Bochaca, 'Caractères généraux des villes portuaires du littoral castillan nord-peninsulaire au Moyen Âge', in *Ports maritimes et ports fluviaux au Moyen Âge* (Paris, 2005), pp. 63–78.

the examples of Vivero, Santa Marta de Ortigueira, Betanzos and Noya.[20] In Asturias, the influence of the estuaries was decisive (figure 3.1).

In the Asturian case, each port was a 'world of its own' that managed to adapt its infrastructure to the needs of commercial traffic. In most cases this was the result of improvised interventions rather than long-term planning.[21] In spite its limitations the Asturian port network was able to respond to local needs by virtue of autonomous, resolute, and tremendously effective operations in simple landing spots formed by docks, quays, warehouses, dockyards and toll houses.[22]

The Asturian fleet was mostly artisanal – employing angles, cords, hooks, or nets – with the humble fisheries becoming points of convergence for fishermen and mariners. As is well known, the type of vessels used depended on the distance of fisheries from the coastline, and the gear used depended on both the type of fleet and the distance. Although the organisation of fishing in Asturias was distinctive given its irregularity, it seems undisputable that traditional fishing and shellfish harvesting concentrated most of the activity of coastal fisheries with direct access to the sea and markets on the docks that facilitated the fiscal oversight of these activities. This simplicity in the organisation of fishing activities might explain the later building of large port infrastructures to channel

20 Solely La Coruña and Pontevedra invested significant resources in the construction of masonry port infrastructures. Cf. María Dolores Barral Rivadulla, *La Coruña en los siglos XIII al XV: historia y configuración urbana de una villa de realengo en la Galicia medieval* (La Coruña, 1998); and Armas Castro, *Pontevedra en los siglos XII a XV*, pp. 58–68.

21 Many Asturian towns were forced to expand, surprised by the unpredictable growth of commercial transactions. We can recall the council discussion that took place in Ribadesella on the need to immediately build a dock 'in stone and mortar', defrayed by the inhabitants through the imposition of a levy amounting to 800,000 maravedis. Margarita Cuartas Rivero, *Oviedo y el Principado de Asturias a fines de la Edad Media* (Oviedo, 1983), p. 123 and pp. 140–141.

22 The first references to the dock of San Sebastián date to 1318, though it took almost a century for the town to conclude it. There are also accounts from Motrico from the thirteenth century, and a second phase of extension of the port in the sixteenth century. In the case of Guetaria and Renteria, they requested a licence from the Crown for the construction of a dock in 1479 and 1495, respectively. This work was carried well into the sixteenth century. A first large port buit in stone, in Bilbao, is found in the accounts from 1402 onwards, as well as the existence of two new docks in 1463. See Arízaga Bolumburu and Solórzano Telechea 'La construction d'infrastructures portuaires dans les villes du nord', pp. 135–140. For analysis of the port of Bilbao, see Beatriz Arízaga Bolumburu and Sergio Martínez Martínez, *Atlas de villas medievales de Vasconia. Bizcaya* (San Sebastián, 2006), pp. 66–70. In the Cantabrian case, Santander would be an exception, with a port infrastructure of moderately significant size, two quays and a shipyard, documented since 1396: Miguel Ángel Aramburu Zabala and Begoña Alonso Ruiz, *Santander: un puerto para el Renacimiento* (Santander, 1994), pp. 53–57. We follow here the information gathered in Álvarez Carvallo, 'Arquitectura y ciudad'.

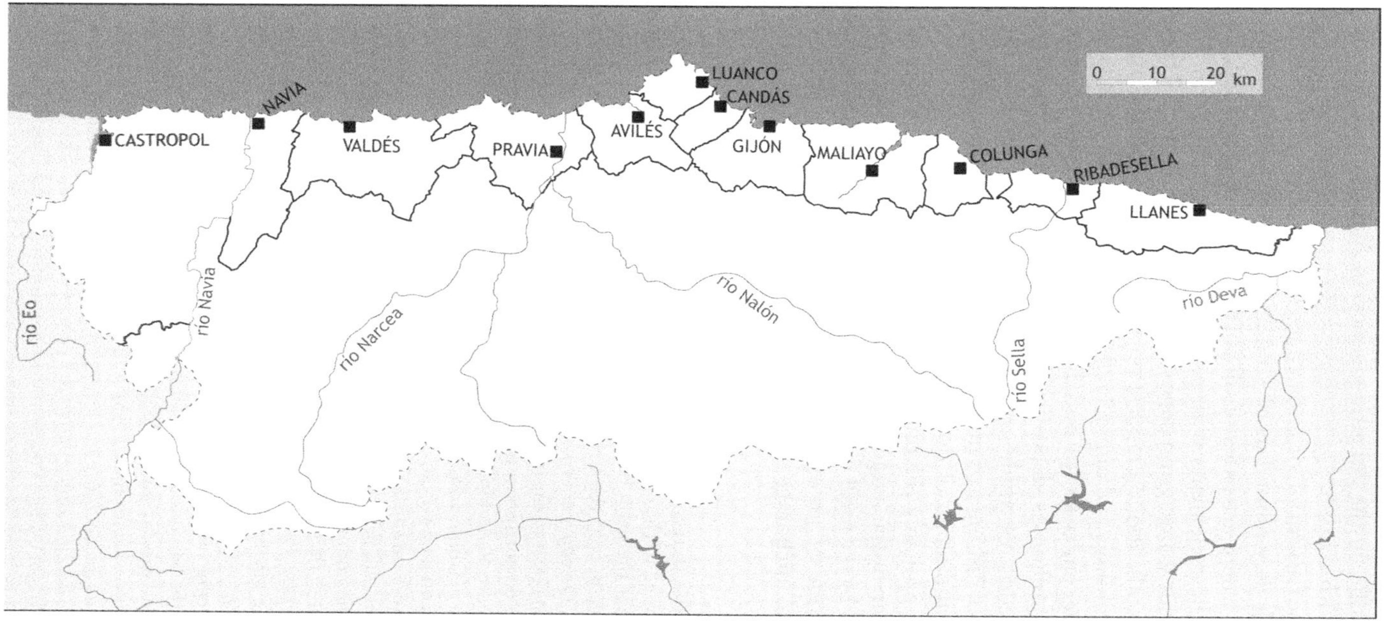

Figure 3.1. Estuaries and port towns with their jurisdictional spaces

mercantile traffic 'in the Atlantic manner' in Asturias, which took place well into the fifteenth century.[23]

Much to the frustration of researchers, sources offer only a handful of terms that, although they remind us of strategic points of contact between the sea and the land where activities of all sorts must have coincided, do not allow us to define these elements with precision: *officinae salinarum*, *piscationes*, warehouses, salt stores, grain deposits, docks, weights, etc. All these are vague terms used to talk about a modest port infrastructure, consisting of a limited number of buildings and annex facilities for the storage of nets, provisioning and victualling; embarkation and disembarkation sites for persons and wares; fishermen's warehouses; deposits; and even, in some cases, naval construction. These infrastructures would crystallise over time as a result of the increasing organisation of fishing activities and the support of the regal licences for the construction and repair of docks.[24]

Avilés was probably the only Asturian town with a significant port infrastructure driven by the burgeoning commerce from the twelfth century onward and animated by the regal fiscal exemptions.[25] If we consider the Avilés estuary as the backbone of an estuarine marshland, the bay must have enjoyed a relatively large anchorage space, with sufficient depth for mooring.[26] Fishing

23 Well into the sixteenth century, we find a rise in construction licences and fiscal exemptions granted to the councils by the Crown for the execution of building work – let us not forget that the main beneficiary of the increase and improvement in commercial transactions was, in fact, the Crown – or the authorisation to exact extraordinary levies. Cuartas Rivero, *Oviedo y el Principado de Asturias*, p. 123.

24 No mentions exist to the markets in Asturias, and the first references to the building of quays and docks do not appear until the mid-sixteenth century. Cf. the excellent monograph by Laura Sampedro Redondo, *Sobre el cay. Libro 2°. Libro de Actas del Ayuntamiento de Gijón, 1560–1577* (Gijón, 2005).

25 The exponential growth in commercial traffic of the town of Avilés is verified from the late twelfth century onwards. This commercial and mercantile wealth, closely linked to the granary of Avilés, will provide the Crown with handsome profits: in 1429, the King's revenue on salt from Avilés amounted to 174,300 maravedis, a considerable amount that will justify the regal interest in the development of the town's port. Miguel Ángel Ladero Quesada, *El siglo XV en Castilla. Fuentes de renta y política fiscal* (Barcelona, 1982), p. 56.

26 In 1488, the inhabitants of Avilés protested before the Catholic Monarchs: '*se cierra la barra y canal por donde las dichas naos han de venir a entrar en la dicha villa a cabsa de un cay que de tiempo inmemorial tenían el cuál diz que se les ha desbaratado e derrocado*' ('the closure of the bar and channel through which said *naos* arrived to said town by virtue of a quay that had existed since time immemorial which is now derelict and ruined'). A bar that was apparently safe for the entry of ships and which at that time was derelict and ruined '*por no tener agua que les baste por estar cerrado de arena*' ('for lack of sufficient water due to silting'), in *Colección diplomática del concejo de Avilés, 1155–1498*, ed. María Josefa Sanz Fuentes, Miguel Calleja Puerta and José Antonio Álvarez Castrillón (Oviedo, 2011), p. 496. Over a century later, Martín de Iturrioz, resident of Saint Jean de Luz (France), granted

ships and small boats for inshore fishing, pinnaces, cogs and larger vessels shared a confined space where the existence of a quay by the town wall is documented since at least 1488.[27]

Although it must have been common usage to sell fish on the pier itself, 'at the water mouth', council authorities strove to limit the trading of goods to the dock and quay of the town [*la plaza del cai*], a relatively ample space where the discharge, sale and salting of fish would take place in the late Middle Ages. In 1488 the town initiated the construction of a quay for the discharge of wares by the gate known as the Seagate, which took several years to complete and required the regal grant of a special tax collection amounting to 280,000 maravedis.[28]

Further down the port hierarchy, Gijón, Candás, Villaviciosa, Llanes and Castropol probably boasted little more than modest infrastructures catering for local needs during the Middle Ages. In the early twelfth century, the chronicle of Rodrigo Ximénez de Rada describes Gijón as a deserted *civitas*, a patent expression of the low economic vitality of the town.[29] Archival sources preserved for the eleventh and twelfth centuries clearly describe a distinctly rural society where wealth was based on the ownership of land, with practically non-existent commercial circulation and monetary exchanges. Little is known of medieval Gijón, of its morphology and urban life, constrained by the old Roman wall of *Gigia*. The fishing character of Gijón is defined by physical space: a hill connected to the sea by a tongue of sand, and two bays that from early on determined the predominant economic activity. The fish quarter or '*barrio de las pescaderías*', La Barquera, the Casa de las Ballenas, and the seamen's guild are the best examples of how the population managed to draw maximum

a letter of attorney to Pedro Bertin, a French resident of Avilés, with the commission of finding the remains of his ship *La María*, '*que se perdió a la barra de esta villa*' ('lost in the bar of this town') having run aground due to lack of sufficient water. Néstor Vigil Montes, *La villa de Avilés en 1602. Estudio del protocolo notarial de Julián de Valdés León* (Oviedo, 2011), pp. 185–187.

27 Ruiz de la Peña Solar, 'Funciones y paisajes urbanos', pp. 699–704 and p. 731.

28 *Colección diplomática del concejo de Avilés*, *passim*, pp. 495–497. The main purpose of the commercial centralisation was purely to facilitate taxation. Buyers and sellers participated in the discharge of fish, both fresh and preserved, leasing baskets from the town council to transport the goods to the urban market. These were probably the same as those found in the food market of Oviedo during the weekly market, whose placement near the meat stalls caused constant conflict between local merchants. Analysed in María Álvarez Fernández, *Oviedo a fines de la Edad Media. Morfología urbana y política concejil* (Oviedo, 2009), pp. 318–336. Also, Juan Uría Ríu, 'Oviedo y Avilés en el comercio atlántico de la Edad Media (siglos XIII al XVI)', *Boletín del Real Instituto de Estudios Asturianos*, 62 (1967), 199–250.

29 Gaspar Fernández Cuesta (ed.), *Vrbe II. La construcción histórica de la ciudad de Gijón* (Oviedo, 2015). We analyse the medieval chapter of the town on p. 32. The full edition is available online: <www.Gijón.es/publicacions/show/7800-vrbe-ii-la-construccion-historica-de-la-ciudad-de-Gijón> [accessed 30 April 2020.]

benefits from the sea: fisheries, salting factories, whale hunting and, later, some wine trade.[30]

From its small anchorage, Gijón initiated its modernisation process as late as the sixteenth century, by virtue of the building of a port to solve the unworkability of the harbour for the discharge of vessels arriving from Portugal, Andalusia and Ireland.[31] Still, with a whale slaughterhouse documented from as early as the thirteenth century, it was not until the sixteenth century that the first information regarding the building of a dock in Candás comes to light.[32]

Founded in 1270, Villaviciosa monopolised the trading of substantial agricultural and livestock produce, and the port activity of the whaling port of Tazones, where a significant fishing and trading activity developed.[33] The port system of the estuary, stretching a little over 10 kilometres, connected Tazones with head of the estuary, the town of Maliayo, with the small anchorage of El Puntal between both. Unlikely as it might seem today, the estuary's depth and navigability were quite different in the past, as manifested by testimonies of deep-draft vessels – *naos*, caravels – navigating these waters in the late Middle Ages. Let us not forget that the difficult landing of Charles of Ghent in 1517 took place at this point, and that his visit brought a full retinue worthy of the regal figure they escorted.[34]

The minute beach of Tazones, formed by the inlet formed on the left bank of the estuary of Villaviciosa, is a space with an intense Roman flavour, where we can envision the existence of a *stationem* port later to become the port of Tazones in the medieval era.[35] We know little of this secluded Asturian port: it must have originated as a very small pier that was later to grow in importance, reaching its apogee in the late seventeenth century. In 1571, the fishermen of Tazones demanded the building of a quay, a demand to be aborted by the

30 Claim presented before the Council of Castile by the master of a *nao* from Gijón that was attacked in the Galician port of Megia by Basque mariners, who had stolen four wineskins with wine from Ribadavia, with an approximate value of 13,000 maravedis. AGS, RGS, marzo 1498, fol. 376.

31 For the analysis of the dock of Gijón, see Luis Adaro Ruiz, *El puerto de Gijón y otros puertos asturianos* (Gijón, 1976), pp. 41–47.

32 Pilar García Cuetos has brought to light the construction efforts undertaken in this town by Juan de Cerecedo, *el Viejo*, who renovated the structure around 1550. Following his death, his nephew, Cerecedo *el Mozo*, continued the enterprise, concluding the project and demanding payment by the town council of the debt owed to his family. Pilar García Cuetos, *Arquitectura en Asturias (1500–1580). La dinastía de los Cerecedo* (Oviedo, 1996), pp. 188–189 and 202.

33 Solano Fernández-Sordo, *De Maliayo a Villaviciosa*.

34 María Álvarez Fernández (ed.), *Quinientos años después. Villaviciosa: 1517–2017. La época en que D. Carlos vino a Asturias* (Oviedo, 2019).

35 Solano Fernández-Sordo, *De Maliayo a Villaviciosa*, pp. 550–556.

neighbouring town of Villaviciosa for fear of potential competition.[36] It is difficult to imagine how this new infrastructure could represent a serious threat to the estuarine transit of Villaviciosa, the final port on the estuary. In any case, it was not until the late nineteenth century that Tazones was declared a 'second order port' and the construction of the port was initiated.[37] Between Tazones and Villaviciosa, we find the landing place of El Puntal, a privileged point given its excellent natural conditions.[38] Upstream, in Villaviciosa, and very near the bridge of Buetes, there must also have been a small dock harbouring little boats to disembark wares from the larger vessels anchored in Tazones and El Puntal.[39]

Ribadesella was also a port of a certain importance. It is defined as a *French port* in several early sixteenth-century documents, which gives a clear indication of the presence of foreign vessels. The commercial success of the town can be deduced from the various petitions of the town council to the Catholic Monarchs, such as the one in 1486 requesting the imposition of a tax on wine trade to fund the building of the parish church (Santa María del Puerto), a hospital for pilgrims (San Sebastián), and the repair of roads and lanes, since the town was a place of many necessary, useful and profitable transactions, and received many foreign pilgrims.[40] We have no evidence of the physical appearance of its port infrastructure, but it is quite probable that the hostilities between Castile and France in the early decades of the sixteenth century meant these enclaves were, in most cases, fortified.[41]

Port development of Llanes was also late to flourish, although, from the granting of town charters by Alfonso IX in 1225, this coastal burgh displayed a vitality and dynamism closely linked to its commercial activity, superior at times to that of Villaviciosa and Avilés. Thus, it was only a matter of time before this marked increase in commercial activity was followed by improvements in the infrastructure of the port to streamline and facilitate its activities, but all

36 Gonzalo Anes Álvarez de Castrillón, *Economía y sociedad en la Asturias del Antiguo Régimen* (Barcelona, 1988), p. 125.

37 A century later, the fishermen of Tazones reiterated this petition, to a different location, the *Punta o Piedra del Cay*. Solano Fernández-Sordo, *De Maliayo a Villaviciosa*, p. 626 *et passim*.

38 The present-day marina has no resemblance to the probable configuration of the port during the Middle Ages. The depth of the port has also changed, as it had the capacity to furnish anchorage to *naos* arriving from Ireland in the mid-sixteenth century. Solano Fernández-Sordo, *De Maliayo a Villaviciosa*, *passim*.

39 *Ibid.*

40 AGS, RGS, febrero 1486, fol. 128.

41 By royal decree of the Catholic Monarchs, the councils of Gozón, Carreño, Villaviciosa, Colunga, Ribadesella and Llanes went on to fortify their ports and arm their merchant vessels. Ciriaco Miguel Vigil, *Asturias monumental, epigráfica y diplomática* (Oviedo, 1887), p. 243.

evidence indicates that the physical conditions of the Llanes coastline did not assist in this enterprise.[42]

A perilous entrance, high mountains, a chasm of hell with large waves roaring impetuously, horrible and frightening to see and hear, a rough sea, steep and dangerous, broken, split and sunken ships. This was how the port of Llanes appeared to the chronicler Laurent Vital in 1517.[43] The first source referring to the building of the dock and quay in Llanes would not appear until 1552, when the king authorised a tax to be levied on imported goods for a total value of 3,000 gold ducats; another source, three years later, documents the appointment of a master of the quay warden and the building of a dock.[44] Despite the repeated references of the Fleming to the destruction of ships, we know nothing of the possible existence of shipyards in Llanes for the building and repair of vessels, or of any possible facilities related to this activity. In the late Middle Ages, Llanes had a 'house of whales', with moulting ovens and all the necessary instruments for the production of whale oil, near the Tazones inlet.[45] The formidable Book of Accounts of the town, with the financial accounts of the late sixteenth century, reveals the magnitude of the initiative, which must have absorbed all the financial and human resources of the small maritime town, and which was to continue well into the seventeenth century.[46]

In the westernmost corner of Asturias, the extensive and rich episcopal lands of Ribadeo incorporated from 1299 an important port hub on the Eo estuary, the natural border with Galicia, and were beneficiary, from early on, of the activity deployed by the *extraneis navibus negociatorum* that had visited Asturian coasts since the previous century.[47] The rights of usage of the estuary produced juicy profits but also numerous conflicts between the burghs on either side: Ribadeo and Roboredo, and later, Castropol.[48]

42 As can be surmised from the description of Llanes by Laurent Vital, chronicler of King Charles V and a direct witness of the fortuitous regal landing. Laurent Vital, *Primer viaje a España de Carlos I con su desembarco en Asturias* (Oviedo, 1992), pp. 178–180.

43 *Ibid.*

44 Álvarez Carvallo, 'Arquitectura y ciudad', from p. 404. The author provides a detailed analysis of the building process initiated in 1555 in addition to the conditions agreed between the town and the architect, the Guipuzcoan, Pedro de Ornieta.

45 *Ibid.*

46 *Ibid.*

47 Santos García Larragueta, *Colección de documentos de la Catedral de Oviedo* (Oviedo, 1962), no. 120.

48 Of particular interest are the conflicts deriving from the nocturnal traffic by the fishermen of Castropol in the Eo estuary, clandestinely transporting their merchandise to Ribadeo. This illicit custom, penalised by the local municipal ordinances of 1376 and 1381, is analysed in Juan Ignacio Ruiz de la Peña Solar, 'Conflictos interlocales por el control de los espacios económicos privilegiados: el ejemplo asturgalaico de las pueblas de Ribadeo y Roboredo (1282)', *Boletín del Instituto de Estudios Asturianos*, 138 (1991), 559–588. There

Despite the splendid local testimonies preserved from the fourteenth century, with highly detailed information of local life, neither the municipal ordinances (1376, 1381), the commercial privileges liberating loading and discharge in the port of Castropol (1386), nor the extant books of taxes and municipal surveys allows us to make a logical reconstruction of the Asturian port area of the Eo estuary. It must have been of a considerable size considering the population involved in maritime activities. Albeit much later, response number thirty-seven of the Survey of the Marquis de la Ensenada (1749–1750) records twenty-four mariners in the town, noting also that there were two ships – of 15 and 20 tuns, respectively – and three barges.[49]

Extant municipal regulations preserved in Castropol certify the taxation on imported goods in the town market – bread, wine, lard – and the formal prohibition, in 1371, of 'clandestine' trade, except for timber, in the ports of La Linera, San Roman, Tapia and Santa Gadea, small adjacent harbours that were to play a significant role in both fish and timber trades.[50] Municipal statutes of 1381 add significant information regarding clandestine trade and contraband, so characteristic of these small enclaves, that escaped urban tax policies and aspired to circumvent feudal levies by disembarking in minor or unguarded inlets and landing the merchandise in smaller vessels or by land.[51]

The Sea as an Opportunity: Men of the Sea and the Handling of Cargo

It would be wrong to assume that port spaces were enclaves frequented exclusively by mariners, whalers, merchants, fishermen, boatmen and shipmasters. Many other occupations related to the sea and maritime tasks were also present in these minute docks, where their services was very necessary: granary owners,

are also frequent documentary references to the clandestine discharge of salt in the ports of Gijón, Cudillero and Pravia, circumventing the duly authorised regal granaries. Isabel González García, Juan Ignacio Ruiz de la Peña Solar 'La economía salinera en la Asturias medieval', *Asturiensia medievalia*, 1 (1972), 11–89.

49 José Luis Pérez de Castro, 'El concejo de Castropol según el catastro de Ensenada', *Archivum: Revista de la Facultad de Filología*, 26 (1976), 261–281, at p. 279.

50 Ruiz de la Peña Solar, *Las polas asturianas en la Edad Media*, *passim*, p. 410. Also, the overall description of the Eo basin by José Antonio Álvarez Castrillón, 'Aproximación histórica a la cuenca del Eo: desde los primeros testimonios a la época medieval', in *En torno al bimilenario del Eo* (Oviedo, 2002), pp. 405–438. In this region, forestry and shipbuilding are still prominent. Joaquín Ocampo Suárez-Valdés, Patricia Suárez Cano and Esteban García Canal, *El caso Astilleros Gondán* (Gijón, 2018).

51 We find a documented complaint, the same year, by Gutierre de Toledo, Bishop of Oviedo and town lord, regarding this fraudulent practice. Ruiz de la Peña Solar, *Las polas asturianas en la Edad Media*, *passim*, p. 410.

sail makers, carpenters, watchmen, tavern keepers, men in charge of the lights on the port mouth or of loading and unloading fish onto boats or the dock for direct sale, muleteers, fish salters, rope makers, blacksmiths, caulkers. All these were men 'of the sea' composing the social landscape of Asturian ports in the late Middle Ages, organising port labour and later protecting their professional interests.[52]

The precious testimony of what could be the first documentary reference in Asturias to stevedoring tasks as salaried occupations is dated 1320. That year, the councils of Oviedo and Avilés agreed that merchants of the former were to assist in the unloading of wine in exchange for merchants of Avilés refraining from intercepting goods en route to the market of Oviedo.[53]

In Asturias, the defence of trade mutualism did not foster the development of supralocal organisations, with the action of their community of interests remaining, at most, within the limits of the confraternities. Contrary to the case of Basque ports, there were no merchant guilds in Asturias and the general tone of the relations between Asturian ports was one of local 'rivalry' and the protection of their privilege against foreign merchants, striving to attract as much traffic as possible to their ports.[54]

Asturian port spaces were directly controlled by urban councils and, in some specific cases, such as Llanes and Luarca, by seamen confraternities.[55] Wherever they existed, these associations channelled all productive sectors involved in maritime activities: merchants, shipowners, mariners, masters and fishermen, in both fishing and commercial activities. A thorough regulation of the institutional organisation of the corporations is revealed in the guild ordinances that regulated the sea trade between Llanes and Luarca, which include in their clauses the rules on admission to the confraternity, the appointment of leaders, the operative regime of the association and its spheres of competence, the regulation of fishing seasons – which varied depending on the marine species – the artefacts employed, the maintenance of ports and ships, risk prevention and associated safety measures, the distribution of profits, the conditions for

52 Jesús Ángel Solórzano Telechea, Michel Bochaca and Amélia Aguiar Andrade (eds), *Gentes de mar en la ciudad atlántica medieval* (Logroño, 2012).

53 *Colección diplomática del concejo de Avilés*, *passim*, pp. 291–294.

54 An overall study in Juan Ignacio Ruiz de la Peña Solar, 'Solidaridades profesionales en las ciudades de la Corona de Castilla. Las cofradías de mareantes', in *J. I. Ruiz de la Peña Solar*, ed. Beltrán Suárez and Álvarez Fernández, pp. 363–383.

55 Of general consensus is the medieval origin of the guild associations of Ribadesella, Lastres, Gijón, Avilés, Cudillero and Luarca: Ruiz de la Peña Solar, *Las polas asturianas*, *passim*, pp. 252–255. For the ordinances of the guild of seamen of Luarca, see María Jesús Suárez Álvarez, 'El nobilísimo gremio de mareantes de Luarca. Ordenanzas del Novilísimo Gremio de mareantes y navegantes fijosdalgos de la villa y puerto de Luarca y Tierra de Valdés, del año 1468', *Asturiensia Medievalia*, 2 (1975), 239–258.

the sale of the produce, sanctions, and welfare actions provided to members, disabled, destitute or ageing mariners, widows and orphans.[56]

The Llanes confraternity of fishermen, mariners, shipowners and merchants of Saint Nicholas enjoyed the regulation and protection of their professional interests related to maritime activities from the approval of their Ordinances by the Catholic Monarchs in April 1480.[57] And, as occurred in San Sebastián, where the powerful confraternity of Saint Peter funded the construction of a lighthouse to aid ships entering the port, it is very probable that in Llanes the confraternity of Saint Nicholas contributed to the cost of building the quay, though the want of documentary evidence for that date prevents us from confirming this.[58]

These associations are a clear sign of the burgeoning maritime activity of the towns where they were established, as we can see in the case of the port of Tazones. Of unknown but probably later date, the guild of seamen of Tazones – documented for the first time in the General Responses to the Survey of 1753, but undoubtedly predating it – was constituted principally, though not solely, to protect the right and collection of the impost on baskets to carry fish, which was set at 300 *reales* per year.[59] Very possibly, the confraternity of Tazones was contemporary with the seamen's confraternity of Saint Catherine of Gijón and the 'Very Noble Guild of Seamen and Fishermen of Luarca', whose ordinances provide a faithful testimony of the organisation of port labour.[60] The guild was of disputed authenticity until recently, but a precious contract of 1477 establishing the birth of a trading company in Luarca confirms the existence of said guild's regulations: on 4 March 1477, a crew of twenty-nine mariners of the guild and of seamen and navigators of Luarca entered into agreement with a Domingo Rochel, '*maestre de mar e dueño de la nao Virxen Branca*', to enrol in a '*campaña de pescaria mayor en mar lontana para la caza de ballenas e pescaria de pixotas e besugos en el mar de Yngalaterra e Flandres e mas allá si a de menester*'.[61] The contract strictly follows the habitual regulations of the

56 Ernesto García Fernández, 'Las cofradías de mercaderes, mareantes y pescadores vascas en la Edad Media', in *Ciudades y villas portuarias*, ed. Arízaga Bolumburu and Solórzano Telechea, pp. 257–294.

57 We follow the conclusions of Álvarez Carballo from the study on the town of Llanes in the late Middle Age, 'Arquitectura y ciudad', *passim*, pp. 424–432.

58 García Fernández, 'Las cofradías de mercaderes', pp. 271–276.

59 Solano Fernández-Sordo, *De Maliayo a Villaviciosa*, *passim*.

60 Luciano Castañón, 'El gremio de mareantes de Gijón', *Boletín del Instituto de Estudios Asturianos*, 107 (1992), 835–858; and Eduardo Núñez Fernández, 'El gremio de mareantes de Luarca. Estado actual de la investigación en torno a esta institución valdesana', *Boletín de la Asociación Asturiana de Bibliotecarios, Archiveros, Documentalistas y Museólogos*, 16.2 (2005), 37–47.

61 'shipmaster and owner of the *nao* Virxen Branca'; 'campaign of deep-sea fishing in distant seas for the hunting of whales, fishing of cod and sea bream in the seas of England and Flanders and beyond if necessary'.

guild, which are included in the document, addressing both the distribution of profits and the responsibilities of each participant in the venture.[62]

Conclusions

In the late twelfth century, Roger de Howden, an erudite English diplomat, compiled a magnificent maritime itinerary that provides us with a fascinating image of the whole Cantabrian coastline.[63] The itinerary, starting in York and sailing along the eastern coast of England to Dartmouth, crossing the English Channel to the Île-de-Batz and continuing south, describes Asturian ports thus:

> Deinde in terra regis de Sancto Iacobo non longe a montibus de Sore est bonus portus qui dicitur Melias. Deinde est portus qui dicitur Giguin – Gijón – sed non est bonus portus, et ibi est mons magnus qui similiter dicitur Giguin. Deinde in terra eiusdem regis est portus et uilla qui dicuntur Abilis – Avilés – et est ibi castellum quod dicitur Gozsun, sed non est ibi bonus portus nisi pro necessitate et cum mare ex maiori parte fuerit ascensum. Et ibi sunt montes qui dicuntur Bumais et tota prouincia illa dicitur Bumais. Et inter Gozsun – Gozón – et Sanctum Saluatorem quem dicunt locum sanctum et requisitum a peregrinis, sunt V leuce. Deinde in terra eiusdem regis est bona anchoratio que dicitur Artede – Artedo – et illa anchoratio est sub castello quod dicitur Caprafiga. Deinde in terra eiusdem regis est portus et burgus bonus qui dicitur Ribadure – Ribadeo – et est portus ille bonus et profundus et bonus ad capiendum, sed melior a sinistra parte.[64]

The chronicle, written in the atmosphere of the *Historia Compostelana*, offers a detailed account of the perception foreigners had of the Asturian coast in the mid-twelfth century, a coast whose limited ports – '*non est ibi bonus portus nisi pro necessitate*' – cannot compare, in the chronicler's opinion, with the neighbouring Galician port of Ribadeo, which he describes as '*portus et burgus bonus*'.

62 This precious contract is edited and analysed in María Soledad Beltrán Suárez, *Marineros de Luarca a la caza de la ballena. El primer contrato conocido, 1477* (Luarca, 2019). We wish to thank the author for granting us access to the conclusions of the study and permission to include the information in this article.

63 Patrick Gautier Dalché, *Du Yorkshire a l'Inde. Une géographie urbaine et maritime de la fin du XIIe siècle (Roger de Howden)* (Geneva, 2005). An analysis of Basque ports through this chronicle in Íñigo Ruiz Arzálluz, 'Vasconia en el siglo XII. Roger de Howden, el De viis maris y la extensión del Vizcondado de Bayona', *Anuario del Seminario de Filología vasca 'Julio de Urquijo'*, LII:1–2 (2018), 697–712.

64 Gautier Dalché, *Du Yorkshire a l'Inde*, p. 184.

Setting aside the analysis of other equally intriguing topics that have been but cursorily discussed in this study, we can draw certain conclusions to sum up this necessarily brief and provisional work. In the first place, from the impressions provided by coetaneous chroniclers of Asturian ports and from the preserved accounts, we can well conclude the modesty of Asturian and Galician port structures in the Cantabrian coast as a whole, except for the specific cases of Ferrol, Pontevedra and Avilés. These port nuclei were minor microcosms striving for survival through fishing activities. Second, and directly related to their limitations, these ports had a simple infrastructure more in keeping with small berths and fisheries than with the large and middling ports of the European Atlantic. Last, this discreet economic activity was mirrored in the modest trade associations that the people of the sea established in their places of origin. Of course, this last statement does not contradict the fact that those 'harvesters of the sea' activated local economies through a common effort that even today strengthens the very evident bonds of solidarity in Galician and Asturian maritime communities.

4

Slave Trade and Northern Portuguese Seaport Operations in the Sixteenth Century

AMÂNDIO J. M. BARROS

Escola Superior de Educação do Politécnico do Porto – CITCEM

ABSTRACT. This chapter aims to identify and analyse the logistics of slave trade from the northern Portuguese seaports in the early modern period. This is a generally unknown topic in Portuguese and European historiographies, which for a long time focused exclusively on the major ports such as Lisbon or Seville. However, when looking at the early modern port traffic on the northern Portuguese coast, the slave trade was one of the main ventures of commercial and mercantile agents and triggered new and potent port dynamics. Analysis of a set of ships chartered from Porto, Viana and Vila do Conde, and numerous mercantile contracts between merchants and ship-owners – from the mid-sixteenth century onwards – allows us to identify the operative logistics and the participants in this complex process. From cargo handling to the fitting of the ships, and from mercantile societies to financial investments, we can uncover a complex and widely spread practice related to the slave trade in these Portuguese seaports, proving that the slave trade depended on many more agents and connections than those studied hitherto by historians.

On 8 February 1526, after a troubled six-month voyage, the ship *Conceição* arrived in São Tomé. On board, in deplorable conditions, it carried 466 slaves bought on behalf of the island's contractors in the Kingdom of Congo. En route, eighty-nine were buried at sea, victims of illness, hunger, accidents and the ultimate and desperate means to avoid captivity: suicide.[1]

In a less dramatic tone, this chapter deals with the same topic: the Atlantic Slave Trade. I will analyse a slightly later chronology, the second half of the

1 Amândio Barros, 'Trato de escravos e economia atlântica. O contrato do navio Conceição', in *Trabalho Forçado Africano. Articulações com o poder político* (Porto, 2007), pp. 15–46.

sixteenth century, and approach the subject from a different perspective: the ports of northern Portugal and their participation in this business, one of the most conspicuous in the history of the early modern era. The main objective is to identify, describe and analyse the slave-trade logistics mobilised by these ports.

This topic remains generally untapped in Portuguese and European historiography, which for a long time has concentrated exclusively on major ports such as Lisbon or Seville. However, when looking at port traffic of the early modern period on the northern coast of Portugal, the slave trade was one of the major business pursuits and became the driving force behind the vigorous new port dynamics.

The accumulation of wealth in early modern Europe was largely dependent on slavery. With their deep involvement in Atlantic trade, Portuguese ports were important players in the process of transferring African forced labour to the New World.[2] As the phenomenon contributed to the development of sugarcane industries and mining in the Americas, and the distribution of wealth and economic growth in Europe, it also shaped the social landscape of the Atlantic ports. This text addresses the second part of the issue: the presence of slaves in Portuguese port societies and the relations between port labour and slavery in early modern times, without neglecting, notwithstanding, the Atlantic Slave Trade mechanisms in these ports and the actors engaged in this traffic.

The examination of a set of chartered vessels from Porto, Viana and Vila do Conde, and a large set of commercial business contracts from the mid-sixteenth century, allows us to gather information on the operative dimension and the actors involved in this complex process. From cargo handling to vessel fitting, mercantile arrangements to financial investments, one can unveil the complex and widespread practices related to the transatlantic slave trade, and prove that trafficking depended on far more actors and connections than those hitherto studied by slave-trade historians.[3] In fact, historians have on most occasions approached the subject from the standpoint of the policies established by the

2 The subject is excellently addressed in Yda Schreuder, *Amsterdam's Sephardic Merchants and the Atlantic Sugar Trade in the Seventeenth Century* (New York, 2019).

3 The bibliography is vast. See, among many others, Philip D. Curtin, *The Atlantic Slave Trade* (Madison, WI, 1969); Stanley L. Engerman and Eugene D. Genovese (eds), *Race and Slavery in the Western Hemisphere* (Princeton, 1975); James A. Rawley (with Stephen D. Behrendt), *The Transatlantic Slave Trade: A History*, revised edition (Lincoln and London, 2005); Barbara Solow (ed.), *Slavery and the Rise of the Atlantic System* (Cambridge, 1991); Milton Meltzer, *Slavery: A World History* (New York, 1993); David Eltis, *The Rise of African Slavery in the Americas* (Cambridge, 2000). Some new perspectives about the subject in Toby Green, *The Rise of the Trans-Atlantic Slave Trade in Western Africa, 1300–1589* (New York, 2012); Linda A. Newson and Susie Minchin, *From Capture to Sale: The Portuguese Slave Trade to Spanish South America in the Early Seventeenth Century* (Leiden and Boston,

central powers, the legislation, and the traffic registers produced by the Crown or its contracting parties, disregarding the fact that the Atlantic projection of early modern economies was mainly driven by the action of ports and the private merchants operating therein. In my view, researchers should expand their focus to include these local processes of port development, as well as the role of the Crown and the permanent interaction between private business and government institutions, in their definitions of economic policies in the early modern period.

Part of the difficulty in doing so arises from the choice of archival sources. Until recently, books and essays produced in Portugal and abroad have been based on documentation drawn up by the Crown or central power institutions, with a predominance of institutional and administrative information, and legislation on the traffic and slave flows controlled by the contractors. So, to fully appreciate the happenings in merchants' houses and ports, we must turn to other sources – notary and municipal records – and buttress this information with that extant in foreign archives, given the international dimension of the activity of these ports from the outset of the transatlantic slave trade.

Drawing from the notary and municipal records of northern Portuguese ports, in the following pages I will elaborate on the diversified character of the slave-trade business from these ports. Most of the information revealed in this chapter has not been published before; nor has it been systematically analysed. First, this data allows us to assess the extent of the participation of each port in the traffic, which, as will be seen, reached a considerable volume at various times during the sixteenth century. Second, this participation had a significant impact on shipbuilding, with shipyards in these ports – namely in Porto – building ships destined specifically for slave transport. Finally, the magnitude of the logistics mobilised, the contacts established, the movement of people, capital, and goods across the Atlantic due to this trade remains yet to be fully assessed. Some important aspects remain open to further discussion. Perhaps the one deserving most attention, given its complexity, is the detailed analysis of the composition, solidarity mechanisms, and scope of the commercial networks involved; some of these elements are identified here and part of their operation will be revealed. However, the main objective of this chapter is to discuss ports and the involvement of their ships, in an attempt to understand their part in the transformation of the early modern world through the Atlantic Slave Trade, and the many consequences it entailed.

2007); Herbert S. Klein, *The Atlantic Slave Trade* (Cambridge, 2010). I will cite further studies throughout this text.

Port Structures and Logistics

One of the questions that we can only partially answer is whether slave trade triggered changes in the physiognomy of these ports. Did the magnitude of slavery require the introduction, modification or adaptation of infrastructures? For example, was there a place to house slaves upon their arrival at these ports, on the assumption that slaves were landed on these docks?[4] Over time, services, administrative offices and bureaucracy would populate these enclaves. But there are further matters to consider: the consolidation of the transatlantic slave trade forced merchants to become familiar with fiscal, administrative and legal procedures, to develop specialised knowledge about the procedures for obtaining licenses, and to develop postal services and information exchange networks; merchants and mercantile networks traced, surveyed and managed slave routes, were familiar with the difficulties slave trading entailed, and developed their expertise to manage their resources accordingly.

October 1590. A caravel with ninety-six slaves arrived in Porto from Bristol;[5] the ship originally transporting the slaves (a *nao*) had been captured by English privateers and taken to England, where the slaves were transferred to a caravel. That vessel entered the Douro river, on her way to call in Porto. The slaves were in as poor a condition as those carried in the ship *Conceição*, evoked in the opening of this text. The final destination was the port-city of Lisbon, but the ship was forced to remain in Porto. Surprise at the arrival of a ship loaded with such merchandise soon gave way to the usual legal procedures with customs officials demanding the payment of duties. After some time detained on board, the slaves were disembarked to continue their journey, by land, to Lisbon, given the poor condition of the ship. We have no record of how long they remained in Porto, nor where they were accommodated until they left the city. They were possibly held in the customs house itself, which had large warehouses capable of accommodating them for a short time, probably amid bales of various wares and surely in squalid conditions.

Two years later, rough seas forced the Captain Francisco Fajardo to seek refuge in this port with the ship *Assunção* when returning from Elmina, laden with gold, slaves, and civet. As in the previous case, the port authorities demanded the payment of taxes, although the ship had entered the Douro river due to unforeseeable circumstances or *force majeure* [*caso fortuito*],

4 There was not; there was only one case of ninety slaves at the end of the sixteenth century. For the rest, they would be quite reduced numbers, since these ports, in essence, were not arrival markets.

5 The story of this ship and this shipment of slaves has been a complicated one. Initially it was a *nao* from Porto/Matosinhos with these slaves, seized by English privateers, taken to Bristol and then 'exchanged' for the aforementioned caravel, offering terrible conditions to those who traveled in her. See the details of this case in Amândio Barros, *Porto. A construção de um espaço marítimo no início dos tempos modernos* (Lisbon, 2016), pp. 483–484.

since the ship's original destination was Lisbon. The lengthy court ruling on the case informs us that the ship was moored at the customs house pier [*hamcorado jumto ao cais d'Allfandegua*], but it is not clear whether the slaves were brought ashore.[6] We can confirm only that the ship was moored in the city's main wharf. This structure, the most relevant of the port, had undergone extensive expansion works some years earlier. This renovation, rather than being driven by the slave trade itself, was fostered by the overall evolution of the port's activity, which included arrivals of slaves, albeit in modest numbers since most were destined for domestic service, and only a few were sent to the city's workshops. Both port traffic and the slave traffic increased in the latter decades of the sixteenth century. In any case, the port enclave was expanded and new businesses requiring slave workforce were established. Several ship-owners and merchants – purveyors of slaves to the Portuguese and Castilian Atlantic domains – benefited from considerable investments made in port structures: Duarte Carneiro Rangel, a Porto citizen, judge [*desembargador*] and well-known slave trader, also owned warehouses, 'with porches and covers' [*com suas logeas e cobertos*], adjacent to the port, that he leased to salt and sugar traders, and which were run by slaves.[7]

The supervision of shipbuilding was another activity in which the growth of the slave trade may have had some influence. Once again, the transatlantic slave trade did not directly cause developments in this area, but it was closely related to them, particularly when it became an attractive business for important merchants who financed the construction of vessels. Such developments led to the establishment of specialists in the assessment of ship tonnage: tonnage surveyors [*arqueadores*], who were appointed officially. Although it is interesting, this topic would divert us from the core subject of this study.[8] Ship tonnage had become a matter of state in the early modern period when the king granted subsidies to shipbuilders. The amount of the subsidies depended on the tonnage of vessels and, initially, the assessment of the tonnage declared by the owner had to be certified in Lisbon.[9] Later, the major ports incorporated the *arqueadores* appointed by the Crown. This interest of ports should not

6 ADP, *Sentenças do cabido*, liv. 768, fol. 297v.

7 ADP, *Po1º*, 3rd ser., liv. 18, fol. 34.

8 It can be studied in Leonor Freire Costa, *Naus e Galeões na Ribeira de Lisboa. A construção naval no século XVI para a Rota do Cabo* (Cascais, 1997), pp. 264–270; Amélia Polónia, *Vila do Conde: um porto nortenho na expansão ultramarina quinhentista*, vol. I (Porto, 1999), pp. 368–369; Amândio Barros, *Porto: a construção de um espaço marítimo nos alvores dos tempos modernos*, vol. I (Porto, 2004), pp. 241–243. See also, for the seventeeenth century, Inês Marinho Osório, 'O transporte de escravos no Atlântico: a arqueação dos navios negreiros' (Masters diss., Universidade Nova de Lisboa, 2016) <https://run.unl.pt/handle/10362/19616> [accessed 18 February 2020].

9 For some time exclusively in this port, it should be noted that the tonnage subsidies' policy in Portugal had its origins and first regulations in the Middle Ages – at least from the fourteenth century.

surprise us, as one of the requirements of maritime traffic was the inspection and assessment of the ship to control the cargo, prevent smuggling and avoid accidents resulting from overloading. In 1584, several ships from Porto (at least four, in an unprecedented episode in the history of the northern ports' participation in the transatlantic slave trade) were chartered to Congo and Angola (and then to Brazil, where the slaves were to be sold); among them, the *nao Nossa Senhora da Batalha*,[10] whose tonnage assessment was presented in 'the certificate issued by the Royal Accounts House of Porto',[11] as in the case of the ship *Espírito Santo*.[12] On other occasions, the certificates were issued by the Royal Accounts House (*Casa dos Contos*) in Lisbon, which also issued the licences to buy the slaves. Although the issuance of these declarations would require that the ships be inspected – those newly built at the shipyard or those moored in the quays – by the Royal Accounting officer, assisted by two recognised specialists, in general, the process was, it turns out, more of a bureaucratic procedure and did not require any modifications in port structures.[13]

What do these facts entail? Although transatlantic slave-trade operations were planned and executed in this port, both by itself and in articulation with other northern Portuguese ports, only exceptionally were they ports of destination and distribution of slaves.[14] Thus, it is almost certain that the Atlantic Slave Trade did not bring about significant structural changes, except those resulting from the increase in maritime traffic, as noted above. For example, it did not require the construction of specific docks for slave landing, barges to transport them from the ships to the shore[15] or buildings to lodge them for

10 The others, the *nao Espírito Santo* and the *nao* of 'Aleixo Jorge'. ADP, *Po 1ª*, 3rd ser., liv. 74, fol. 65.

11 *Ibid.*

12 *Ibid.*, liv. 75, fol. 47.

13 Not just at the shipyard. An older ship, in order to carry out this type of function (which necessarily involved the fitting of artillery – which also was subsidised), was required to undergo this inspection.

14 In contrast to Lisbon, as seems to be evident, even from the information in the latter documents. However, we should not think that the capital city absorbed a large number of slaves. The larger contingents were to be taken elsewhere: to Seville, for example. In the case of the slaves who came from England in the aforementioned caravel, it was stated that they would be discharged (then transferred) in/to Lisbon, at the 'house of estates' ('Casa das Herdades'). Here, there is mention of the discharge at 'the contractor's house', that of João Baptista Rovelasca, also called 'the contracting house'. It is known that at least between 1582 and 1589 Rovelasca held the São Tomé slave trade contract. See Rafael Moreira and Luís de Albuquerque, *Portugal no mundo: Tentativas para uma ocupação efectiva em Africa no século XIX. A Europa e a Africa na segunda metade do século XIX. O colonialismo português na primeira metade do século* XX (Lisbon, 1989), p. 54, and Vitorino M. Godinho, *Os Descobrimentos e a economia mundial*, vol. II (Lisbon, 1981), p. 575.

15 As stated in by D. Manuel I's regulations on wages paid in ports (Lisbon was the model). ADP, *Cabido. Sentenças*, liv. 728, fol. 191. However, it should be noted that the

shorter or longer periods; at most, it may have prompted the construction or adaptation of customs houses and port buildings to temporarily house slaves who were traded in the city or were to be sold elsewhere.

There is no doubt that the slaves went through customs. Sometimes they were 'second-hand' merchandise, that is, not obtained directly in one of Africa's well-known markets – Benin, Congo or Angola – but purchased elsewhere. Seafarers bought many in Brazil, for instance from a master who no longer needed the one or two he had on board, or sold them for whatever reason. This was common in these port societies; when the *nao Jesus* was sold in the port of Rosas, near Barcelona, in 1565, two slaves serving on board were included in the bargain; at the end of the sixteenth century, two seafarers from the maritime neighbourhood of São João da Foz bought 'two little boys' in Brazil, who were then registered in the customs house.[16] Also, the crew members seized any opportunity to invest their modest capital in the purchase and sale of a few slaves as a means to increase their earnings during the voyage. Again within the sphere of maritime and port societies, throughout the notarial records we come across this type of information: everyone, from the most opulent merchants and the wealthy shipmasters, to the modest sailors and craftsmen of any kind, had slaves at home, on their ships or in their workshops.

There is hardly any further information on the presence of slaves in the daily activity of the city and ports. To be clearer: slaves were everywhere, and we know they were workers in the main cities and ports, but we lack details about their work, the proportion of slaves working in shops or crafts, their wages or working conditions. However, that same presence and the consolidation of this business forced the agents to familiarise themselves with the legal and administrative procedural frameworks – not surprisingly, the regional Customs Accounts' House of Porto, as the local representation of Crown administration and tax mechanisms, was ruled by the royal legislation approved for Lisbon.[17]

Finally, and as has been stated, the merchants and the shipowners were familiar with the Atlantic Slave Trade routes and with all the requisites of this business, which we know to have been extremely complex. Trading slaves by leasing and commissioning ships was part of a port business that became increasingly aware of the significance of the Atlantic for its trading horizons, and of the requirements for increased material and operative resources to accomplish their goals. The investments mobilised in port cities such as

---

boat service, crossing and boat leasing to assist in the handling of goods existed and was very active.

16 ADP, *Cabido. Redízima*, liv. 113, fol. 16v.

17 As an example of tax legislation on slaves: ADP, *Contadoria da Comarca do Porto*, liv. 3 (0008), Ms. 'Provisoys dos escravos pera paguarem dizyma a Sua Alteza' (1563), fol. 210; or the same year's license, 'Allvara de Sua Alteza per que mamda que se pague dyzima de todalas cousas que forem pera fora deste Reyno pelos portos sequos', *ibid.* fols 225–227.

Porto, Viana and Vila do Conde during the early modern era bear witness to this evolution.[18]

Slave Presence in Ports and Port Operations: Cargo Handling and Black Sailors

Regarding the transatlantic slave trade, further and richer data is available, particularly concerning the integration of forced labour in the northern merchant shipping ventures, as described above. The existence of slaves in ports and in ships is noted, though scarcely studied in depth, except in very rare cases.[19] As stated earlier, the regular inflow of slaves is well known, as a consequence of the maritime routes and of the merchants' operations in these ports, which led them, and their agents, to expand across the Atlantic and the existing slave markets. Slaves were present and active in early modern Portuguese societies. To a lesser extent than in Lisbon, where they were a considerable part of the social landscape,[20] it was not unusual to find Chinese [*chinas*], Indians [*índios*], Javanese [*jaus*], Japanese [*japões*] and Brazilians [*brasis*] serving as slaves in Porto, Vila do Conde and Viana. These were exceptions among the slaves living in these ports and were a sign of distinction and exoticism for their owners and households. But of course, unsurprisingly, Africans (from São Tomé, Cape Verde, Guinea, Congo, Angola and Mozambique) were greater in number.[21] This indicates that if the Atlantic Slave Trade shipping charts are much more spectacular and inform us of the integration of the Portuguese ports in the construction processes of the so-called 'Atlantic system'[22] – verifiable

18 See the cited bibliography, in particular, Barros, *Porto. A construção de um espaço marítimo no início dos tempos modernos*; Polónia, *Vila do Conde*; Manuel António Fernandes Moreira, *O porto de Viana do Castelo na época dos descobrimentos* (Viana do Castelo, 1984).

19 Polónia, *Vila do Conde*, cited in Francisco Araújo and Sandra Alves, 'Escravos e libertos em Leça da Palmeira (1560–1836)', *Africana Studia*, 7 (2004), 53–72. Barros, *Porto. A construção de um espaço marítimo no início dos tempos modernos*, cited by Jorge Fonseca, *Escravos e senhores na Lisboa quinhentista* (Lisbon, 2010).

20 Fonseca, *Escravos e senhores*, cit. Ana M. Rodrigues (ed.), *Os negros em Portugal: sécs. XV a XIX* (Lisbon, 1999).

21 They were, of course, also worthy of praise – owning slaves, and having, above all, many slaves, was a sign of social power.

22 Not so much in the traditional sense, which here we intend to nuance, of the triangular trade that gave rise to the Industrial Revolution, but above all in the sense of a more complete and inclusive Atlantic history. See a more traditional interpretation of the subject in Solow (ed.), *Slavery and the Rise*; and a recent overview of the theme in Filipa Ribeiro da Silva, *Dutch and Portuguese in Western Africa: Empires, Merchants and the Atlantic System, 1580–1674* (Leiden and Boston, 2011). Bearing in mind what this researcher posits about

through their involvement in the development of milling economies (namely sugarcane plantations in Brazil) and mining in Spanish America – the fact is that, residually, but consistently and repeatedly, some slaves were directed to these maritime communities, as evidenced by the notarial and parish records used to support this study.

At this point in the analysis I wish to turn our attention to the slaves in the ports and their participation in the ports' operations: mainly, those who were employed in shipyards (as carpenters or caulkers' assistants), as undifferentiated workers on the docks (in cargo handling), and as sailors. The slave appears as a professionally integrated social type in the occupations normally found in a port and in a city. He moved freely within the urban space[23] and seldom ran away;[24] he worked for his master, to whom he handed over most of his wages (we are unaware of the exact amounts he earned); and, according to sources, slave labour in the city was not exploited intensively.[25] To sum up, although we have many references regarding slavery in the various shipbuilding activities, the general impression is that this was not widespread, and it followed the general pattern regarding the presence of slaves in the city: not very many and never exceeding the number of free workers (for instance, in craftsmen workshops).

Beyond the shipyard, but in functions related to shipbuilding and shipping support, rope makers were a highly active group, and slaves were employed in the port ropewalks and workshops. This was the case with Eva Afonso, recognised in Porto in the late sixteenth century as an active cordage business-woman, whose slaves produced rigging for local ships and export. She leased their work abroad, for instance in Alicante.[26]

In the shipyards, and as part of the shipbuilding 'industry', we find slaves working as caulkers; as multifunctional labourers they could be found both on the shipyard and on ships serving as caulkers; and they worked as sailors or cabin men too.

---

the merchants' initiative ('Furthermore, private entrepreneurship across the borders of the European Empires is usually disregarded', p. 13), the present text seeks, to some extent, also to contribute to filling this gap.

23 This is a circumstance known to researchers but unknown by the general public, influenced by social types pictured by cinema and literature, which give an image of the prisoner and incarcerated slave taken to work by harsh foremen and living through severe privations, which in fact would happen in tropical environments where they worked on the plantations. In European cities this did not happen.

24 Evidence of slaves escaping has been found but these events were documented following their capture elsewhere in the country, which suggests that episodes of this kind would not abound.

25 In the Early Modern Portugal, this was not the case. A. C. de C. M. Saunders, *História social dos escravos e libertos negros em Portugal (1441–1555)* (Lisbon, 1994).

26 According to some sources she had also placed one of her slaves in Seville. Barros, *Porto. A construção de um espaço marítimo no início dos tempos modernos*, pp. 438, 441, 442.

In Porto there are reports of at least two slaves serving as caulkers; one was called Francisco, 'Cape Verdean black, caulker', owned by Miguel Martins (also a caulker, and a resident in the maritime quarter of Miragaia). Francisco divided his time between work on the shipyard and service on board a small caravel (*caravelão*) of which Martins was a shareholder.[27] The other slave, of unknown name, belonged to the seaman Pedro Mateus, and was raised by his father, Mateus Afonso, caulker, resident 'in Lavandeira, near Fonte das Virtudes', also in Miragaia, and by his wife Genebra Pires. He remained at least ten years in their household, during which time his owners 'taught him to be a caulker', with good results it seems, for it is stated that 'he was a very good worker' [*bom hofficial*].[28]

Outside the shipyard but still involved in the port services, there are references to undifferentiated workers loading and unloading ships, carrying goods to the customs house and to the warehouses, where we find evidence of the presence of slaves.[29] They could also be found in another occupation related to the port's operation: guarding their owners' merchandise while it was quarantined by the port's health service, remaining in the lazaretto until the goods were cleared for dispatch.[30]

The presence of the slaves should also be noted in another aspect of port life. With the increased flow of incoming and outgoing ships, loading and unloading of goods, storage and transport, activity on both banks of the Douro river became more dynamic, with the extension of barge services. On 9 January 1549, the City Council revoked a license that it had exceptionally granted to a certain André Afonso, the holder of barge service lease, authorising him to employ slaves in the barges. Users complained that one of his slaves could not understand what they said because he did 'not speak the Portuguese language', and was disobedient, and should, therefore, be removed because he compromised a service that was fundamental to the prosperity of both river margins.[31]

Accounts of the presence of slaves serving on ships are abundant. Traditionally, historiography has not paid much attention to this fact, except in later chronologies, and has reduced their presence to the advantage Europeans could obtain

27 ADP, *Po 1º*, 3rd ser., liv. 38, fol. 20. In 1571 he was in Lisbon, where he had been taken by his owner; he was expected to return to the shipyard.

28 ADP, *Po 1º*, 3rd ser., liv. 42, fols 95–95v.

29 In the town council minutes, for example, where mention is made of port workers and of those who worked, for example, in the expansion of the city wharf. Slave labour was used in this large-scale public work. Barros, *Porto. A construção de um espaço marítimo no início dos tempos modernos*, p. 62.

30 Of course, at their owners' service, keeping their goods and not exactly as port workers. See this case of slaves guarding goods in the lazaretto (exposed to illnesses carried in ships and bales), in the second half of the sixteenth century, at Barros, *Porto: a construção de um espaço marítimo nos alvores dos tempos modernos*, vol. I, p. 210.

31 AHMP, *Vereações*, liv. 17, fol. 3.

from their knowledge of certain routes and markets.[32] In the sixteenth-century Portuguese seaports, slaves were employed as sailors for all types of navigation. They worked side by side with the Portuguese and European sailors, serving on the same ships, performing the same duties, earning the same wages. Living and dying on board, moving from one ship to another, departing for other ports in search of work, and sharing misfortune and adventures.

In a single sample taken from notarial documentation, I found almost two dozen slaves on duty on board, serving as cabin crew and sailors, as in the following examples. Gonçalo Dias Ponte was one of the last examples of Porto citizens, a man of privileged status, who earned a living with his ship, the *Jesus*. In 1565 he had travelled to the Italian port of Civitavecchia, carrying alum. He died on the return voyage at the Catalan port of Rosas, where the ship was to be sold including, as mentioned earlier, the two slaves he had serving as sailors.[33]

In 1572, Diogo, an Indian slave [*escravo índio*] owned by Mateus Afonso, served as cabin crew on the ship of which his owner's father, Pedro Mateus, caulker, was a shareholder, and he participated in at least three crossings to Brazil on the ship. The wages he earned were used to support his owner's parents in old age, in return for which he received the promise of a letter of manumission;[34] perhaps he never exercised this right to be a freeman: the Indian Diogo died in São Tomé in 1577 aboard the ship on which he 'was earning for his master'.[35]

An illustrative story is that of Mateus, a sailor slave, who, after serving on the ship owned by Maria Pires and her son-in-law Francisco Dias until it was shipwrecked in Bahia – during a voyage to Brazil between 1577 and 1578 – became part of the crew on another ship (owned by Manuel Fernandes and the same Francisco Dias), later to be transferred to a Lisbon ship. In 1584 he returned to Brazil on this vessel, a voyage for which he would receive around 18,000 *reais*;[36] he had earned the same amount for each crossing in the previous ships, making him a well-paid sailor.[37]

We find slaves on board ships, as sailors, in other Portuguese ports and on Castilian ships, as is abundantly documented for the Spanish Americas Route. Moreover, and proving that there were many transnational interests in

32 Peter Linebaugh and Marcus Rediker, *The Many-Headed Hydra: Sailors, Slaves, Commoners, and the Hidden History of the Revolutionary Atlantic* (Boston, 2000), p. 130.

33 ADP, *Po 1º*, 3rd ser., liv. 21, fol. 162v.

34 ADP, *Po 1º*, 3rd ser., liv. 42, fol. 95.

35 ADP, *Po 1º*, liv. 58, fol. 103v. Also, Domingo Pires, a black sailor on the Cape Verde route, between the end of the sixteenth century and the beginning of the following century, accepting orders from merchants. M. E. Madeira Santos, *História Geral de Cabo Verde*, vol. II (Lisbon, 1995), pp. 234–244.

36 More precisely, 17,350 *reais*, because of the 18,000 were deducted the expenses with clothes of his equipment.

37 ADP, *Po 1º*, 3rd ser., liv. 76, fol. 133.

the Atlantic business, some of these slaves had Portuguese owners, who would monetise their property. This reveals a pattern that appears to be a common trait of these Iberian maritime societies – and might illustrate a shortage of manpower on board. At every stage of the venture we come across forced labour on board, with slaves sharing tasks alongside free sailors.[38] Finally, at home – that is, in the ports – there is evidence that the slaves moved without restrictions. There is scant information about the actual conditions on board the ships, so we do not know whether the slaves were 'monitored' or if their movements were restricted at sea or during stopovers.[39]

An important aspect for this narrative would be to question the value of this slave labour: was it more or less valuable than labour raised locally? Were they trained (after being brought to Portugal), or were they already experienced sailors when they were captured? Were they on the ship because, as I suggested earlier, there was a shortage of local sailors? Or was the lack of sailors never felt, and the slaves were employed on board only when their owners held an interest in the ships? Or would employing them on ships be part of the usual hiring processes of the city, which additionally brought advantages to the

38 Royal License addressed to the royal officers of Tierra Firme, at the request of Andrés Guerrero, owner and pilot of the ship *Concepción*, who declared that a black slave named Andrés Godino hired as a sailor in the ship, on arriving in Nombre de Dios had refused to return to 'these kingdoms' of Castilla. Guerrero, with the permission of the said officers, had sold the slave. Archivo General de Indias (AGI), Panama, 235, L.8, F.126R-127R. 1595: On board the Portuguese galleon San Martín at the service of the navy of Castile, Jerónimo Francisco, a slave owned by Marina Roldán, of Seville, worked as cabin boy on the fleet's flagship in New Spain in 1593 commanded by General Marcos de Aramburu, dying on the same galleon San Martín. AGI, Contratación, 242, N.1, R.3. 1596. A list of passengers to the Americas: Antón de Vejel, cabin boy, black slave owned by Francisco García, of Sanlúcar de Barrameda. AGI, Indiferente, 2048, N.62. 1608: Death records: Number 32. Information about the justification of Antón Sardina's death, slave and cabin crew, on board. AGI, Contratación, 941B. 1610: in another list of items of property of the deceased, there is reference to Antonio Moreno, slave, sailor, born in Tavira, Portugal, and dead at sea on board the ship commanded by Captain Juan de Vergara. AGI, Contratación, 296A e 296A, N.2, R.5. 1621: On the ship *Our Lady of the Rosary* (now in Castile, another coincidence in the name of the ship and the invocation of a devotion linked to the slaves), when travelling between San Juan de Ulúa and Vera Cruz in 1621, three slaves (or former slaves) died: Juan Rosell, Creole, cabin boy, died in San Juan de Ulúa; Mateo, black slave, cabin boy, dead in Veracruz; Antón, black slave, cabin boy, dead in Veracruz. AGI, Contratación, 5709, N.218, R.23.

39 This is a very complex subject to address in this chapter. Many factors must be taken into account, in particular issues related to uprooting. A slave brought from Africa to a European port could hardly succeed if he ran away. Even in Africa – assuming the ships were trading on that continent, which they did – they could not be expected to find safe refuge anywhere. In 1526, on a voyage to buy slaves in Congo, faced with a deadlock in the delivery of the slaves by the African authorities, one of the contractors' slaves had to go alone to the King of Congo's court to negotiate the order. Barros, 'Trato de escravos e economia atlántica', p. 38.

owners, who received a large part of their wages? How were they received by the other sailors? To what extent, if any, was there exchange of knowledge in crews that included slaves? Although none of these questions can have a definite answer, I would posit some suggestions. If it is true that the Portuguese found experienced pilots and sailors in the seas they travelled, making intensive use of them, learning routes and techniques, the cases reported here do not fit this reality;[40] rather, they fit in with the reality of local apprenticeship (as we know it in these European maritime societies), because many of the slaves were very young and, for the most part, had been born in Portugal; they generally served in modest positions in the ship's hierarchy (as did young Portuguese sailors, who had to spend years going through various stages of apprenticeship to learn the trade), as servants or cabin boys, but with the expectation of moving up in the hierarchy to the category of sailor. There are no references to racial conflict between white and black sailors in the accounts of daily life on board, but these records are extremely laconic regarding social relations on the ships.[41] Finally, and equal to medieval and early modern craftsmen, these slaves could prove competent at their trade, earn a reputation as good workers (sailors), be well paid for their services and even 'offer' their services on several ships and ports, as we have seen with the sailor Mateus's case.

As in the previous examples collected in Porto, an identical reality can be observed in other ports. Such is the case of the neighbouring port of Vila do Conde, where it was common to find slaves earning for their masters as seamen.[42] In this aspect, the Iberian Peninsula clearly distinguished itself from most European ports, where the presence of slaves in these activities was either non-existent or has not yet been noted by historians. While further considering the participation of ports in the Atlantic Slave Trade, James Rawley speaks of a late London connection to this business, and an even later one of Liverpool and Nantes, and found no evidence of the presence of slaves in port labour.[43]

40 In general, with the following exception, which the chronicles themselves confirm: about the slave Diogo Fernandes, who 'walked on the sea [...] a slave of Indian nation that was his captive' ('*andava sobre o mar [...] hum escravo cativo indio de naçam que era seu cativo*'). In this case, we find the connection between the slave collective (here as a supplier of slave labour) and the Atlantic traffic, where this captive had mobility, serving on several ships. ADP, *Po 1°*, liv. 24, fols 92v–93.

41 This does not necessarily mean they did not occur. Aggressiveness was one of the most evident traits of seafarers, and cultural differences could trigger confrontations. However, we find no documented evidence in the records of the Northern Portuguese merchant navy.

42 Polónia, *Vila do Conde*, pp. 784–785. She identifies at least three occurrences of slave sailors – to whom wages ('marinhagens') were owed for their journeys serving on board as sailors – but admits that the phenomenon is deeper and more widespread. Porto's documentation, as we have seen, confirms this conjecture.

43 David Eltis, 'Foreword', to James A. Rawley, *London, Metropolis of the Slave Trade* (Columbia & London, 2003), pp. xi–xii.

But even in those with a longstanding relationship with slavery (and specifically regarding slave labour in the docks and on the ships), the connection differs significantly and is considerably less vigorous than that displayed in the port cities of Portugal and the Iberian Peninsula. From the Middle Ages, the largest concentrations of slaves were centred in the more commercially active cities, such as Genoa and Venice (and on the Iberian Peninsula, but with Mediterranean 'features', Barcelona). These were slaves of different origins, acquired in established markets such as Laiazzo, Pera, Caffa, Chios or Famagusta. The medieval Ottoman incursions compromised some of these businesses and the Iberian markets began to emerge, supplied by sub-Saharan slaves. The Italians needed them for their galleys, while domestic work, where they had hitherto been employed (mid-fifteenth century), suffered from their now diminished presence. In general, purchases declined and, when possible, the purchase of female slaves was favoured. It was only in the Iberian Peninsula where a balance between the numbers of men and women existed, since tolerance for slave ownership lasted longer, as we have observed. Few slaves worked in crafts workshops; however, in Venice, and like the situation observed in Porto albeit, of course, at a much smaller scale, a considerable number of slaves were employed in barge services. The remaining slaves in the city seemed to be employed exclusively in domestic work.[44] In Florence, slaves were usually bought in Lisbon through commercial companies, such as the Cambini, who operated there for many years; women (the 'females') were predominant and light-skinned slaves were preferred, also for domestic services.[45]

Nothing, therefore, is comparable to the incidence of slavery in the Portuguese seaport societies. For instance, there is no evidence of slaves on board ships serving as seamen, which seems to be a particular feature of the early modern Iberian maritime societies, as was the fact that some slaves were able to progress socially. Certain cases show the extent to which slaves had risen in social status to serve as representatives of contractors and merchants in Portugal and overseas, a practice that would continue throughout the history of Portuguese slavery.[46] Such was the example of Antonio 'Brazil', owned by Garcia Gomes Vitória (in 1576), who served his master on the slave procurement

44 Judith M. Bennett and Ruth M. Karras (eds.), *The Oxford Handbook of Women and Gender in Medieval Europe* (Oxford, 2013), pp. 288–289. See also the classic work of Jacques Heers, *Escravos e servidão doméstica na Idade Média no mundo mediterrânico* (Lisbon, 1983) (1st edn in French, 1981).

45 Sergio Tognetti, 'The Trade of Black African Slaves in Florence', in *Black Africans in Renaissance Europe*, ed. Thomas F. Earle and Kate J. P. Lowe (Cambridge, 2005), pp. 213–224, at p. 217.

46 'Evidence exists of Africans on board ships acting as overseers of the cargo and representatives of freighters. Prior to 1642, Luís, slave of António Bruto, completed two voyages to Brazil accompanying a few hundred captives on behalf of his master'. Arlindo M. Caldeira, 'Angola and the Seventeenth-Century South Atlantic Slave Trade', in *Networks*

voyages he was involved in.[47] Or the four slaves who, in the following year, accompanied Tomás Jorge, Pantaleão Ribeiro, Afonso Fernandes, Manuel Cardoso, Francisco Tomás, Pantaleão Lopes and Manuel Guterres in Africa and Brazil, to guard their merchandise and assist in all travel arrangements.[48] The mulattos, such as António Rodrigues, 'grey man' [*homem baço*],[49] hired to bring black slaves from São Tomé [*negros de São Tomé*] to Brazil, enjoyed a special and differentiated status among the shipboard personnel. These were, however, special cases, and as such deserve to be mentioned[50] even though their participation differed from the routines of the city's specialised agents, continuously engaged in shipping, trade and slavery circuits at the service of merchants and their trading networks, which had been established to exploit the transatlantic slave trade. In any case, these slaves represent a little known and to some extent unexpected behaviour in master–slave relations.

As an example of a specialised slave-trade agent – simultaneously operating on his own, at the service of New Christian commercial networks, and with slaves at his service – it is worth mentioning Gaspar Colaço, of high social status, a citizen commissioned in 1584 by Miguel Leão and Gaspar Cardoso to buy slaves in Angola and sugar in Brazil ('*e dise o dito Guaspar Collaso que se hobrigava a comprar e acondicionar os escravos na presente vyagem [e] vyr em boa ora dar conta com entrega do propio e procedido da dicta armaçam*

and Trans-Cultural Exchange: Slave Trading in the South Atlantic, 1590–1867, ed. David Richardson and Filipa Ribeiro da Silva (Leiden and Boston, 2015), pp. 101–142, at pp. 128–129.

47 ADP, *Po 1°*, 3rd ser., liv. 55, fol. 185v.

48 'And as for the slaves, who were four, namely: one named Pedro, of Tomas Jorge, and Pedro, of Manuel Cardoso, and Nicolau, of Pantalião Lopes, and Simão, of Pantalião Ribeiro, as stated by the aforesaid merchants who left them in the aforesaid lazaretto to guard their goods'. ('*E coanto aos escravos que eram coatro convém a saber: hum per nome Pedro de Tomas George, e Pedro de Manuel Cardoso, e Nicolao de Pantalião Lopez, e Simão de Pantalião Ribeiro diseram os ditos mercadores que pera garda de suas mercadorias os deixavam no dito degredo*'). AHMP, *Livros de visitas de saúde*, liv. 1, fol. 49.

49 On the ship *Santa Clara*, from Lisbon, whose master was a native of Vila do Conde. Rodrigues had also been a sailor and had come to Porto to serve as such. He had been at sea at least between 1569 and 1573, where he died. This is a complex case. The man was the son of a 'black slave', from out of town, and was perhaps a free man, since his condition of captivity is not stated. He died in the middle of the ocean, as it was said, and his goods, as was customary at sea, were auctioned off among the crew members. ADP, *Po 1°*, 3rd ser., liv. 47, fol. 186.

50 Polónia, *Vila do Conde*, p. 785, identifies a slave in charge of collecting what was due to his owner: 'in 1596 [...] Maria Carneira issues a power of attorney to Belchior, her slave, in order to collect all her debts and income'.

dentro a esta dicta cidade do Porto sem fazer houtra vyagem nehua'[51]), whom we find repeatedly performing this type of function in the Atlantic Slave Trade.

The Greatest Slave Trader

In the previous pages I have attempted to describe port labour performed by slaves rather than the transatlantic slave trade itself. However, one was influenced by the other. In my studies on the subject, shipping and the Atlantic Slave Trade from these northern Portuguese ports was recurrent and one can identify a large group of merchants participating in it, as evidenced by the numerous contracts they negotiated, and the ships dedicated to that trade. The complexity of the dynamics surrounding this business called for intricate port operations that I will soon share in a forthcoming longer study. To close this chapter, I have chosen a significant character as an example. He did not belong to the group of merchants we usually identify as the protagonists of the transatlantic slave trade and of general trade in these ports – the New Christian merchants and their networks – nor was he isolated from them. He was a powerful and influential actor in the economic and political life of Porto, given his connections with the institutions of power of the Hispanic Crown.

Porto's leading slave trader in the latter years of the sixteenth century was Luís Álvares de Távora, owner of a fleet dedicated to the Atlantic Slave Trade and Brazilian sugar trade. He was a member of one of Portugal's most powerful noble families, a Knight of the Order of Malta, *Balio* (*commendator*) of the Hospitaller Order's Monastery of Leça, and served the Crown in several important functions in Porto and the surrounding territory, where he had much influence. He was the owner of important vineyards and a producer of Douro wines, especially from his farm of Vacaria, which was administered by the Jesuits, and exploited the port's potential by investing in shipbuilding to accumulate a vast fortune from trading slaves and sugar. The documents demonstrate that he possessed a small fleet, an extensive staff of secretaries, masters, pilots and seamen at his service, as well as the operative capacity to guarantee supplies (of Douro wines, for example) for the voyages and victualling of his vessels. He owned, as far as we know, a galleon, a *nao* and a small galleon (*patacho*), all devoted to the Atlantic Slave Trade and all fitted with artillery. In this brief note about this character it must be said that the power he wielded resulted from his being part of or very close to influential

51 It must be said that the three were business partners and leaders of a comercial network. ADP, *Po 1º*, 3rd ser., liv. 74, fols 154–154v ('and the aforesaid Guaspar Collaso that he was commissioned to buy and pack the slaves in the present voyage [and] arrive in good time to give account with delivery of the cargo and proceeding to the aforesaid warehouse in the city of Porto without making any further voyage').

political, economic and social networks, which, among other things, granted him access to weaponry, equipment and capital. Moreover, he was one of the main suppliers of the *armadas* and the Hispanic royal navy. On several occasions his role as importer of artillery from Biscay facilitated the acquisition of cannons for his own ships – the shipwright Pero Franco was commissioned to build a ship (*patacho*) in four months, with a structure prepared to receive pieces of artillery. The contract for this commission specified that he was to include hatches to mount the cannons.[52]

The voyages made by this vessel demonstrate that, from the outset, it was intentionally designed to be a slave ship, and was often thus employed throughout its existence.[53] I highlight this information because it is rare in the history of the Portuguese merchant navy, allowing us to asses tonnage, model, specifications, characteristics and performance. And if that ship was prepared to receive artillery, it was also fitted to accommodate slaves. When it was chartered in 1598, the *patacho*, by then named the *São Rafael*, transported 290 slaves from Angola (and/or Congo) to Brazil on behalf of the *Balio* (250 slaves) and the crew (40 slaves); the responsibility for the ship and business was with the master, and in his absence with the pilot, Antonio Pires.[54] Further, the existence of a charter on a ship owned by him reveals how he managed this activity in a highly sophisticated manner, separating the different lines of business,[55] and keeping his private property separate from the company's assets. It is worth mentioning that he spent approximately seven million *reais* to purchase those slaves, a sum he would recoup through their sale in Brazil.

Confirming the trend described earlier, this ship, and most of the other ships belonging to the *Balio*, seldom sailed directly to Africa; they would sail first to Brazil and then on to Angola. Anchored and properly fitted in Porto, ready to sail, the master of the ship was commissioned to load, 'below the deck', all the goods necessary for the journey, 'and then unload them in Rio de Janeiro'. At this port he would load the ship with flour and continue his journey to Angola to buy slaves, using the flour to feed them once purchased; then the ship would return to Brazil to deliver the slaves. The return would be in three months, which was considered a reasonable time to buy the slaves and embark them, and this time frame is frequent in charters involving other northern Portuguese vessels.

52 ADP, *Po 10*, 3rd ser., liv. 106, fols 145v–148v.

53 Although we know that these ships, as well as their crew, participated in multiple activities; however, the preference was for the transport of slaves; it suffices to realise that a low-tonnage ship such as this (70 tonnes) had carried the largest number of slaves – see the following note for the archival reference – which indicates that from the construction stage the ship had been prepared for such a function.

54 ADP, *Po 2º*, 1st ser., liv. 11, fols 105–108.

55 For example, by chartering his own ship himself – possibly for maritime insurance reasons or liability with regard to the contract.

Beyond acting as administrator of the vessel, the master had to plan the route to buy the slaves in Angola or Congo. In terms of the ship and its use, this vessel was designed to complement the slave cargo with carrying other merchandise in the return voyage – to ensure that the ship did not travel 'empty', to cover expenses and, eventually, make some profit: however, 'if there is cargo to return, from Brazil, a new freight charter must be issued'.[56]

This example seems to reveal a pattern in the history of Portuguese navigation in the late sixteenth century: that of the responsibilities of masters and seafarers. Arlindo Caldeira proves this later but quite significant reality:

> the ship captain or master had sole commercial responsibilities on board the slave ship. He was in fact committed by surety to the ship owner and was to be held responsible for the outcome of the voyage, whether good or bad. In some cases, masters were joint owners of the ships. The ship pilot's responsibilities, by contrast, were confined to navigational matters. In delegating his tasks, the captain or master was often assisted by a deputy master (*contramestre*) and a steward (*despenseiro*). As for the rest of the crew, their number depended on the ship tonnage, varying between 15 and 30 sailors. To them might be added several cabin-boys (*grumetes*), mostly of African descent and some enslaved. In 1708, the *Nossa Senhora do Cabo*, carrying 742 slaves, had nearly 50 'black and white men serving on board'.[57]

Conclusion

In the ports that prospered from the Atlantic business, the influence of the transatlantic slave trade would inevitably influence their operations and dynamics. In this chapter I have gathered some research notes on these matters. Despite my wish to provide further information regarding the presence of slaves in the ports, the documentation is scant and mostly silent as to how slaves and the Atlantic Slave Trade impacted port operations as we would call it today.

I believe that this chapter does, however, provide some useful data, thanks to the quality of the information collected mostly from notary records. These show us that in the Portuguese port societies of the early modern era, the slave was an inescapable social type, and that forced labour existed in the different sectors supporting the maritime business, through different expressions, in both port services and shipyards, and, as has been seen, with a strong impact on board ships.

56 ADP, *Po* 2°, 1st ser., liv. 11, fols 105–108.

57 Arlindo Caldeira, 'Angola and the Seventeenth-Century', p. 128.

This capacity of the slave to intervene in maritime societies, in my opinion, should be emphasised: for instance, the fact that the slave performed tasks which we were not aware of until recently – and which, as we have seen, most of the European spaces were unaware of. The time has come to reflect on the meaning of such intervention and on such data. Throughout the chapter, I have tried to demonstrate the significance of the presence of slaves in the ports, because historiography, for decades, has ignored slave labour in Portugal's port societies and communities. I would have liked to probe further in this analysis, but I believe that the way has been opened up, or at least a path has been signalled: one reminding us that the history of the slaves in seaports is another element to enrich the social and economic history of these structures and, as a result, to decisively assist in clarifying fundamental aspects of the construction of the early modern world. Once again, the explanation of this period of deep changes will not make sense if the local historiographic element is not accounted for.

Another aspect to expand upon is the extent of the Atlantic Slave Trade, the interest it generated within maritime communities and the resources available for such research. For many, the numerous documented journeys, the vast numbers of slaves bought and sold, and the commercial companies created for this purpose will come as a surprise, as will the number of vessels deployed for this purpose: *naos*, *patachos*, galleons and ships were mobilised in ports and then chartered by merchants and commercial societies. A new insight into port shipping history is provided by the information on ships sailing to Africa on their own or in small fleets, properly organised and regulated before departure in the presence of a notary and the municipal authorities. The fact that some of these vessels were built on purpose for the transatlantic slave trade is also a novelty, and this has been adequately highlighted. This was the case of the *patacho São Rafael* owned by the Balio de Leça, the most important slave trader in Porto, which, properly equipped, 'keel-tight and side-tight, and with its artillery seated', as stipulated in the ship's charters, carried in its holds the human cargo to which the Atlantic world created by the Iberians largely owes its birth.

Figure 4.1. The royal customs house in Vila do Conde

Figure 4.2. The medieval royal customs house, 'Casa do Infante' (House of Henry the Navigator), in Porto

Figure 4.3. Warehouses by the medieval wall in Porto

Figure 4.4. Ship mooring stone by the medieval wall and customs house in Porto

5

Transport and Shipping in the Portuguese Northern Border in the Sixteenth Century

SARA PINTO

CITCEM, University of Porto (Portugal)[1]

ABSTRACT. Commercial relations in the Portuguese northern border has been a fruitful subject in Portuguese and Spanish historiography. A common background concerning natural landscape, population mobility and sharing of resources – the sea and the river – connected both margins of the Minho river and moulded their stories and people. On this matter, we know a lot about product circulation – the importance of salt, wine, fish or textile routes – the seasonality of migrations around labour offers, or the sharing of neighbourhood privileges in each other's towns. However, in what concerns the logistics of transport and shipping, as the operations concerning loading and unloading, there is a lot of work to be done. This chapter aims to approach transport and shipping operations in the Portuguese northern border in the sixteenth century, setting the focus on the seaport of Caminha, and the relations established between border communities. The analysis is settled on detailed empirical work that uses different data sources, such as historical cartography, travel memories and descriptions, appeals to the Crown, customs house records and council minutes. The chapter will assess the following topics: maritime landscape, port infrastructures and navigation constraints; navigation and trade circuits, considering competitive and cooperative behaviour between border communities; and customs and port administration.

A border has the important purpose of creating relationships, allowing territories and communities to establish contact with their neighbours. It

1 Sara Pinto, CITCEM – Transdisciplinary Research Centre 'Culture, Space and Memory', University of Porto, Porto, Portugal.

defines their interactions of rivalry, exchange or cooperation.[2] Commercial relations along the northern border of Portugal have been a fruitful subject for Portuguese and Spanish historiography.[3] A common setting including the physical environment, the mobility of the population, and shared resources – the sea and the river – connected both margins of the river Minho, shaping their history and people.

Much is known of the circulation of products – the importance of salt, wine, fish, or textile routes – the seasonality of migrations following employment opportunities, or the shared local privileges between towns. There remains, however, much untapped potential for the research of shipping logistics such as cargo handling operations. This chapter aims to approach transport and shipping operations in the Portuguese northern border during the sixteenth century, centred on the seaport of Caminha, and the relations established between border communities. The analysis is based on detailed empirical work including various data sources, such as historical cartography, travel memories and descriptions, appeals to the Crown, customs house accounts and council minutes. I will discuss the following topics: maritime landscape, port infrastructures and navigation constraints; navigation and trade circuits; competitive

2 Juan Manuel Trillo Santamaría and João Carlos Garcia, 'Galicia-Minho: el cuestionamiento de una frontera. Debates en el discurso geográfico ibérico', *Revista de historiografia*, 23 (2015), 159–189.

3 Elisa Ferreira Priegue, *Galicia en el comercio marítimo medieval* (La Coruña, 1988); José Armas Castro, *Pontevedra en los siglos XII a XV. Configuracion y desarrollo de una villa marinera en la Galicia medieval* (Pontevedra, 1992), and 'Mercaderes portugueses en Pontevedra en el siglo XV. Sobre algunos problemas de abastecimento urbano', in *Actas do Congresso Internacional Bartolomeu Dias e a sua época*, vol. III (Porto, 1989), pp. 217–230; José Marques, 'A fronteira do Minho, espaço de convivência galaico-minhota, na Idade Média e Relações económicas do Norte de Portugal com o Reino de Castela, no século XV', in *Estudos em Homenagem a Luís António de Oliveira Ramos*, vol. 2 (Porto, 2004), pp. 697–712; Paz Romero Portilla, 'Relaciones entre Portugal y Galicia Siglo XIV–XV', *Revista da Faculdade de Letras. Historia*, 9.1 (2008), 217–270; *eadem*, 'La singular relación Portugal-Galicia y su reflejo en la documentación medieval', *Revista de Ciências Históricas*, 15 (2000), 53–70; Oscar Fangueiro, 'Relações pesqueiras e comerciais luso-galegas', in *Colóquio de etnografia marítima* (Santiago de Compostela, 1984), pp. 251–276; Amélia Aguiar Andrade, 'Vilas, poder régio e fronteira: o exemplo do Entre Lima e Minho medieval' (PhD diss., Universidade Nova de Lisboa, 1994); Isabel M. D. Braga, *Península Ibérica: um espaço, dois reinos: interrelações na época de Carlos V* (Lisbon, 2001); Humberto Baquero Moreno, 'Relações entre Portugal e a Galiza nos séculos XIV e XV', *Revista da Faculdade de Letras. Historia*, 7 (1990), 34–46; Francisco Ribeiro da Silva, 'Intercâmbios comerciais entre o norte de Portugal e a Galiza na viragem do século XVII para o século XVIII', *Douro – Estudos & Documentos*, 2.4 (1997), 173–213; Antonio Meijide Pardo, 'Aspectos del comércio gallego de exportacíon a Portugal en el siglo XVIII', in *Actas de las I Jornadas de Metodología Aplicada de las Ciencias Históricas*, vol. 3 (Santiago de Compostela, 1975), pp. 803–824.

and cooperative behaviour between border communities; and customs and port administration.

For a full understanding of the Portuguese northern border some variables must be considered first. One must understand, for example, the great changes in coastal landscapes during the Middle Ages and the sixteenth century.[4] In terms of the effects of geomorphological variations, some studies – centred on the Atlantic façade – remark on the decisive influence waterfront configurations and climate conditions had on the activities and progress of ports.[5] Obstacles to navigation, in particular sandbars, were very common and are frequently mentioned in historical records, as was the lack of adequate moorings.

Well into the sixteenth century, numerous port town councils of northern Portugal were still struggling with the implementation and development of port infrastructures. Local studies suggest that smaller boats were the predominant mode of transport for the unloading and transfer of goods to land.[6] The sandbar and the port could, in fact, be set in different locations. The port, as a gateway for import and export business and tax collection, was based within the customs facilities, often occupying several buildings. In this sense, a port would operate wherever it could. This meant that, should a ship be unable to reach port, customs officers had to go on board to control and supervise incoming goods.[7]

Another challenge arises from historical records. For this subject, information can be drawn from different types of sources: council records, customs regulations, and freight charters or merchant deeds. Unfortunately, in our case study – Caminha – council records and contracts for early periods have not survived. An alternative research path was the analysis of customs regulations and practices of the port of Viana, since the two towns shared customs

4 Sara Pinto, 'Caminha no século XVI: estudo sócio-económico dos que ganhão suas vidas sobre as agoas do mar' (MA diss., Universidade do Porto, 2008); and Assunção Araújo, 'A evolução do litoral em tempos históricos: a contribuição da Geografia física', in *Actas 'O Litoral em Perspectiva Histórica (séc. XVI a XVIII)* (Porto, 2002), pp. 73–91.

5 Ana María Rivera Medina, 'La construcción-reconstrucción de un espácio portuário. El canal y ría de Bilbao en los siglos XIV–XVI', in *La gobernanza de los puertos atlánticos, siglos XIV–XX: políticas y estructuras portuarias*, ed. Amélia Polónia and Ana María Rivera Medina (Madrid, 2016), pp. 171–191; and *eadem*, '"Por tanto reparo y adereço". Las infraestructuras portuarias y la red de intereses de las villas vizcaínas medievales en la ejecución de las obras', in *Gentes de mar en la ciudad atlántica medieval*, ed. Jesús Solórzano Telechea, Michel Bochaca and Amélia Aguiar Andrade (Logroño, 2012), pp. 345–357.

6 Manuel António Fernandes Moreira, *O porto de Viana do Castelo na época dos descobrimentos* (Viana do Castelo, 1984); Amélia Polónia, *A expansão ultramarina numa perspectiva local: o porto de Vila do Conde no século XVI* (Lisbon, 2007); Amândio Barros, *Porto. A construção de um espaço marítimo no início dos tempos modernos* (Lisbon, 2016); Inês Amorim, *Porto de Aveiro: entre a terra e o mar* (Aveiro, 2008).

7 *Ibid.*, p. 42.

administration. In fact, their customs house was designated by the combined name of Viana de Caminha. Comparisons with other nearby seaports, such as Porto and Vila do Conde, which have been studied in depth, will also be addressed to further enrich the analysis.

Maritime Landscape: Port Infrastructures and Navigation Constraints

> Comment ne pas s'interroger sur les poids des contraintes naturelles, muables ou immobiles, qui provoquent au dynamisme ou au repli, qui définissent ou non les caractères maritimes d'une population, qui conditionnent une part des relations sociales des hommes de la mer?[8]

Considerations of the design and functions of a port, in addition to its logistics (workforce and devices employed in its operation), require a previous analysis of the natural setting and its geomorphological profile.

Data collected from historical records, namely maps (figures 5.1 and 5.2), clearly reveals that the river Minho was navigable by vessels of a significantly greater size than the shallow-draught boats we can find there today. In the mid-fifteenth century, Valença do Minho – 30 kilometres upstream – was visited by foreign ships and boasted a fleet of its own which participated in active trade ventures with other ports.[9] The river Minho was navigable for over 50 kilometres from the river mouth, beyond Valença.[10] However, the sixteenth century witnessed extreme weather conditions in the form of intense winds, with significant repercussions on the Portuguese waterfront.[11] The passage by the sandbar, once deep and straight, was obstructed by the formation of spits and sand deposits in and around the city walls. Human interventions in response to these alterations did, in many cases, more harm than good. In Caminha, a particularly poor decision involved the planting of a pine forest on the sand dune, ordered by the king, D. Dinis, in 1284, to prevent the sand from invading agricultural lands. The effects proved disastrous, solidifying the sand

8 'How not to ponder over the consequences of natural constraints, whether variable or immobile, whether driving dynamism or withdrawal, as a determinant or as a deterrent of maritime characteristics of a population, which condition part of the social relations of the men of the sea?' Alain Cabantous, *Dix mille marins face á l'océan. Les populations maritimes de Dunkerque ao Havre aux XVIIe et XVIIIe siècles (vers 1660–1794): Etude sociale* (Paris, 1991), p. 55.

9 António Caetano Alves, 'Causas e processos da dinâmica sedimentar na evolução actual do litoral do Alto Minho' (unpublished PhD diss., Universidade do Minho, 1996), pp. 31, 143 and 296.

10 Antonio H. Oliveira Marques, 'Portugal nas crises dos sécs. XIV e XV', in *Nova História de Portugal*, vol. 4 (Lisbon, 1987), pp. 115–121, at p. 128.

11 Alves, 'Causas e processos da dinâmica sedimentar', pp. 80–285.

Figure 5.1. (left) The mouth of the Minho's river and Caminha. From Pedro Texeira, *Descripción de España y de las costas y puertos de sus reinos* (1634)

Figure 5.2. (below) Water depth in Caminha's maritime bar entrance. From Willem Jansz. Blaew, *De Zeecusten van Galissen Tusschem de Cabo Finisterre en Camino* (1638)

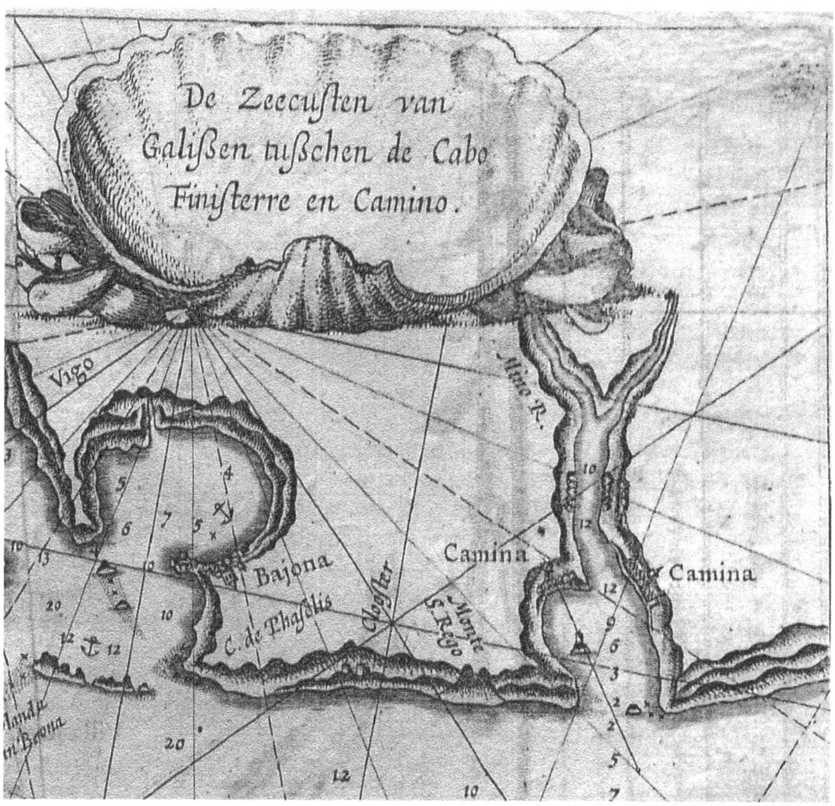

dune irreparably to become a permanent obstacle to the entrance of medium-draft ships and aggravating the penetration of the bar by the sand dune.[12]

One of the most essential historical records for the study of the sixteenth-century landscape is the survey of the Portuguese fortifications by Duarte d'Armas in 1509.[13] Despite not recording silting or river depths, it depicts the presence or absence of vessels, which, combined with an observation of their number and dimension, become suitable indicators of navigability of this waterway. In the depictions of Caminha, we observe large ships and caravels at the river mouth: one of the *naus* is sailing to the ocean, while another, with two caravels, remains anchored at the river mouth, near the village, and a third one is shown near the castle of Vila Nova de Cerveira (figure 5.3A). Upstream, in Valença do Minho, three big *naus* are anchored, with their three masts, forecastles and aftercastles, as well as two small caravels, with two masts and two lateen sails (figure 5.3B). Fifty kilometres upstream, in Monção, the artist depicted a single boat on the river, a small barge, with a boatman and a single sail (figure 5.3C). These depictions seem to confirm the interrupted navigation in Valença, and that from this point cargo was to be transported by land.[14]

Another phenomenon witnessed by observers were the rough tides by the Caminha sandbar. In 1532, the travel writer Claude de Bronseval describes his arrival in Portugal:

> praça forte de Caminha situada sobre a margem do rio. Foi preciso atravessar aqui e não sem perigo, as águas do mar, que refluíram ao conter as do rio. Mas um bateleiro fez-nos atravessar com toda a segurança as ondas profundas e caprichosas. Desta cidade, vê-se o mar que bate duas vezes por dia as muralhas com as suas ondas potentes.[15]

To tame the sea, the town council ordered the building of a stone quay in 1612, demanding contributions of the county by taxation.[16] This is one of the rare mentions we found regarding the building of port infrastructures in

12 Luis Felipe Aviz de Brito, *A Desembocadura do Rio Minho nos Tempos Antigos* (Caminha, 1987), p. 92.

13 Duarte de Armas, *Livro das Fortalezas, Fac-simile do Ms. 159 da Casa Forte do Arquivo Nacional da Torre do Tombo* (Lisbon, 1997).

14 Suzanne Daveau, 'Caminhos e fronteira na Serra da Peneda: Alguns exemplos nos séculos XV e XVI e na actualidade', *Revista Geografia*, 1st ser. 19 (2003), 81–96.

15 'the stronghold of Caminha located on the riverbank. One had to cross here the sea water, and not without danger, which refluxed by containing the ones from the river. Then a lighter made us cross the deep and capricious waves safely. From this city one can see the sea that strikes the walls twice a day with its powerful waves'. In Claude de Bronseval, *Peregrinatio Hispanica 1531–1533*, t. 1 (Paris, 1970), p. 309.

16 Biblioteca Nacional de Portugal, Reservados, Ms. 8750: Rocha de Morais, *Grandezas da Villa de Caminha* (1722).

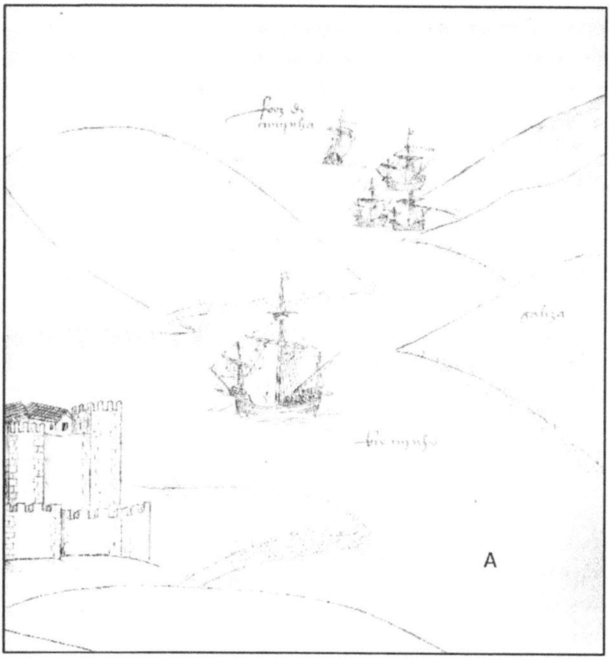

Figure 5.3. Presence of ships along the course of the river Minho: A, river mouth to Vila Nova de Cerveira (15 km upstream); B, Valença (30 km upstream); C, Monção (50 km upstream). Códices e documentos de proveniência desconhecida, no. 159 PT/TT/CF/159

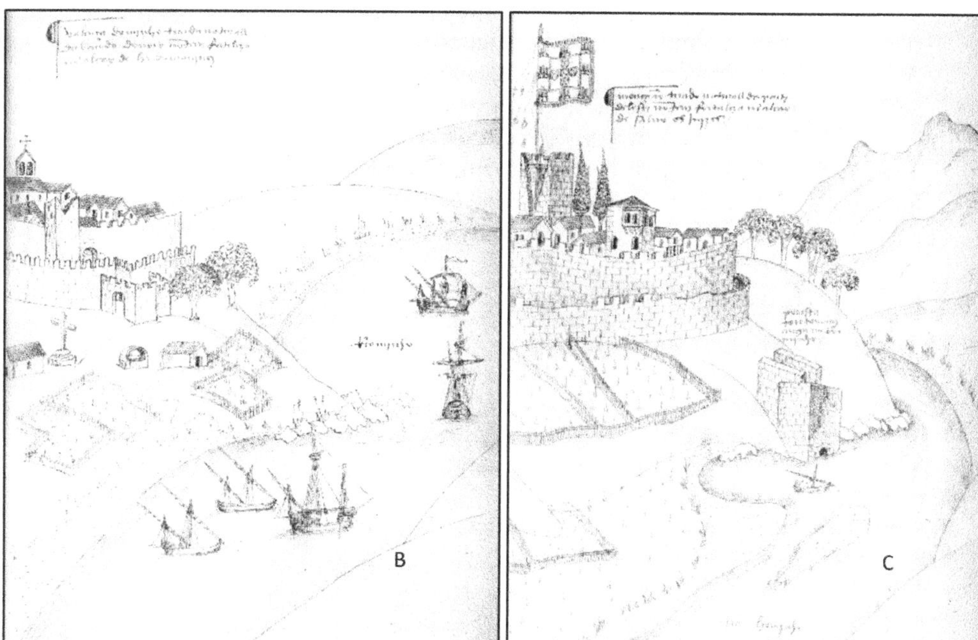

Caminha. However, the results of geomorphological changes were rapidly felt. A map of 1705 describes a town wall in Caminha: '*que em outro tempo foi de grande serventia para os navios que junto a ela estavam no rio Minho com um cais muito grande de cantaria; porém como as areias tudo cobriram, se perdeu o uso desta porta*'.[17] Although this reference dates from the seventeenth century, we must consider the possibility that the stone quay was built on a previous structure. We can also posit the existence of two wharves: one called the 'Vau' – located at the mouth of the Coura, a tributary of the Minho (see figure 5.1) – used mainly by fishermen (given its proximity to their houses); and another pier, facing the ocean and located at the end of 'Areinho do Ouro' street, of predominantly commercial use. One source explains that its name was:

> Arinho do Ouro, porque antes destes muros ia dar ao areal, que nesta terra se chama arinho, e se chamava de ouro tanta era a riqueza do comércio que aqui ouve em tempos passados, que aquela areia das praias do nosso Minho, em que encalhavam as embarcações dos negociantes.[18]

Navigation and Trade Circuits: Competitive and Cooperative Behaviours

Textile manufacturing activated a triangular trade between northern Europe (England, Flanders and France), Portuguese northwestern seaports, and the Atlantic islands of Azores and Madeira. Northwestern seaports served as gateways for the inland redistribution of textiles. Caminha and Viana were particularly relevant within this circuit, as evidenced by the many privileges and special status granted by the Crown. From the thirteenth century their inhabitants were exempt from paying the *diezmo* [tithe], a privilege that was to become the main driver of commercial dynamics of the region. Caminha and Viana gradually assumed their position as nodal points in the routes connecting the Mediterranean and the Atlantic.

17 'that once served the ships nearby in the river Minho, with a very large pier built of stone; however, as the sand covered it all, the use for this wall was lost.' In Antonio Carvalho da Costa, 'Da Villa de Caminha', in *Corografia portugueza, e descriçam topografica do famoso reyno de Portugal* (Braga, 1868–1869), p. 246.

18 'Arinho do Ouro [Sandbank of Gold] because one could pass the wall and reach the sandbank, locally called "arinho", and it was named of gold because of the rich trade practised here in past times, and the sand of the Minho beaches as landing spots for merchant ships'. In Biblioteca Pública Municipal do Porto, Reservados, Ms. 543: Miguel da Purificação, *Descripção da villa de Caminha*, fols 55–63v.

> São de pescadores as primeiras viagens a relativa distância – do Porto à Galiza, da Pederneira ao Algarve, do Algarve à costa andaluza. Viagens modestas, de pura cabotagem, em que a actividade piscatória e o transporte de mercadorias dão as mãos e assentam numa mesma base.[19]

From the fifteenth century, there were interdependent economic activities within the integration of Galicia and the Portuguese northwest region (Entre-Douro-e-Minho).[20] As described by Elisa Ferreira Priegue, the width of the Minho river was not a barrier to border trade between Portugal and Galicia. Rather it developed into a channel of communication that was difficult for the authorities to control and was subject to repeated regulation, both by Spanish and Portuguese kings.

In the early modern age, the movement of goods between Galicia and Portugal was characterised by a modest, highly diversified traffic, with an insignificant international trade. Indeed, excluding trade in salt, wine, fish and wood, this was a small-scale traffic, between the villages on the margins of the Minho, united by ancient privileges of vicinity and a placid disregard of fiscal barriers. Both kingdoms acted as complementary elements in overcoming the scarcity of goods.[21] For this same reason, maritime and fluvial trade with other ports, Iberian and European, and gradually overseas, became a crucial driver of urban development, initially in Caminha, Viana and Baiona, and later in Vigo.[22]

From at least the fourteenth century, Portuguese and Galicians shared a status of vicinity, on occasions sanctioned by royal privileges, on others simply as the result of ancient customs. These privileges linked the communities from both margins: La Guardia with Caminha; Monção with Salvaterra; the whole of Galicia with Valença; Tui and Baiona shared contacts throughout the Portuguese kingdom.

In Portugal, the demand for wood, fish and imported fabrics was satisfied by Galicia; in the opposite direction, the Portuguese supplied their salt, wine and fruit, for both consumption and distribution. This free trade caused harsh losses in tax revenue, since – except for long-distance goods such as salt – most of the traffic developed by these communities was practised directly, disregarding fiscal restraints.

19 'The first cabotage routes – from Porto to Galicia, Pederneira to Algarve, Algarve to Andalucia, were exploited by fishermen. Modest routes, from port to port, with fishing and transportation as simultaneous activities under the same framework', in Fernanda Espinosa, *Escritos históricos* (Porto, 1972), p. 151.

20 Leonor Freire Costa, 'O transporte no Atlântico: as frotas do açúcar (1580–1663)' (PhD diss. Universidade Técnica de Lisboa, 2000).

21 Ferreira Priegue, *Galicia en el comercio marítimo medieval.*

22 Carminda Cavaco, *A região de fronteira do rio Minho. Projecto de Estudos de Geografia Humana e Regional: Relatório no. 1* (Lisbon, 1973), p. 54.

It is therefore not surprising that royal and private officers repeatedly attempted to obstruct Portuguese and Galician cross-border traffic.[23] Proof of this is the complaint brought before the Lisbon royal courts in 1456 by representatives of Viana, Vila Nova (Cerveira), Valença and Caminha:

> Senhor em cada huu anno se carrega no rrio de minho pera frandes e pera aragam huu navyo e aly se ajuntavam as mercadorias de toda riba de minho comprando os mercadores da comarca a mayor parte das mercadorias asy as de hua parte como da outra de galiza e as traziam a esta parte e as carregavam no dicto navyo e despois que eram carregadas as davam em rrol ao almoxarife e asy dadas faziam novimento pera meyo do rio e ali tomava as outras mercadorias que alguus galegos que as queriam caregar e seguia sua viagem e ase custumou de sempre atee ora avera dous annos que gonçalo afonso voso coontador mandou que nenhum navio deste reino nom fretasse no dicto rio nem em galiza alguua mercadoria levasse nele nem trouxesse em o que recebemos grande agravo e vossas rendas e dizima nom rendem nada praza a vosa alteza mandar husar como se atee quy husou.[24]

Interestingly, the similarity in goods imported and exported by both territories caused episodes of competition for external markets, or situations where Portuguese and Galicians cooperated in foreign trade ventures. Both were direct competitors in the Mediterranean from the end of the fourteenth century and throughout the fifteenth. Of the Portuguese travelling to Mediterranean ports with fish and leather, these were mainly from Caminha, Viana, Ponte de Lima and Vila do Conde.

Portuguese and Galician ships arrived in Valencia and Barcelona in convoys, departed together, and partnerships were established to compensate for the low capacity of individual ventures.[25] One of the most interesting features of this commercial dynamic is related to fish trade. Portugal, one of the major fish exporters, was also a market for Galician fish, especially the northern villages

23 José Marques, *Relações entre Portugal e Castela nos finais da Idade Média* (Braga, 1994); *idem*, 'A fronteira do Minho'.

24 'Sir, every year one ship is loaded in the river Minho for Flanders and Aragon and here goods from all Minho are collected, bought by the county's merchants in both kingdoms and once the ship is loaded, they present the record of items to the *almoxarife* [customs officer], and then they sail to the middle of the river to load the goods from the Galicians and then it continues sailing, and thus is how it used to be, but two years ago your agent has ordered that no ship from this kingdom be freighted in this river neither in Galicia, which was a big penalty for us and for your dues and taxes, whereby we request that you allow the usual practice'. Torre do Tombo, Chancelaria de D. Afonso V, livro 36, fl. 197; published in João Martins da Silva Marques (ed.), *Descobrimentos Portugueses. Documentos para a sua história publicados e prefaciados por João Martins da Silva Marques* (Lisbon, 1988), doc. no. 1171.

25 Ferreira Priegue, *Galicia en el comercio marítimo medieval*.

engaged in fish salting activities. In the months that Portuguese *naus* set sail to the Mediterranean with sardines, conger eel and hake, Galician small-tonnage vessels would sail upriver, combining on-board sales with overland transport, and supplying inland villages with fish. Indeed, Portugal was the main market for south Galician fisheries.[26]

A complementary circuit in which both kingdoms participated was salt trade. A significant salt traffic is recorded in the Tui customs house, at least since 1170.[27] The fourteenth century witnessed a boost in salt production in Aveiro and Setúbal, supplying Galician *alfolíns* [storehouses] abundantly with Portuguese salt. This trade displayed two characteristic features: a direct trade with Aveiro (salt in exchange for bread) and the importance of Valença do Minho,[28] to the extent that, in 1378, the Portuguese king abolished the *alfolim* [salt tax] of this town.[29] In 1459, before the royal council in Lisbon, the representative of Valença described the '*muito intenso tráfego comercial entre Valença e Galiza [...] a vila possuía um bom tráfego de sal oriundo de Aveiro e vendido aos galegos que para ela se dirigiam com as suas montadas desde as terras de Limia, Orense e outros lugares*'.[30] Here, the agent explains that most Galicians travelled through Castro Laboreiro and Lamas de Mouro, as it was the straightest and safest route.[31] However, the mayor of Melgaço ordered the arrest of all Galicians, seizing their goods and forcing them to cross Melgaço for tax collection.[32] This traffic produced important taxes, tolls and revenue for the royal coffers. The representative ended his complaint with the warning that, to avoid these actions, Galicians chose to buy salt in Redondela and Pontevedra, hence diminishing royal revenue. At the same royal council, the representatives of Ponte de Lima complained about the 2 *reis* tax they were levied per beast of burden. They stated that:

> os galegos de Monterrei e de Milmanda e de Araujo e doutras partes, que costumavam vir à feira trazendo suas bestas e mercadorias e levando muito

26 Francisco López Capont, *El desarrollo industrial pesquero en el siglo XVIII* (La Coruña, 1998), p. 150.

27 Ferreira Priegue, *Galicia en el comercio marítimo medieval.*

28 José Marques, 'A fronteira do Minho'.

29 João Marques, *Descobrimentos Portugueses*, p. 414.

30 'very intense traffic between Valença and Galicia [...] the village receives the good salt trade, produced in Aveiro, and sells to Galicians who arrive in Valença with their beasts, from the lands of Limia, Orense and other places'. Daveau, 'Caminhos e fronteira na Serra da Peneda', p. 82.

31 Humberto Baquera Moreno, *Relações entre Portugal e a Galiza nos séculos XIV e XV* (Lisbon, 1996), pp. 78–79.

32 This imposition was the result of a royal charter from the king, D. Pedro I, dated from 28 May 1361, 'forcing all who came from from Portugal to Galicia or from Galicia to Portugal to pass through Melgaço'.

> sal e outras coisas, ocasionavam com isso grande beneficio para as sisas e para o bem comum da terra.[33]

Hence, we find two parallel routes within the two main valleys of the Minho river, a complementary downstream traffic by boat and an upstream traffic by hauling beasts.[34]

Customs and Port Administration: 'Viana de Caminha'

In the early sixteenth century, Portugal had an integrated customs structure with a regular and efficient royal officer corps. Common regulations were applied throughout the national territory and a general tax – the *diezmo*, a royal tax on international trade dating back to the foundation of the monarchy – was collected. Occasionally, a tax was levied on specific goods, such as those imposed on cloth in northern seaports. Portuguese customs tax innovations were significant in terms of border reinforcement, the structure of the national territory, and State cohesion. Moreover, it was a precocious endeavour, especially when compared with the Castilian situation. Here, in the northern border bishoprics, the only tax levied was the *salín de la frontera de Portugal* [salt levy on the Portuguese border], proving salt was the only imported product with fiscal significance. It was not until 1559 that customs were established along the border with Portugal, where they collected the *diezmo*.[35]

The existence of customs did not imply administrative autonomy. In fact, some of these had their own facilities, but did not have a permanent officer corps. In some circumstances, the customs house was contingent on a more ancient and larger structure. This was the case in Caminha, which operated in association with Viana under the general name of 'Viana de Caminha'. The Viana customs house was one of the oldest in the northwest, functioning as early as 1402. In the same county, concurrently with these royal customs houses, private collection offices operated, namely those devoted to the collection of feudal rents owed the Marquis of Vila Real. In 1499, the king donated all Caminha revenues and duties to the house of Vila Real, which boasted its own gate in the town walls, called 'the gate of the Marquis'; facing

33 'the Galicians from Monterrei and Milmanda and Arauxo and other places used to come to the market with their beasts and goods and took much salt and other things, bringing good profits to the local finances and for the common welfare of the land'. Daveau, 'Caminhos e fronteira na Serra da Peneda', p. 83.

34 Daveau, 'Caminhos e fronteira na Serra da Peneda', pp. 81–96.

35 João Cordeiro Pereira, 'Para a história das alfândegas em Portugal no início do século XVI (Vila do Conde – organização e movimento)' (PhD diss., Universidade Nova de Lisboa, 1983).

Table 5.1 Caminha Customs Officers

Officer	Functions
Judge	Heads customs clearance. Sets merchandise prices to calculate and collect the tax. Judges minor cases regarding smuggling.
Almoxarife	Officer in charge of the finances, collecting customs rents. Surveys ship inspections and unloading operations, assisted by the *requeredores* and customs men.
Requeredor	Performs ship inspections, before and after unloading the cargo, receiving one third of any smuggled goods.
Clerks	In charge of accounting. Supervise unloading operations.
Customs men	A generic name for minor employees performing ship inspections and assisting in the overall process of unloading and dispatch.
Doorman	Keeps the key of the customs house, certifying that during tax collection only the owner of the goods could enter, and watches over goods waiting for dispatch. He was one of the most highly paid customs officers.

the harbour it was the point of entry for all commodities subject to this tax.[36] Hence, under a common administration, enjoying identical privileges, and holding a special status for textile trade, the customs of Caminha and Viana must be analysed together.

The Caminha customs house exercised its jurisdiction throughout the county, controlling the waterfront between the rivers Minho and Âncora. In the early sixteenth century the customs house relocated between different locations and town officers seemed to struggle in finding an adequate building. After being located at a spot known as Alfandegua da Gandara, in 1532 it was moved to the private shop of Guiomar Martins, only to be moved three months later to another private shop, because the previous one lacked a threshing floor and proper space to unload goods.[37]

In 1532, the Caminha customs house had a judge, an *almoxarife* [customs officer], a *requeredor da marçaria e sisa* [collector], clerks, a doorman and guards (also referred to as customs men) (table 5.1).[38] The senior officers worked in both houses – Viana and Caminha – alternating office days.

36 Manuel António Fernandes Moreira, *A Alfândega de Viana e o comércio de importação de panos no séc. XVI* (Viana do Castelo, 1992); and Cordeiro Pereira, 'Para a história das alfândegas em Portugal', p. 9.

37 Torre do Tombo, Livro da Dízima de Caminha, 1532, fol. 3.

38 For documents mentioning these officers, see *ibid.*, and Moreira, *A Alfândega de Viana*, pp.11–16. Their duties are described in Pereira, 'Para a história das alfândegas em Portugal'.

Accounts of the customs house include the payment of salaries, building leases, office supplies, transport, overtime pay and hiring of couriers. In Caminha, these include expenses for the leasing of boats carrying officers to inspect incoming ships or for boats used in merchandise transhipment and unloading. The use of boats to transfer cargo from ship to land was particularly necessary in Caminha given the absence of an adequate quay. Running costs were covered by the *pelo conto* [house budget], while extra costs required the prior authorisation of the *feitor-mor* [factor]. Two account books from the Caminha customs house have survived: one for the *sisa dos panos* [tax on fabric imports] in 1527, and another recording the collection of the *dízima* [tithe] in 1532. We only find accounts regarding unloading operations in the latter.

Caminha customs house expenses in 1532:[39]

– For a boat transporting customs officers to the *trincado* [clinker boat] arriving from Valença – 20 *reis*
– For the officers sleeping and eating on a ship – 120 *reis*
– For a boat transporting the officers to the *nau* [carrack] arriving from Valença – 20 *reis*
– To carry a door lock to the customs house – 20 *reis*
– For a boat that carried the officers to the *trincado* [ship] arriving from France – 20 *reis*
– For the *barca* [lighter] to unload the *trincado* arriving from France – 260 *reis*
– For the oxen carts to carry these goods to the customs for tax collection – 100 *reis*
– For a boatman who carried the officers to a ship – 80 *reis*
– For the *requeredor* [customs officer] to sleep and eat on the ship – 20 *reis*
– For a *pinaça* [pinnace] to bring cargo (cloth) from a ship arriving from France – 250 *reis*

In the documents analysed, references to unloading operations mention the devices employed, especially the means of transport, rather than the human operators involved. This allows us to confirm the presence of different types of boats employed in the unloading of ships, depending on the volume of the cargo – from lighters to pinnaces – and boats to carry customs officers, in the first stage of dispatch; in the second stage, on land, ox-drawn carts were used. However, we find no mentions of the men involved in these activities. This is a common feature in other studies of Portuguese seaports. Indeed, some authors state that insufficient resources required the participation of the crews in cargo handling operations.[40] However, one can suppose that whenever a ship arrived at port, with the merchants waiting for their cargo, a group of men, undifferentiated workers, would be waiting to offer their services. In Porto, the customs

39 Torre do Tombo, Livro da Dízima de Caminha, 1532, fols 112–113v.

40 Barros, *Porto. A construção de um espaço marítimo no início dos tempos modernos.*

house guard, responsible for supervising the tax collection process, resorted to these men, paying in advance for boats, carts and carriers. On some occasions, the merchants were then charged these expenses when they went to the customs house, while on others these were paid by the town council.

In another northern seaport, Vila do Conde, studies also show that loading and unloading operations took place by the sandbar. In the customs quay, the only boats allowed to dock were small vessels transferring cargo from larger vessels. The larger ships, the *naus*, remained off the coast in deeper waters. In freight contracts from Vila do Conde, the merchant was accountable for all expenses concerning dispatch operations. He was to provide lighters to unload the ship, and in some contracts it was established that the ship's lighter was to be employed for this task. Documents mention two types of vessels: the ship's lighter and *batéis da terra* [land lighters].[41]

Customs regulations as applied throughout the kingdom[42] established that from the moment ships entered the harbour, they were subject to the control of the customs authority and the surveillance of customs officers. Sailors were not allowed to disembark before the dispatching process was finalised. The master was to present the list of goods, identifying owners and the value of each item. Only then, and under strict surveillance, could the cargo be discharged. Regarding these operations, regulations inform us of a concerted effort between sailors and customs agents. Indeed, it is said that the shipmaster and his *companha* [companions] were to unload the ship promptly, but it also establishes that the *almoxarife* and the clerk should bring the men needed to assist in the dispatch. Custom regulations also reveal the extreme caution exercised during discharge operations. Shipmasters were required to proceed effectively and promptly. Otherwise, they could be fined with a penalty of 500 *reis*, plus the cost of the barges. These costs were to be deducted from the freight and the salaries of the shipmaster and seamen. If they were unable to cover it, the *almoxarife* was to lend him the money. Additionally, should the *almoxarife* or the scrivener consider that more boats were required to speed up the dispatch, they should provide those. In this scenario, the king would pay the cost of extra boatmen and loaders, who 'should be well paid, so they would work diligently'. The *alcaide do mar* [sea governor] was to provide the required lighters, by compelling the boatmen for this task. Once unloaded, the merchandise was to be brought to land immediately, to the toll house, or at least to the quay. If the barge docked elsewhere, outside the pier, without declaring at customs, the cargo and the boat would be seized. The same penalty was applied to cargo unloaded during the night, which was forbidden. Regulations also established that merchandise should always be carried uncovered and penalised

41 Polónia, *A expansão ultramarina numa perspectiva local.*

42 Francisco Salles Lencastre, *Estudo sobre as portagens e alfândegas em Portugal (séculos XII a XVI)* (Lisbon, 1891), pp. 98–99.

individuals for hiding goods under their jackets or in their sleeves. The cargo was to be transported from the wharf to the customs house by the most direct and shortest route and was to be supervised throughout the whole process by two customs guards. Expenses for officers sleeping and eating on board is explained by customs regulations, which established that when ships were unable to pass the sandbar, due to rough seas, the *almoxarife* was to send one or more customs agents to remain on board until conditions improved. Further, as unloading at night was forbidden, when a ship docked, the *almoxarife* and the clerk were to seal the goods and leave customs agents on board to guard the cargo.[43]

Council minutes of Viana contribute to the analysis of the process of unloading and transportation, in addition to costs. Here are some of the prices charged in Viana for carriers and cartloads, from 1526 to 1572:[44]

– *Carreteiros* [carters] from the *ribeira* [waterfront] to the city centre – 3 to 5 *reis*
– *Caminheiros* [carriers] – 100 *reis* per day
– Worker – 70 *reis* per day
– Cartloads from Viana to Caminha – 50 *reis*
– *Carreto* [cartload] from the pier to the *postigo da ribeira* [city wall gate] – 3 to 5 *reis*
– Carrying a wine cask to Caminha – 60 *reis* (40 *reis* for two empty casks)
– Cartloads of wine, firewood or stone – 15 reis per *légua* [league][45]

In Caminha, customs house accounts reveal that boat owners charged 20 *reis* to transfer officers to the incoming ships, or 260 *reis* for unloading services. Then, if needed, ox-carts transported the cargo to the customs house for 100 *reis*. In Viana, short-distance conveyance records reveal the work of the *carreteiros* – owners of small two-wheel carts – who transported the goods to the town centre; and the cartloads, transporting cargo from quay to town gate. For longer distances, the cartloads sent to Caminha completed maritime routes by land. The council minutes of Viana reveal a particularly important reference to 'workers', which appears to verify the existence, and relevance, of unspecialised labour in the ports sector – groups of men who provided services, such as cargo handling, as required. As a direct result of their lack of expertise they are not represented as an organised group, a characteristic shared – at least in Portuguese maritime history – with other maritime occupations.[46] As such,

43 *Ibid.*
44 Moreira, *O porto de Viana do Castelo*; *idem*, *A Alfândega de Viana*.
45 *légua* is approximately 5 kilometers or 3 miles.
46 Amélia Polónia, 'L'historiographie portugaise sur les gens de mer et les communautés littorales: une approche de synthèse', *Revue d'Histoire Maritime – Numéro thématique: La Recherche Internationale en Histoire Maritime*, 11–12 (2010), 175–194.

much maritime labour and many port services were provided by a workforce characterised by its heterogeneity, precariousness, seasonality, mobility and a significant foreign presence.[47]

Conclusions

Although much has been written concerning trade routes involving the Portuguese northern seaports, there remains much to study regarding port logistics and infrastructures.[48] Regarding the men who remained on land and in harbours, assisting in shipping operations, details are even scantier. In writing about this topic in connection to the Portuguese northern border and surrounding coastal villages, it has been challenging to contribute to the understanding of transport logistics and cargo handling.

As a case study, a border provides an exceptional vantage point, especially when the focus is not on the geographical division *per se*, but rather on the relations arising and developed around it. In this broader sense, a border territory forces its neighbours to interact, whether through rivalry, exchange or cooperation. Hence, this setting explains the development of regional dynamics – truly, the construction of an integrated and complementary regional system – within two of the most prominent maritime powers in the sixteenth century. Transport and shipping were the main vectors in this relationship. As observed, Portuguese and Galicians interacted, ignoring political borders, either in collaboration – compensating their low individual enterprise capacity – or as competitors sharing the same routes and offering the same products.

A second feature one should be aware of when studying these matters is the impact of environmental variations on port dynamics. We have demonstrated that ports were highly influenced by changing coastline features during the Middle Ages and the sixteenth century. Geomorphology played an important role in defining logistic procedures; sea conditions or the location of sandbars determined loading and unloading operations. Thus, both the historical cartography and the depictions analysed here demonstrate the constraints on navigation in the Minho estuary, such as sand deposits or rough seas. This

47 Sara Pinto, 'Os homens do mar de Caminha no século XVI. A pluriactividade nas comunidades marítimas', *Revista Estudos Regionais*, 8 (2014), 13–22.

48 An extended analysis on these matters – geomorphologic features, seaport infrastructures evolution, technological innovations, etc. – was developed within the research project 'Hisportos: A Contribution to the History of NW Portuguese Seaports in the Early Modern Age'. See Amélia Polónia, 'HISPORTOS – A Research Project on Portuguese Seaports in the Early Modern Age', in *European Seaports in the Early Modern Age – A Comparative Approach: Proceedings/International Workshop European Seaport Systems* (Porto, 2007), pp. 28–41. Results of the project are available at http://web.letras.up.pt/hisportos/.

scenario explains why it was so difficult to implement, and maintain, proper port infrastructures, such as stone quays, and why small boats were the main vehicles for loading and unloading tasks.

This led us to focus on a case study, the accounts of the customs house of Caminha, where we observed periodic payments for barge services. Small boats approached the incoming ships, carrying officers to inspect and assist in the unloading process. On the quay, men – 'workers' as mentioned in the council minutes of Viana – carts and ox-carts, depending on the volumes to be transported, completed the process. We long for more knowledge about the workers but the lack of documentation and their own ambiguous profile as a workforce preclude more profound insights. This is a common obstacle for those writing about the history of coastal communities.

Despite being able to present and develop some of the main features regarding transport and shipping in the Portuguese northern border, this remains a stimulating historical region and a challenge for researchers.

6

Anchorages, Infrastructures and Stevedoring in Medieval Atlantic Andalusia

ENRIQUE JOSÉ RUIZ PILARES

University of Cádiz

ABSTRACT. During the Late Middle Ages port infrastructures were, for the most part, very precarious. Landing and cargo handling facilities were in many cases limited to fragile timber structures or beaches and riverbanks. These were frequently poorly fitted and dangerous sites, chiefly due to the persistent silting of waterways that was aggravated by the negligence of operators. On the Andalusian Atlantic littoral, this situation became a great nuisance for communities throughout the fifteenth century in their bid to partake in the economic prosperity stemming from the flourishing mercantile activities. Extant documentation for some of these port enclaves has allowed us to analyse the interventions of the different authorities –including the monarchy, seigneurial nobility, municipal councils and ecclesiastic institutions – to mitigate these deficiencies.

Port Infrastructures in the Late Middle Ages

The fifteenth century witnessed the flourishing and development of maritime commerce on the coast of Atlantic Andalusia.[1] From that moment on, the region became one of the more dynamic and attractive markets in Europe.[2]

1 This work is part of the research project funded by the Spanish Ministry of Education titled 'El mar como frontera. Transgresiones legales en el Atlántico bajomedieval' (PGC2018-095719-B-I00).

2 Antonio Collantes de Terán Sánchez and Antonio García-Baquero González (eds), *Andalucía 1492: razones de un protagonismo* (Seville, 1992); Enrique Otte Sander, *Sevilla y sus mercaderes a fines de la Edad Media* (Seville, 1996); and Eduardo Aznar Vallejo, 'Andalucía y el Atlántico Andalucía y el Atlántico Norte a fines de la Edad Media', *Historia. Instituciones. Documentos*, 30 (2003), 103–120.

This scenario was determined by several interconnected factors.[3] First, the strategic position along the international commercial routes made this area an obligatory stopping point for merchants connecting the Mediterranean and the Atlantic.[4] Second, rich fertile lands made this area one of the main exporters of staple goods for the European medieval markets: cereal from the countryside of Seville and Jerez de la Frontera; oil, mainly from the Sevillian Aljarafe region; and wine, in particular from Jerez and the Sierra Norte mountains of Seville.[5] Finally, another element that stimulated the development of the Andalusian littoral was the establishment of numerous foreign communities, attracted to this region for the reasons mentioned above. The majority hailed from other regions within the Iberian Peninsula. They were people of the sea, mostly shipmasters from the Cantabrian seaboard and the Portuguese Algarve, and merchants from the Crown of Aragon.[6] Others came mostly from the Italian peninsula (namely Genoa), Flanders or England. They were fewer in number but highly influential in terms of the development of credit and the export of Andalusian goods.[7]

3 Juan Manuel Bello León, *Extranjeros en Castilla (1474–1501): notas y documentos para el estudio de su presencia en el reino a fines del siglo XV* (Tenerife, 1994), pp. 41–42; *idem*, 'El Reino de Sevilla en el comercio exterior castellano (siglos XIV y XV)', in *Castilla y Europa. Comercio y Mercaderes en los siglos XIV, XV y XVI*, ed. Hilario Casado Alonso (Burgos, 1995), pp. 57–80.

4 Raúl González Arévalo, 'Comercio exterior del reino de Sevilla a través de los manuales de mercaderías italianos bajomedievales', *Historia. Instituciones. Documentos*, 38 (2001), 219–253.

5 Miguel Ángel Ladero Quesada and Manuel González Jiménez, *Diezmo eclesiástico y producción de cereales en el reino de Sevilla (1408–1503)* (Seville, 1979); Emilio Martín Gutiérrez, 'El viñedo en la zona de Jerez a finales de la Edad Media', in *Historia de Andalucía. VII Coloquio*, ed. Antonio Malpica Cuello, Rafael Peinado Santaella and Adela Fábregas García (Granada, 2009), pp. 287–300; Mercedes Borrero Fernández, *La organización del trabajo. De la explotación de la tierra a las relaciones laborales en el campo andaluz (siglos XIII–XVI)* (Seville, 2003).

6 Manuela Ronquillo Rubio, *Los vascos en Sevilla y su tierra durante los siglos XIII, XIV y XV. Fundamentos de su éxito y permanencia* (Bilbao, 2004); Natalia Palenzuela Domínguez, *Los mercaderes burgaleses en Sevilla a fines de la Edad Media* (Seville, 2003); Juan Manuel Bello León, 'Mercaderes del siglo XV de Jerez de la Frontera', *Historia. Instituciones. Documentos*, 41 (2014), 11–44; *idem*, '¿Quiénes eran los mercaderes de Sevilla a finales de la Edad Media?', in *Gentes del mar en la ciudad atlántica medieval*, ed. Jesús Ángel Solórzano Telechea, Michel Bochaca and Amélia Andrade (Logroño, 2012), pp. 249–274.

7 Juan Manuel Bello León, 'Mercaderes extranjeros en Sevilla en tiempos de los Reyes Católicos', *Historia. Instituciones. Documentos*, 20 (1993), 47–84; Raúl González Arévalo, 'Presencia diferencial italiana en el sur de la Península Ibérica en la Baja Edad Media. Estado de la cuestión y propuesta de investigación', *Medievalismo*, 23 (2013), 175–208; José Antonio Mingorance Ruiz, 'Los extranjeros en Jerez de la Frontera a fines de la Edad Media' (PhD diss., University Pablo de Olvide, Seville, 2013), pp. 80–228, <http://hdl.handle.net/10433/755> [accesed 20 January 2020].

The vast Andalusian littoral, with an extension of almost 300 kilometres from the river Guadiana on the border with Portugal, to the Strait of Gibraltar, possessed natural features that favoured the establishment of significant port enclaves.[8] Of importance were the bays of Cádiz and Algeciras, the Guadalquivir estuary, and the Tinto and Odiel estuaries in Huelva.[9] A large port system developed, with its own dynamic and hierarchies, where the city of Seville, in spite of being located further inland on the banks of the Guadalquivir river, 80 kilometres from the seashore, played a leading role as a large financial centre and the seat of the principal international commerce companies of the southern Peninsula.[10] This prominence did not imply that the neighbouring port cities and towns, both coastal and fluvial, played a secondary role within this port complex.[11] The latest research blurs the binary distinction between Seville and its 'anteports', and proposes historical readings informed by notions such as 'connection' and 'interdependence'. This is evidenced through analysis of freight contracts which portray the fierce competition and conflicts between the different ports for the benefits of growing commerce and the development of fishing activities.[12] This is particularly so if we consider the complex jurisdictional reality of the littoral. The Castilian monarchy had granted the nobles the largest portions of their lands after the Christian conquests of the thirteenth

8 An environmental reading of this coastal space in Emilio Martín Gutiérrez, 'Los paisajes costeros interpretados desde la riparia. Reflexiones sobre el Golfo de Cádiz a finales de la Edad Media', *Riparia, Suplemento* 2 (2019), 47–79; and *idem*, 'El Estrecho de Gibraltar durante el siglo XIV: medio ambiente y redes comerciales en Algeciras', *Revista del Centro de Estudios Históricos de Granada y su Reino*, 30 (2018), 51–69.

9 On the main ports of this coastal space see, Víctor Muñoz Gómez, 'Para el conocimiento de la costa de Andalucía atlántica (siglos XIV–XVI), descripciones, relaciones y documentación náutica', *Historia. Instituciones. Documentos*, 40 (2013), 179–205; and *idem*, 'Puertos, abras, cabos e islas: la topografía medieval de la costa atlántica de Andalucía a través de las cartas portulanas', in *De mar a mar. Los puertos castellanos en la Baja Edad Media*, ed. Eduardo Aznar Vallejo and Roberto J. González Zalacain (San Cristóbal de La Laguna, 2015), pp. 179–221.

10 Antonio Miguel Bernal Rodríguez and Antonio Collantes de Terán Sánchez, 'El puerto de Sevilla, de puerto fluvial medieval a centro portuario mundial (siglos XIV–XVII)', in *I porti come impresa economica*, ed. Simoneta Cavaciocchi (Florence, 1988), pp. 779–824.

11 Roberto J. González Zalacain, 'De Puerto a Puerto. Las relaciones entre los puertos de la Bahía de Cádiz (Siglos XV–XVI)', in *De mar a mar*, ed. Aznar Vallejo and González Zalacain, pp. 147–177.

12 This follows from the analysis of the outstanding demographic weight of the foreign communities of the Bay of Cádiz: 'a situation of equality, if not of superiority with respect to Seville' at the end of the Middle Ages. Raúl González Arévalo, 'La integración de los italianos en las sociedades portuarias andaluzas (siglos XIII–XV)', in *Las sociedades portuarias de la Europa Atlántica en la Edad Media*, ed. Beatriz Arízaga Bolumburu and Jesús Ángel Solórzano Telechea (Logroño, 2016), pp. 337–364, at p. 272.

century (figure 6.1), giving rise to a complex tax structure marked by differing privileges and fiscal fees.[13]

Focusing on the subject of this chapter, within this context of economic expansion, Andalusian Atlantic ports – beyond their privileged natural conditions as harbours – boasted hardly any artificial infrastructures to facilitate the loading and unloading of merchandise. When these infrastructures were present, in most cases they were very precarious. This is the case, for example, of timber wharves, which were exposed to both the harsh effect of the climate and the bad practices of the mariners, as we shall see in this chapter. These installations in many cases could not guarantee efficient stevedoring and stowage activities. This scenario did not differ greatly from that of other European spaces. To mention a very relevant case in Cantabrian ports, despite the intense and flourishing maritime traffic with the north of Europe from the thirteenth century onwards, they did not possess solid infrastructures until the late Middle Ages, as can be surmised from the chronology of the construction of stone quays in the main port enclaves: Bilbao, 1402; Santander, 1434; San Sebastián, 1440; Laredo, 1460; Pasajes, 1497.[14] In neighbouring Portugal, we find a similar situation, as one of its principal port enclaves, Oporto, did not have a stone quay until 1449.[15] The situation on the Mediterranean coast of the Crown of Aragon was hardly better: Barcelona did not have a dock until the fifteenth century and, on the Valencian coastline, only Alicante had a wharf and a crane.[16] This reality contrasted with the development of infrastructures in the large port centres of northern Europe, with solid port facilities that buttressed

13 Juan Manuel Bello León, 'El marco jurídico y fiscal en los puertos andaluces a finales de la Edad Media', in *De mar a mar*, ed. Aznar Vallejo and González Zalacain, pp. 17–58. For more information on the population of this region, see Antonio Domínguez Ortiz, 'La población del Reino de Sevilla en 1534', *Cuadernos de Historia. Anexos Hispania*, 7 (1977), 337–355; Carlos Flores Varela, 'La evolución de la población urbana de Andalucía en los siglos XV y XVI', *En La España Medieval*, 28 (2005), 97–125.

14 Beatriz Arízaga Bolumburu and Jesús Ángel Solórzano Telechea, 'La construction d'infrastructures portuaires dans les villes du nord de la péninsule ibérique à la fin du Moyen Âge', in *Ports et littoraux de l'Europe atlantique. Transformations naturelles et aménagements humains (XIVe–XVIe siècles)*, ed. Michel Bochaca and Jean Louis Sarrazin (Rennes, 2007), pp. 121–140.

15 Amândio Barros, 'A construçao de um centro portuário atlântico: O Porto nos séculos XVI e XVII', in *La gobernanza de los puertos atlánticos, siglos XIV–XX: políticas y estructuras portuarias*, ed. Amélia Polónia and Ana María Rivera Medina (Madrid, 2016), pp. 193–218.

16 José Ramón Hinojosa Montalvo, 'Ciudades portuarias en la Corona de Aragón durante la baja edad media: los ejemplos de Mallorca, Valencia y Alicante', in *Città portuali del Mediterraneo. Storia e archeologia*, ed. Ennio Poleggi (Genoa, 1989), pp. 151–165.

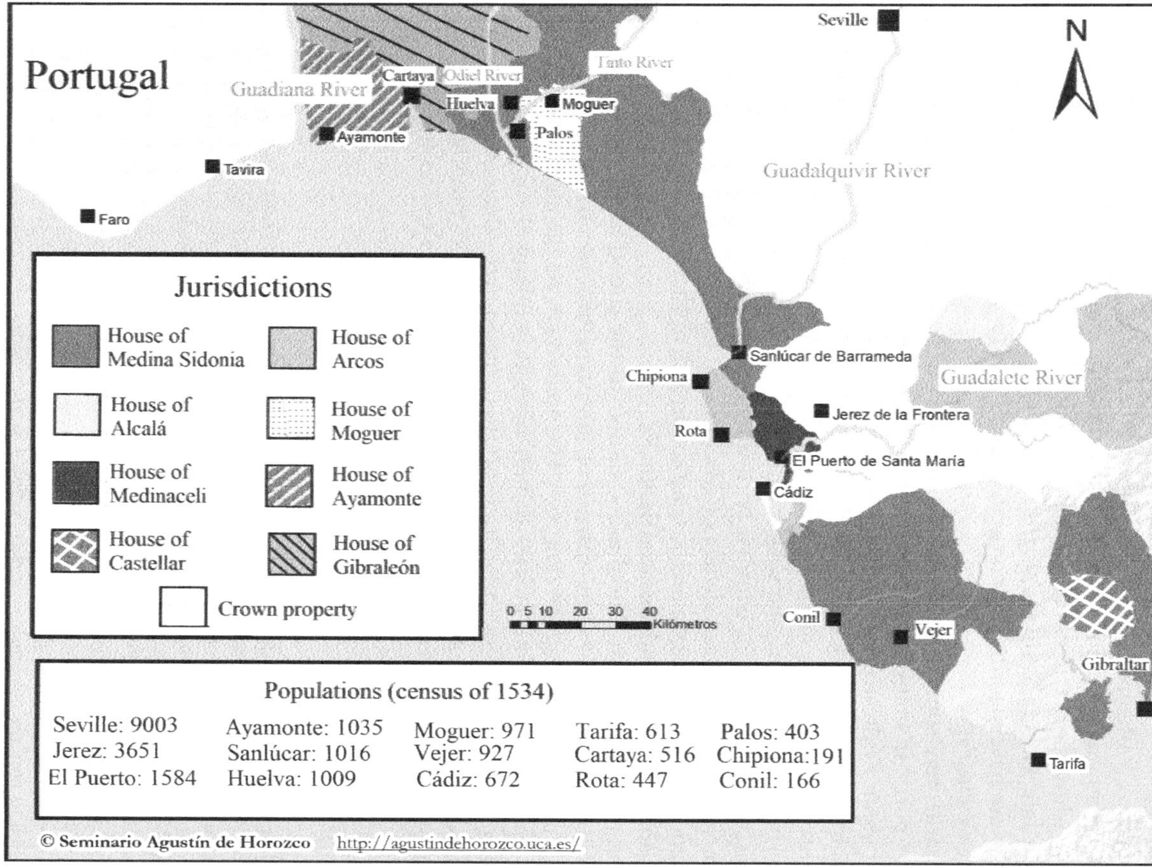

Figure 6.1. Principal ports on the Andalusian Atlantic littoral: location, jurisdiction and population. The data included in the map refer to the number of neighbours – not inhabitants – according to a census conducted by the Castilian Crown between 1528 and 1534. Although somewhat late for our study framework, it is the only one offering complete data that covers all surrounding populations. *Censo de Pecheros: Carlos I, 1528* (Madrid, 2008), t. II

the commercial growth they experienced throughout the latter centuries of the Middle Ages.[17]

In the majority of port spaces, a habitual practice was the use of beaches or riverbanks sheltered from winds and possible pirate raids as landing sites, requiring the use of smaller boats to connect larger ships with the shore. This was common practice, even in towns with significant maritime traffic such as Valencia, whose port – *el Grao* – was described by an anonymous Milanese merchant late as 1519: '*non ha portto alcuno, ma solo spiaggia*'. The larger vessels, as we have mentioned, '*non si accostano alla terra, ma stano in mare meza lega o circa*'.[18]

Shipyards were some of the rare infrastructures to become common in late medieval ports, in many cases as remnants of the Al-Andalus era. This was brought about by the need for facilities to repair the frequent damage suffered by the ships from the heavy swells, inclement weather, and technical difficulties of all sorts. However, the majority of port enclaves did not have permanent access to installations or to a shipwright with the necessary wood and fastenings to repair smaller vessels, in contrast with the large shipyards extant, in the Spanish case, in Barcelona, Valencia or Mallorca on the Mediterranean, that of Santander or San Sebastián on the Cantabrian Sea, or that of Seville, which we will analyse, on the Andalusian Atlantic.[19]

In the ports of Atlantic Andalusia – similar to the situation of ports in the neighbouring Portugal – the absence of infrastructures was the common standard until the mid-fifteenth century.[20] The need to attract the increasingly intense maritime traffic and greater volume of trade explains the initiatives implemented by the different authorities governing these ports – the monarchy, feudal lords, urban elites, and even ecclesiastical institutions – to promote the building of infrastructures as a means to reap the benefits of this new economic

17 Philippe Contamine, 'Équipements et installations portuaires en France, de la fin du Moyen Âge aux Temps modernes', in *I porti come impresa economica*, ed. Simonetta Cavaciocchi (Florence, 1988), pp. 7–20; Maryanne Kowalkeski, 'Port Labor in Medieval England', in *The Sea in History – The Medieval World*, ed. Christian Buchet and Michel Balard (Woodbridge 2017), pp. 619–628.

18 'it has no port but only a beach'; 'do not berth by land but remain at sea half a league or so away'. David Igual Luis, 'Non ha porto alcuno, ma solo spiaggia. La actividad marítima valenciana en el siglo XV', *Aragón en la Edad Media*, 25 (2014), 101–134, at p. 102.

19 For the state of the art and bibliographic summary of peninsular shipyards, Juan Manuel Bello León and Alejandro Martín Perera, *Las atarazanas de Sevilla a finales de la Edad Media* (Madrid, 2012), pp. 10–16.

20 Amélia Polónia and Sara Pinto, 'Harbour Construction Policies and Funding Agency in Early Modern Portugal (1400–1800)', in *La gobernanza de los puertos atlánticos*, ed. Polónia and Rivera Medina, pp. 9–24.

reality.[21] This building of facilities went hand in hand with the specialisation and development of the 'people of the sea', as historiography has described the individuals participating in this type of venture.[22] Their different categories have been described by Maryanne Kowaleski for the English case.[23] It is not the aim of this chapter to delve into the proliferation of a series of maritime professions in Andalusian port enclaves since this has recently received ample attention from various specialists.[24] We cannot, however, separate analysis of the shipyards from the profession of the shipwright, or the docks and warehouses from the carters, porters and all sorts of professions involved in cargo handling activities, as I will show in this chapter.[25]

The Ports of the Coast of Huelva

The westernmost region of the Andalusian Atlantic littoral, the modern-day province of Huelva, is bordered to the north by the river Guadiana and the Portuguese frontier, and to the south by the estuary of the river Guadalquivir. It is a very straight coastline, with hardly any inlets or headlands to provide shelter from winds and storms. Consequently, only the inland banks of the rivers flowing into the sea offered the necessary conditions for the establishment of port spaces.[26] However, the area's coastal populations were less dense and commercial traffic was considerably more modest than in other enclaves on the Andalusian Atlantic coast. This did not discourage the local lords – the land belonged to seigneurial estates – from investing in the development of infrastructures to increase the economic impact of commerce in the area.

Palos de la Frontera, although it was one of the less densely populated settlements – around 2,000 inhabitants recorded in the early fifteenth century – boasted the most important port on the Huelva littoral. It was located on the mouth of the river Tinto, a short distance from the coast. When ships commanded by

21 Jesús Ángel Solórzano Telechea and Javier Añíbarro Rodríguez, 'Infraestructuras e instalaciones portuarias, fluviales e hídricas en las villas del norte peninsular a finales de la Edad Media: las obras públicas como instrumento de poder', in *Musulmanes y cristianos frente a lagua en las ciudades medievales*, ed. María Isabel Val Valdivieso and Olatz Villanueva Zubizarreta (Santander, 2008), pp. 277–280.

22 Jesús Ángel Solórzano Telechea, Michel Bochaca and Amélia Aguiar Andrade (eds), *Gentes de mar en la ciudad atlántica medieval* (Logroño, 2012), pp. 13–16.

23 Kowaleski, 'Port Labor', pp. 620–627.

24 Eduardo Aznar Vallejo, 'La regulación de los oficios del mar en Andalucía', in *Gentes de mar*, ed. Solórzano Telechea, Bochaca and Aguiar Andrade, pp. 95–122.

25 Emilio Martín Gutiérrez and Enrique José Ruiz Pilares, *El viñedo en Jerez durante el siglo XV. Un mercado de trabajo en torno al vino* (Jerez de la Frontera, 2019).

26 Antonio González Gómez, *Moguer en la baja edad media (1248–1538)* (Huelva, 1977), p. 136.

Christopher Columbus sailed from this port to the Americas in 1492, Palos de la Frontera enjoyed a prominent position among other surrounding towns thanks to its better port facilities, which according to sources could accommodate fifty mid-sized vessels in the harbour.[27] It is thus not surprising that the Catholic Monarchs purchased part of the town to prepare for this voyage, since all the ports on the Andalusian Atlantic littoral were under feudal dominion except for the small town of Puerto Real, founded in the interior of the Bay of Cádiz in 1483.[28] The latest archaeological interventions, carried out in the context of the fifth centenary of Columbus's crossing, have exposed the physiognomy of the port space between the fifteenth and the sixteenth centuries. It was located in a wetland area, a natural harbour providing shelter from tides and winds. Since there was no wharf, a lack common to most ports of the time, all merchandise was loaded and unloaded directly onto the shore by boats and small vessels.[29] A shipyard was erected in the vicinity,[30] by a ceramic factory and a warehouse or *alota*, with a series of associated infrastructures.[31]

The main port installation is the abovementioned warehouse or *alota*, a term employed exclusively in ports of Huelva.[32] These infrastructures, whose main function was to serve as port tolls, included cellars and inns for the purchase and consumption of food, a storage facility, another for accommodation, a fountain and a series of secondary facilities such as wells, water conduits and dumpsites. The complex also included an industrial compound related to maritime economy, with ten different types of kiln to produce bricks, tiles, lime, ceramic and houseware. The *alota* was created around the mid-fifteenth

27 Juan Manuel Campos Carrasco, 'El descubrimiento arqueológico del Puerto Colombino de Palos de la Frontera', in *Actas de las Jornadas Historia sobre el Descubrimiento de América*, t. IV (Seville, 2019), pp. 443–462.

28 At the end of the Middle Ages the town of Palos was an estate in shared ownership, 11/12 belonging to the Count of Miranda, and the remainder to the Dukes of Medina Sidonia. However, the Catholic Monarchs acquired the Miranda estate in June 1492, while preparing Columbus' voyage. Years later Carlos I resold it to its former owners, Miguel Ángel Ladero Quesada, 'Los señoríos medievales onubenses. Período de formación', in *Huelva en la Edad Media 20 años después*, ed. Juan Luis Carriazo Rubio and José María Miura Andrade (Huelva, 1998), pp. 203–227, at p. 226.

29 Examples from other port spaces in Kowaleski, 'Port Labor', p. 624.

30 David González Cruz and Julio Izquierdo Labrado, 'Astilleros, barcos y construcción naval en tiempos de los descubrimientos: Palos de la Frontera y puertos del litoral onubense (Huelva, Saltes y San Juan del Puerto)', in *Barcos y construcción naval entre el Atlántico y el Mediterráneo en la época de los descubrimientos (siglos XV y XVI)*, ed. David González Cruz (Madrid, 2018), pp. 51–88.

31 Campos Carrasco, 'El descubrimiento arqueológico del Puerto Colombino', p. 464.

32 This specificity is confirmed by its unique appearance in the documentation and ordinances of the coast of Huelva, as was the case of the regulation of the Ayamonte riverbank in 1552: Juan Luis Carriazo Rubio, 'Pesca, frontera y señorío: Ayamonte de la Edad Media a la Edad Moderna', *Huelva en su Historia*, 8 (2001), 41–66, at pp. 57–61.

century, in the context of the soaring commercial development and demographic growth of the town until well into the sixteenth century, when Palos suffered a demographic crisis due to the migration flow to America, as can be seen in the ordinances of 1488.[33] These norms described a series of mercantile activities such as the disbursements of the merchants to the *alota* depending on the volume and quality of their goods.[34]

The nearby town of Huelva, with twice the population of Palos, was less significant in terms of port infrastructure in the late Middle Ages. The most graphic representation of this reality is the later building of an *alota* in the town in the early sixteenth century.[35] The town was is located on the Odiel river, a few kilometres from the Atlantic. We have no evidence of facilities connected with cargo handling activities in this port. However, the ordinances promulgated in 1503 describe a paved platform, known as La Calzada, leading to the shore of the Odiel. Fish stalls were installed here for the sale of fresh fish arriving in the town.[36]

In northern Huelva, connected to the ocean through the estuary of the river Piedras, we find the town of Cartaya, under the domain of the Marquis of Gibraleón. It was accessible for larger vessels, as described in the town ordinances of 1509. However, as stated in the document, the inhabitants of the town complained that, with the increase in traffic and maritime commerce, navigability toward the interior of the estuary had become increasingly difficult. They accused shipmasters – foreigners in particular – of jettisoning ballast (stones, gravel or sand used to stabilise ships) with the risk that the waterway 'could be clogged in such a manner that the ships would not be able to access the port'.[37] From these sources, we know that the port had a very precarious wharf for loading and unloading. An ordinance of 1516 states that:

> algunos marineros y personas de la mar [...] acostunbran amarrar sus barcos e caravelas a los maderos e travesones [...] que estavan en el dicho

33 Alberto Bermejo Meléndez and Javier Bermejo Meléndez, 'Las instalaciones del puerto de época colombina de Palos de la Frontera (Huelva): la alota y el campo de hornos', in *Actas de las Jornadas Historia sobre el Descubrimiento de América*, t. IV (Seville, 2019), pp. 513–541.

34 Antonio González Gómez, 'Las Ordenanzas Municipales de Palos de la Frontera (1484–1521)', *Historia. Instituciones. Documentos*, 3 (1976), 249–280.

35 Julio Izquierdo Labrado, 'Análisis demoeconómico de la costa de Huelva (1510–1530)', *Huelva en su Historia*, 2 (1988), 347–358, at p. 351.

36 María Auxiliadora García-Arreciado Batanero, 'La villa de Huelva en la Baja Edad Media', *Huelva en su historia*, 2 (1988), 175–230.

37 María Concepción Quintanilla Raso, 'La reglamentación de una villa de señorío en el tránsito de la Edad Media a la Moderna. Ordenanzas de Cartaya (Huelva) (Fines s. XV–primera mitad s. XVI)', *Historia, Instituciones, Documentos*, 13 (1986), 189–259, at p. 231.

> muelle, de lo qual dis que viene mucho daño e perjuysio al dicho muelle y edefiçio dél.[38]

To prevent this practice a fine of 200 maravedis was established for those who insisted on attaching their ships, of any type, even small boats or skiffs known as *cópanos*, in such a manner. Half the amount collected was allocated to repairs and the other half to pay the person in charge of the facilities, the *arrendador del muelle* [dock warden].[39]

Other significant port towns on the coast of Huelva were Ayamonte and Moguer. The latter, belonging to the estate of Portocarrero, was located on the river Tinto. The port was located in a harbour, described in the documents as *pozo de navíos* (ship well), providing anchorage for mostly mid-sized vessels such as caravels. In order to prevent the clogging of the waterway, as described in the case of Palos, ordinances were issued in 1538 banning the jettison of ballast into the sea and ordering the continued upkeep of the waterways. Small skiffs were employed to connect with the river.[40] The enclave included small facilities for shipbuilding and repair, inherited from the fishing tradition of these towns, as occurred in Ayamonte, in the Estúñiga estate domain.[41] We know that this burgh, bordering Portugal on the mouth of the river Guadiana, had an *alota* in the early sixteenth century, located by the wetlands on the riverbanks. As in the case of Moguer, only small vessels could unload here, while the larger vessels had to moor '*en el rio largo*' [on the long river].[42]

Seville and the Guadalquivir

The most important town on the Andalusian Atlantic littoral was, undoubtedly, Seville. Despite its location approximately 80 kilometres from the shore, the town was perfectly connected with international maritime routes through the river Guadalquivir, which was navigable by larger ships all the way to the

38 'mariners and seamen [...] have the habit of attaching their boats and caravels to the pillars and crosspieces [...] of said dock, which is said to cause much damage and harm to said dock and building', *ibid.*, p. 250.

39 *Ibid.*

40 González Gómez, *Moguer en la baja edad media*, p. 139.

41 David Ropero Regidor, 'Barcos y construcción naval en Moguer en la era de los descubrimientos', and Antonio Manuel González Díaz, 'Barcos y carpintería de ribera en el marquesado de Ayamonte', both in *Barcos y construcción naval entre el Atlántico y el Mediterráneo en la época de los descubrimientos (siglos XV y XVI)*, ed. David González Cruz (Madrid, 2018), pp. 89–118 and pp. 153–172, respectively.

42 Carriazo Rubio, 'Pesca, frontera y señorío Ayamonte', p. 60.

town, the final stretch of the routes of international traffic.[43] This did not mean that navigation was easy. In contrast with coastal towns of the bays of Cádiz or Huelva, Seville did not have adequate port services to become the most important port town on the Andalusian littoral. As gathered in complaints of shipmasters and merchants of larger ships in 1509, the port was inconveniently located, and access was arduous. The main problem was found at the river mouth, with areas of shallow draughts and a series of shoals and sandbars impeding fluvial navigation. A similar problem was documented in other contemporary fluvial ports, such as Oporto.[44] These areas underwent constant transformation due to natural and human impacts on the area,[45] in addition to climate variations, as evidenced in the geomorphological transformations of the Portuguese northeastern littoral during the sixteenth century.[46] This explains the habitual practice of unloading part of the cargo onto auxiliary boats to lighten the main ship. This problem was aggravated by the lack of upkeep of the riverbed, which caused notable problems during the sixteenth century.[47]

To the problematic navigability must be added the scant port equipment. One of the few exceptions was the shipyard, constructed in 1253 by order of the Castilian king Alfonso X to build the fleet of galleys destined to participate in the conquest of western Andalusia. In 1440, the shipyard boasted, among other officials, 35 shipwrights, 32 caulkers, 38 sawyers and 30 weavers. However, by the end of the fifteenth century, with the decline of this type of vessel in favour of the more versatile *naos* and caravels for Atlantic crossings, these infrastructures were repurposed to become warehouses, toll houses, fish markets, and even a jail or a hospital.[48] The vessels lacked sufficient dry docks for repairs and the number of shipwrights available was insufficient to cover the volume of ships arriving in the town.

The actual port of Seville was located by the Torre del Oro, in an area known as El Arenal. It was named Puerto de las Muelas de la Torre del Oro. The port had barely any facilities by the end of the Middle Ages. Until the early

43 This river also connected Seville with another important city of Andalusia, Córdoba. However, the stretch between both locations was travelled by smaller vessels. See Eduardo Aznar Vallejo, 'Barcos y barqueros en Sevilla', *Historia. Instituciones. Documentos*, 21 (1994), pp. 1–12.

44 Barros, 'A construçao de um centro portuário', pp. 193–218.

45 Louic Ménanteau, 'L'influence des facteurs naturels et anthropiques sur l'evolution des ports de Basse-Andalousie (XIIIe–XVIe siècles): études de cas (Palos de la Frontera, Séville et Sanlúcar de Barrameda)', in *Ports et littoraux de l'Europe atlantique. Transformations naturelles et aménagements humains (XIVe–XVIe siècles)*, ed. Michel Bochaca and Jean Louis Sarrazin (Rennes, 2007), pp. 167–187.

46 Polónia and Pinto, 'Harbour Construction Policies and Funding', pp. 15–20.

47 Bernal Rodríguez and Collantes de Terán Sánchez, 'El puerto de Sevilla', p. 781.

48 Bello León and Martín Perera, *Las atarazanas de Sevilla*; and Pablo Emilio Pérez-Mallaína Bueno, *Las atarazanas de Sevilla* (Seville, 2019).

fifteenth century it had only some paved platforms serving as landing docks for the small fishing boats connecting the harbour with the ships moored in the *Pilares* [Pillars] of the river estuary. In 1477, the Catholic Monarchs, who were in Seville, granted the cathedral chapter a licence to build:

> un molle en término de mis Atarazanas con el río Guadalquivir, cerca de la Torre del Oro, en el qual e por el qual pudiesen cargar e descargar la cantería e otras cosas necesarias para la edificación de la dicha Yglesia [...] asy como toneles de aceyte, como de vino e pescado.[49]

The Admiral of Castile was also granted a regal licence in 1477 to build another dock, but the construction never materialised.[50]

The dock of the cathedral chapter was built in timber, and we know it provided 15 metres of berthing space in the eighteenth century. This facility was also leased to private individuals by the ecclesiastical institution. In 1508 this landing place was replaced by another, though its conditions remained precarious.[51] Likewise, during the same period, another dock was built – it was portrayed in a 1500 painting – this one with a crane owned by the municipal council, which was leased to carriers. The crane had a solid circular stone base, a wooden shaft holding a swivel axle on a large wheel and radiating spokes used to stow merchandise by means of pulleys.[52]

From Seville to Sanlúcar, and throughout the Sevillian jurisdictional area, we can identify a series of minor landing spots, again with precarious facilities, used in the loading and unloading of Sevillian agricultural produce. In descending order from Seville to the Atlantic, the most prominent were the docks of El Copero, Gelves and El Rincón, for fruits and vegetables; Coria, for oil from the Aljarafe area; and Horcadas, in Lebrija, the most important of all. This landing site was located halfway between the town and the sea, and was where the large ships were moored and the heavier merchandise discharged.[53]

Despite the difficulties described, Seville became the most relevant port town on the Andalusian littoral until the eighteenth century by compensating for its lack of port infrastructure and distance from the coast with a series of human and economic resources. It was the most important royal town in a region where the littoral was practically under full seigneurial domain until Cádiz returned to the Crown in 1493. It was, moreover, the most densely populated settlement –

49 'a dock by our shipyards on the river Guadalquivir, by the Torre del Oro, to load and unload the stones and other necessary wares for building of the church [...] and oil barrels and wine and fish'. Juan Clemente Rodríguez Estévez, *Los canteros de la catedral de Sevilla. del gótico al renacimiento* (Seville, 1998), pp. 217–218.

50 Bernal Rodríguez and Collantes de Terán Sánchez, 'El puerto de Sevilla', p. 781.

51 Otte Sander, *Sevilla y sus mercaderes*, p. 105.

52 Rodríguez Estévez, *Los canteros de la catedral*, pp. 218–223.

53 Otte Sander, *Sevilla y sus mercaderes*, pp. 105–106.

some 50,000 inhabitants according to a 1534 census – and enjoyed the most extensive hinterland. This position was contested, albeit at a great distance, only by the second largest town of royal domain on the littoral, Jerez, with 20,000 inhabitants.[54]

Regarding port workforce, we know that from the end of the fourteenth century, the Sevillian council authorised Genoese, Venetian and Castilian consuls to hire fourteen carriers to perform loading and unloading tasks. In 1479 there is mention of the employment of twenty-six for the whole city. These seem to be the foremen of larger loading gangs employing slaves and paid workers. By that time, their appointment was done by the city council and the members of the trade.[55]

The Ports of Cádiz: From the Guadalquivir Estuary to the Strait of Gibraltar

The town of Sanlúcar de Barrameda is located at the mouth of the river Guadalquivir, guarding the only fluvial entry connecting Seville with the Atlantic Ocean. From 1297 it was a seigneurial domain of the Guzmán lineage, and these powerful lords, Dukes of Medina Sidonia from the mid-fourteenth century, developed the city to become the focal point of their territories by the end of the Middle Ages. The navigational significance of this port is justified by the privileged location as port of entry and departure for the ships that negotiated in Seville. Moreover, the lords of Sanlúcar enjoyed a unique privilege on the Andalusian Atlantic coast: by a royal grant, they collected taxes on all merchandise traded in the city – the *almojarifazgo*.[56]

There is no evidence of any significant docking structure that might serve as a reference point for cargo handling tasks. As in the majority of ports, the boats moored at the river mouth and unloaded their cargo onto boats which were landed on the beach known as *playa de la Ribera*. This beach was located 4 kilometres from the harbour, on the outskirts of the commercial suburb formed in the mid-fifteenth century which carried the same name. We know that, on 17 December 1528, the Duke paid 1,950 maravedis to boatmen hired to transport 855 barrels of tuna from the shore to a Portuguese caravel moored in deeper waters. This scene was portrayed in an engraving by the painter Anton van de

54 Bernal Rodríguez and Collantes de Terán Sánchez, 'El puerto de Sevilla', p. 782.
55 *Ibid.*, pp. 790–792.
56 Antonio Moreno Ollero, *Sanlúcar de Barrameda a fines de la Edad Media* (Cádiz, 1983); Antonio Moreno Ollero and Alfonso Franco Silva, 'Datos sobre el comercio del puerto de Sanlúcar de Barrameda en el primer tercio del siglo XVI', in *Hacienda y comercio: actas del II coloquio de Historia Medieval Andaluza* (Seville, 1982), pp. 283–296.

Wyngaerde in 1567.[57] By the beach, there is evidence of warehouses where the aforesaid merchandise was stored, and the ducal toll house whence all maritime traffic was controlled. For the repair of vessels, we know these sailed further upriver to the nearby Henares stream. A small shipyard was located here, next to an inn, known as *de Zanfanejos*, providing accommodation for travellers and mariners.[58]

In the locality of Sanlúcar, on the northernmost limits of the town of Rota, the house of Ponce de León, feudal lords of Arcos de la Frontera, founded the town of Chipiona in 1477. This foundation was intended to hinder and control the maritime traffic of their greatest enemies and competitors, the Dukes of Medina Sidonia. In order to promote maritime business in this new locality, they ordered the building of a dock, probably a timber construction, similar to the one in Cartaya. The purpose of this dock was to '*entrar desde tierra en la mar*' [enter the sea from land]. The building of this structure to facilitate cargo handling in the town was described by the local council as '*una de las más honradas cosas que puede aver en los lugares de la costa de la mar*'.[59] They viewed this as a fundamental structure, describing it as '*un molle donde los navíos puedan estar, porque de su venida a los tales lugares redunda mucha utilidad y provecho e ennoblecimiento*'.[60]

Further south along the coast of Cádiz we find the Bay of Cádiz, the most important natural harbour on the Andalusian Atlantic waterfront. On its northernmost and outermost area was the abovementioned town of Rota, belonging to the Ponce de León estate from 1303. Despite scant research on this enclave,[61] we know that it had a stone pier built before 1517, as portrayed in the description of the place by Ferdinand Columbus, the son of Christopher Columbus: '*Rota es villa de quinientos vezynos. Está riberas de la mar, en llano, bate la mar con los muros della. Puerto de mar. Es de don Luis Ponçe de León e tiene un muelle: lo mejor que ay en aquella costa.*'[62]

57 Richard L. Kagan, *Ciudades del Siglo de Oro: las vistas españolas de Anton van den Wyngaerde* (Madrid, 1986), p. 324.

58 Antonio Moreno Ollero, 'Los nombres del Puerto de Sanlúcar en el siglo XVI: Barrameda, Zanfanejos y Bonanza', *Cartare*, 8 (2018), 1–11.

59 'one of the most honest things that can be in the places on the seacoast'.

60 'a dock where ships can berth, because their arrival to such places redounds to much profit and benefits and ennoblement'. Alfonso Franco Silva, *Estudios sobre ordenanzas municipales (siglos XIV–XVI)* (Cádiz, 1999), p. 261.

61 One of the few exceptions is that of Alfonso Franco Silva, *Rota en la Edad Media* (Rota, 1983).

62 'Rota is a town of five hundred inhabitants. It is on the coastline, is on a flatland, the sea pounds on its walls. Sea port. It belongs to Don Luis Ponçe de León and has a pier: the best of its kind on that coast', Hernando Colón, *Descripción y cosmografía de España por Fernando Colón* (Madrid, 1910), t. II, p. 296.

A document from 1527 reveals that prior to that date, the building work on the '*muelle de la Villa de Rota*' [the pier of the Town of Rota] had concluded, with good workmanship, paid by Luis Ponce de León: '*está asentado que yo hiziese de labrar y hedificase vn molle en la villa de Rota [...] porque de hazerse se esperava mucho provecho en las rentas de aquella villa e cresçimiento de los vecinos*'.[63] The total cost amounted to 6,743,642 maravedis, of which the town council, keenly interested in the successful conclusion of this project, advanced 800,000.[64] Apparently, larger vessels were unable to unload merchandise on this dock, as stated in a document of 1524 which described how they moored in the area known as Playa de los Galeones, near the pier. It was a walled and defended site, with embrasures for protection against Berber attacks.[65]

The interior of the Bay of Cádiz was one of the most relevant port and maritime enclaves on the European Atlantic coastline. It was a large harbour where bulkier vessels could moor when the operators of the association of Biscayan pilots (*Colegio de Pilotos Vizcaínos*) of Cádiz guided them through the appropriate fairways. This institution, dating back to the participation of Basque pilots in the conquest of the Andalusian coast in the thirteenth century, was fully organised by the end of the fifteenth century, as shown in the confirmation of their ordinances and privileges by the Catholic Monarchs in 1500.[66]

Larger vessels had to remain at a distance of several dozen metres from the shore to avoid running aground. The ships and the port were connected by a series of small batels, as occurred in the other enclaves described above. There is no evidence of any construction to serve as a mooring and unloading site. To this purpose, the beach on the outskirts of the town was the landing site for these smaller boats, as portrayed in an anonymous engraving from circa 1513.[67]

By the end of the fifteenth century, Cádiz had become a commercial city of great importance in the Atlantic circuit by virtue of its privileged natural features. This circumstance prompted the need to improve port installations to '*responder a las necesidades de las embarcaciones en el caso de averías y desperfectos antes de afrontar el Océano Atlántico*'.[68] In Cádiz, although there

63 'it is established that I order the work and building of this pier in the town of Rota [...] because in doing so much profit is expected in the revenue of said town and growth for its citizens'.

64 Although paid by Luis Ponce de León, the sum was to be reimbursed to his heir, his firstborn, the Duke of Arcos and future lord of the town at the death of his father. AHN, OSUNA, box 183, doc. 81.

65 AHN, OSUNA, box 183, doc. 78.

66 Fernando Txueka Isasti, 'El Colegio de Pilotos Vizcaínos de Cádiz. La otra historia marítima de los vascos: del Mare Nostrum al Pacífico', *Itsas Memoria. Revista de Estudios Marítimos del País Vasco*, 8 (2016), 591–645.

67 The original is held in the Archivo General de Simancas, MPD, 35, 047.

68 'respond to the demands of vessels in case of damage and deficiencies before embarking on the Atlantic Ocean'. Daniel Ríos Toledano, 'La bahía de Cádiz a fines de la Edad Media:

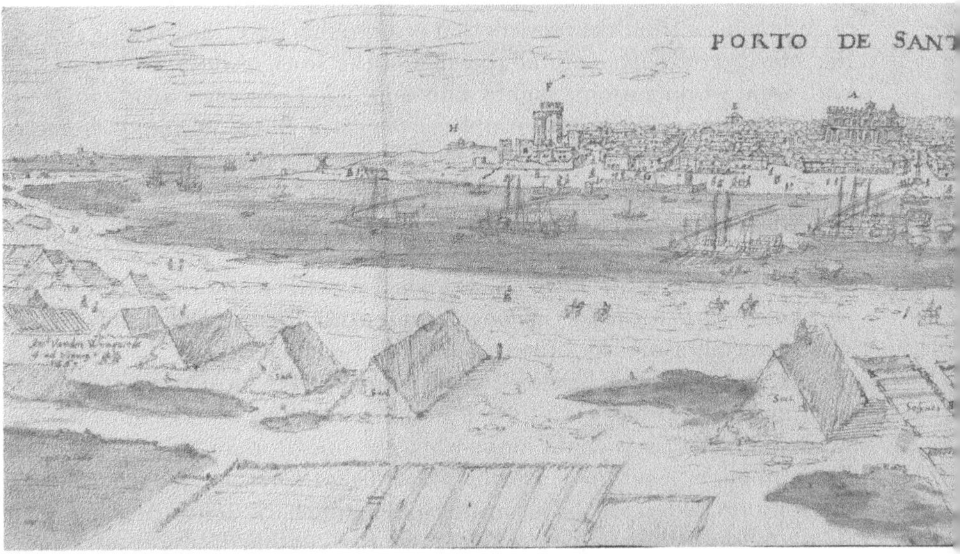

Figure 6.2 Anton van de Wyngaerde, *El Puerto de Santa María* (1567)

must have existed a series of port infrastructures from the Al-Andalus period, the first clear documentary evidence is not found until the fourteenth century. The existence of a fully a functioning shipyard in 1339 has recently been established, according to a document from the Archive of the Kingdom of Mallorca. It was likely of Muslim origin and was probably restored for use during the conquest of Alfonso X in the mid-thirteenth century. This yard was located in the area facing the bay, at the foot of the medieval town wall.[69]

The increase in maritime traffic was parallel to the development of infrastructures. In the year 1500, the town council of Cádiz petitioned the monarchs for a monetary contribution to defray the building of a lighthouse to prevent ships from deviating from their routes and running aground during the night. The construction was done on the tower of the hermitage of the islet of San Sebastián, in the northernmost area of the city, the entry to the bay. To pay for the construction, the monarchs imposed a levy on all vessels loading merchandise in Cádiz and Puerto de Santa María, exempting only fishermen. In addition to the shipyard and the lighthouse, a series of infrastructures were built in reaction to the commercial development, '*tales como depósitos para almacenar mercancías*

paisaje, navegación y comercio' (MA diss., University of Cádiz, 2018), p. 56. I wish to thank the author for providing access to this text.

69 *Ibid*. See also Daniel Ríos Toledano, 'Cádiz y el comercio marítimo genovés en el siglo XIV', *Medievalismo*, 28 (2018), 271–293.

u hospederías para albergar mercaderes, viajeros o marinos'.[70] Likewise, in the fifteenth century, there was a toll house – as there was at the port in the province of Huelva – for trade control and tax collection. In depictions of this city from the early sixteenth century (the first is dated in 1513), we can already glean this type of installation in the vicinity of the port area.[71]

Facing the Island of Cádiz, on the mouth of the river Guadalete, we find the burgh of El Puerto de Santa María, second in importance in the bay interior. This area did not have a designated space for cargo handling tasks, and both banks of the river were used for the purpose, as portrayed in the painting from 1567 by Wyngaerde (figure 6.2). Merchandise was transferred by means of small batels or boats, while the ships anchored in deeper waters. A series of marks designated restricted areas, as evidenced in local regulations. Moreover, damaged and unrepaired vessels were not allowed to remain in this space for more than fifteen days, '*porque los otros navyos puedan adobar y dar carena y este la rybera desempachada para la servidumbre de los otros navyos*'.[72] In the mid-sixteenth century, the erudite Pedro de Medina indicated the existence of

70 'such as deposits to store merchandise or inns to accommodate merchants, travellers or mariners'.

71 Ríos Toledano, 'La bahía de Cádiz', pp. 53–59.

72 'so other vessels can berth and be repaired, and the banks remain clear for the service of other ships'. Raúl Romero Medina, 'Documentos inéditos para el estudio de la temprana

'*unas grandes atarazanas cerca del río*' [large shipyards by the river], which, in his opinion, had been built three centuries earlier by order of Alfonso X.[73]

The significance of the river for the town economy justifies the permanent concern of the Duke of Medinaceli and his council with preventing any detriment to ship transit and the exchange of goods.[74] This explains the drafting of ducal ordinances in 1525 with the purpose of mitigating prior failed attempts for the preservation of the riverbanks of the Guadalete as a port space. This regulation included thirteen provisions with the main purpose of banning ships and citizens from throwing ballast into the river.[75]

The scarcity of extant infrastructures in El Puerto, as in the rest of the Bay of Cádiz and the Andalusian coast, motivated the building by the mid-fifteenth century of one of the most complex port facilities of the littoral. This was located a few kilometres upriver, on the limit between the estate of the Dukes of Medinaceli and the jurisdiction of Jerez de la Frontera – where in 1504 the Dukes founded the Monastery of La Victoria. The motive for this was the need of the Sevillian cathedral charter to extract stones from the quarry they had acquired in the Sierra de San Cristóbal, near the river, for the construction of Seville's gothic cathedral in the early years of the fifteenth century. In order to make the most of 'stone freightage' tasks, as described in 1467 documents, the ecclesiasts commissioned the building of a stone dock on a pre-existing and more fragile structure. Over thirteen days, this project involved the work of '*dos carpinteros e quatro peones labrando los palos que se pusieron en el dicho molle*'.[76] The cost of this project amounted to at least 30,000 maravedis according to extant accounts. By the second quarter of the sixteenth century this dock included a *cargador* or crane to facilitate the hoisting of stones onto the vessels. This structure had disappeared by 1567, when Wyngaerde visited the town, and was not portrayed by the artist. After an intense period of extraction activity between the 1530s and 1540s, with constant repairs to the dock, from the second half of the century the quarries and the port installations were abandoned.[77]

Downriver on the Guadalete – we shall describe the fluvial port of Jerez in detail in the following section – leaving the Bay of Cádiz to the south, were a series of minor docks, extant, as in the case of Vejer, since the time of Alfonso

Edad Moderna en El Puerto de Santa María (1515–1525)', in *El legado de Jano*, ed. Antonio Aguayo Cobo (El Puerto de Santa María, 2016), pp. 155–175, at p. 173.

73 Leopoldo Torres Balbás, 'Atarazanas hispanomusulmanas', *Al-Andalus*, 11 (1946), 175–209, at p. 164.

74 Juan José Iglesias Rodríguez, *Monarquía y nobleza señorial en Andalucía: estudios sobre el señorío de El Puerto (siglos XIII–XVIII)* (Seville, 2003), p. 77.

75 Romero Medina, 'Documentos inéditos', pp. 160–161.

76 'two carpenters and four hand-workers carving the shafts placed on said dock'.

77 Rodríguez Estévez, *Los canteros de la catedral*, pp. 206–209, 388–389.

X. This dock was still functioning at full capacity in the early sixteenth century when it became one of the habitual sites of departure for the cereal purchased by the Portuguese, with permission from the Duke of Medina Sidonia, to provision their North African territories.[78] Conil was also a site with significant traffic, where the tuna fished in the *almadrabas* of the Guzmán estate were shipped.[79] Notwithstanding, the most important port spaces of the area, and where most interventions were practised on the infrastructure during the fifteenth century, were located in the vicinity of the Bay of Algeciras and the Strait of Gibraltar.

Tarifa, on the southernmost edge of the coast of Cádiz, located on a cape or foreland marking the limit of the Strait of Gibraltar, enjoyed a privileged position for maritime traffic. It is the nearest point on the Iberian Peninsula to the North African coast. A significant drawback of this site was that it did not provide adequate locations for port structures, lacking any appropriate harbour shelters from the strong and constant winds on its beaches. It was finally captured from the Moors in 1292, and its border location and the abovementioned problems discouraged the establishment of a large population. Neither archival sources nor archaeological remains have confirmed the existence of relevant port infrastructures in the area. This explains why the Castilian monarchy did not hesitate to cede the territory to the Admiral of Castile and the Enríquez lineage in 1447, hoping the area would develop under seigneurial dominion.[80]

Of greater significance was the port of Gibraltar, on the easternmost edge of the Bay of Algeciras. When Castilian troops conquered the settlement in 1309, Fernando IV ordered the construction of shipyards for the maintenance of his fleet.[81] In 1374 it was again reconquered by the Nasrids, who shortly after (in 1379) destroyed the neighbouring Algeciras and blocked the harbour, in reaction to the impossibility of controlling what had been until then the most important port of the bay.[82] From that moment on Gibraltar became the principal port of the region. In 1462, after several attempts to recapture it, the port finally returned to Christian hands. Castilians were aware of its geostrategic value for protection and naval traffic between the Atlantic and the Mediterranean, and of its excellent natural conditions as a haven against the

78 Manuel Henrique Corte-Real, *Feitoria de Andalucía. A feitoria portuguesa na Andaluzia (1500–1532)* (Lisbon, 1967), pp. 185–188.

79 Juan Manuel Bello León, 'Almadrabas andaluzas a finales de la Edad Media', *Historia. Instituciones. Documentos*, 32 (2005), 81–114.

80 Fernando Villada Paredes, 'Los puertos del estrecho de Gibraltar en los siglos XIV y XV. Una perspectiva arqueológica', in *De mar a mar*, ed. Aznar Vallejo and González Zalacain, pp. 213–253, at pp. 231–233.

81 Francisco Giles Pacheco, Francisca Piñatel Veram and María Isabel Gómez Arroquia, 'Las atarazanas medievales de Gibraltar', *Almoraima*, 25 (2001), 221–238.

82 *Ibid.*, pp. 229–230.

Levant wind. A key motive was the connection with Castilian and Portuguese territories in northern Africa. There is evidence of the existence of a series of warehouses and a dock to facilitate cargo handling tasks and ship repair. In the sixteenth century, the shipyard became obsolete and, as occurred in Seville, the building was put to other uses.[83]

Case Study: El Portal, the Fluvial Harbour of Jerez de la Frontera

In the fifteenth century, at the height of the commercial development of the Andalusian Atlantic façade, the city of Jerez, led by its chivalric and landholding elite, became keenly aware of the opportunities offered by the new maritime routes. Without abandoning cereal farms and large cattle holdings – sources of large profits through the meat and, particularly, leather trades – they invested heavily in the creation of vineyards, wine being highly coveted in the northern European markets, particularly England and Flanders.[84]

Jerez was not a port city, forcing it to depend on overland transport and fluvial ports to provide an outlet for surplus wares. However, the city played an essential role in the port system of the Bay of Cádiz and became a large productive centre for exports and a large redistribution hub for imports to inland markets. Its fluvial waterways, in particular the river Guadalete, connected the different port spaces of the bay.[85]

The council of Jerez was aware of the need to maintain its network of roads and port infrastructures in order to reap the important economic benefits provided by the export of their products.[86] From the mid-fifteenth century, multiple sources report numerous complaints from vintners, carters and merchants – some of the main players of the new times – about the poor condition of the town's infrastructures, a clear sign of the flourishing

83 Villada Paredes, 'Los puertos del estrecho de Gibraltar', pp. 231–233.

84 Emilio Martín Gutiérrez, *Paisajes, ganadería y medio ambiente en las comarcas gaditanas. Siglos XIII al XVI* (Cádiz, 2015); Roberto J. González Zalacain and Víctor Muñoz Gómez, 'Jerez y el Mar en la Baja Edad Media', in *750 aniversario de la incorporación de Jerez a la Corona de Castilla: 1264–2014*, ed. José Sánchez Herrero and Manuel González Jiménez (Jerez de la Frontera, 2014), pp. 351–372; and Enrique José Ruiz Pilares, 'La sociedad jerezana y su implicación en las actividades comerciales. La producción y la comercialización del vino. (finales s. XV–inicios s. XVI)', in *Las sociedades portuarias*, ed. Arízaga Bolumburu and Solórzano Telechea, pp. 337–364.

85 Enrique José Ruiz Pilares, 'Jerez de la Frontera: el gran centro productor del complejo portuario de la Bahía de Cádiz a finales de la Edad Media', *Estudios sobre Patrimonio, Cultura y Ciencias Medievales*, 20 (2018), 355–386.

86 On the importance of roads and their connections with maritime traffic, see Eduardo Aznar Vallejo, 'La conexión marítimo-terrestre en la baja Andalucía. El ejemplo de Sevilla', in *De mar a mar*, ed. Aznar Vallejo and González Zalacain, pp. 125–146.

merchant class in the region. Similar petitions are documented in northern Castile regarding the connections between port spaces and inland markets and production centres.[87] The main focus was on the roads connecting the areas of extraction and elaboration of the resources with the city, such as the road running to the south, from Jerez to El Portal, located 4.5 kilometres south of the city, which was the main site of fluvial export by the Guadalete. This port is our main interest in the present chapter.[88]

This road connected the city of Jerez with El Portal, towards the course of the river Guadalete, from a gate in the southwestern corner of the city wall, the *Puerta Real*. As the main point of entry for merchandise, within the city walls this area contained the principal commercial spaces of the town, such the Ropa Vieja street, where old clothes dealers traded, or the Alcaicería, a focal point of economic activity in the late Middle Ages. Outside the wall, the gate opened onto a square known as Plaza del Arenal and the San Miguel suburb, an area that gradually displaced *intra muros* locations as the principal trading site of the city. It was the place of passage of carts and oxen returning from the river.[89]

Outside the walled area, the road ran toward the wharf, crossing vineyards and olive orchards.[90] The steep terrain, mostly wetlands, marshes, and floodable lowland, belonged to the primitive course of the Guadalete river. Beside the road, several streams discharged in the port. Among these, the most important was the Guadabajaque, which during rainy seasons overflowed and flooded the area. From the fifteenth century, there are records of frequent complaints by locals and transients, in particular carters, about the need to pave the road.[91] Despite council investments and the constant participation of different parties such as carters, merchants and owners in the repair and maintenance of the road, communications between the city and its port did not improve in the sixteenth century. In 1530 the carters of the city complained about the poor condition of the road thus:

> el mayor trato que ay esta çibdad es las mercaderías e vinos e otras cosas que se llevan e sacan desta çibdad para el río del Portal della, y a cabsa de estar

87 Jean-Pierre Molenat, 'Chemins et ponts du Nord de la Castille au temps des Rois Catholiques', *Melanges de la Casa de Velázquez*, 7 (1971), 115–162.

88 A more extensive study of the road network of Jerez is Enrique José Ruiz Pilares, 'La política viaria municipal a finales de la Edad Media (1430–1530): el caso de Jerez de la Frontera', *Norba. Revista de Historia*, 25–26 (2012–2013), 207–226.

89 Raúl Romero Medina and Manuel Romero Bejarano, 'Un lugar llamado Jerez. El Maestro Alonso Rodríguez y sus vínculos familiares y profesionales en el contexto de la arquitectura del Tardogótico en Jerez de la Frontera', in *La Catedral de Sevilla después de Carlín*, ed. Alfonso Jiménez Martín (Seville, 2010), pp. 175–280, at p. 240.

90 Emilio Martín Gutiérrez, *La organización del paisaje rural durante la Baja Edad Media. El ejemplo de Jerez de la Frontera* (Seville, 2004), pp. 199–201.

91 Ruiz Pilares, 'La política viaria municipal', pp. 212–217.

> el camino malo y pasadas y pasos muy peligrosos, a las veses se ahogan los bueyes [...] e se llevan las mercaderias a más preçio que si estuviese bueno el dicho camino.[92]

If the conditions of thoroughfares were less than adequate for the circulation of carts and persons, the situation was not much better in terms of the facilities on the river wharf. El Portal, whose existence is documented prior to the conquest of the territory by the Castilians in the thirteenth century,[93] was during the late Middle Ages a small village under the jurisdiction of Jerez and characterised by a scattered population sustained by activities related to commerce, fishing and vineyards, olive orchards or smallholdings.[94] By the wharf were some buildings and warehouses where the *almojarife* (the guard of El Portal) and the men under his command lived.[95] Here was also the house of the lighterman, the only person who could own a boat authorised to cross the Guadalete until the end of the fifteenth century.[96] This official was also granted a house – an inn of sorts – to lodge travellers in the area. Although it was a privilege exclusively the lighterman could exploit, the inhabitants of the area tried to profit from the constant arrival of travellers. In 1466 it was notified that '*algunos vesinos de la çibdad han fecho agora nuevamente casas en sus viñas e heredades onde asimismo vende vino e pan e otros mantenimientos e acogen gente*'.[97] Disregarding the complaints, the locals were still providing these services in the early sixteenth century.[98]

In terms of cargo handling tasks, there is no record of the profession of organised carriers as there was in Seville. In spite of the demographic significance of Jerez and its important maritime traffic, the large distance between the urban centre and its port explains why these tasks were carried out by a heterogeneous group of individuals: the carters themselves, mariners who enlisted in

92 'the largest business of this city is wares and wines and other things brought to and from this city to the Portal river, and given the bad road and very dangerous passages, sometimes the oxen drown [...] and wares are carried at a higher cost than if the road were in good condition', AMJF, Actas Capitulares (AC), 1530, fol. 153r.

93 Emilio Martín Gutiérrez, 'Análisis de la toponimia y aplicación al estudio del poblamiento. El alfoz de Jerez de la Frontera durante la Baja Edad Media', *Historia. Instituciones. Documentos*, 30 (2003), 257–300, at pp. 288–289.

94 Martín Gutiérrez, *La organización del paisaje rural*, pp. 75 and 191.

95 González Zalacain and Muñoz Gómez, 'Jerez y el Mar', pp. 359–362.

96 It was exploited according to a royal privilege by the council. Its benefits swelled the meager municipal coffers. The Cartuja Bridge began its decline in the mid-sixteenth century. Ruiz Pilares, 'La política viaria municipal', pp. 207–226.

97 'some neighbours of the town have built houses in their vineyards and farms where they sell wine and bread and other goods and they lodge travellers'. AMJF, AC, 1466, fol. 131r.

98 AMJF, AC, 1516, fol. 628r.

the ships, and, in all probability, inhabitants of the area who combined their farming tasks with port services.[99]

We have evidence of the existence of a small timber wharf by the mid-fifteenth century. Its poor condition was denounced by the maintenance officer in 1466. He demanded before the council that a '*molle de piedra*' [stone dock] be built in El Portal.[100] The urban government ignored repeated petitions and complaints during the second half of the century, since the town coffers were empty due to the continuous demands of the monarchy for financial contributions to assist in the conquest of Granada. Once the conflict ended in 1492, the town was able to embark on construction of the dock. Finally, in 1500 the city requested the Catholic Monarchs' permission to levy extraordinary taxes to build '*un muelle de piedra* [...] *como en Sevilla*' [a stone dock [...] as in Seville]:

> por donde se puedan cargar e descargar de los nauíos donde vienen y van, [porque muchas mercancías] se pierden e mojan e dannan e avn los bueyes de los carreteros de las carretas que aquellas cosas lleuan a cargar e descargar al dicho río se pierden e afogan porque entran al descargo de las carretas dentro del agua del dicho río.[101]

Although all the representatives of the council and all the social actors involved agreed to initiate the construction as soon as possible, it was apparently not carried out until well into the sixteenth century. The delay in the execution of this necessary infrastructure can explain the near absence of freight contracts for large ships – caravels – in El Portal until 1514. Until this date, there is evidence only of small ships catering for the interconnections within the Bay of Cádiz.[102]

The full operation of the wharf did not entail the end of cargo handling difficulties. Constant complaints from carters and merchants in the following decades led to the implementation of different projects to solve these problems and recondition facilities. It appears that none of these initiatives was wholly successful and the improvements degraded rapidly due to the low skill of operators or the lack of planning by master builders. Another problem was caused by winter run-offs from the river Guadalete and nearby streams that

99 Enrique José Ruiz Pilares, 'El paisaje portuario en la bahía de Cádiz a finales de la Edad Media: los muelles fluviales', *Riparia, Suplemento* 2 (2019), 173–210, at p. 189.
100 AMJF, AC, 1466, fol. 131r.
101 'where the incoming and outgoing ships can be loaded and unloaded, [because many wares] are lost and get wet and damaged and even the oxen of the carters that are brought to load and unload at said river are lost and drown because they drive the carts into the water of said river', Mingorance Ruiz, 'Los extranjeros en Jerez', pp. 2153–2154.
102 Ruiz Pilares, 'El paisaje portuario en la bahía de Cádiz', p. 190.

soaked the soil by the wharf and eroded the structure's foundations.[103] This was the effect of human activity on aquatic ecosystems, caused by widespread tree felling and agricultural development in the late Middle Ages.[104] In 1597, the council announced that due to the lack of adequate roads and port infrastructures and the silting of some stretches of the river which the larger ships avoided, '*muchos navíos iban a cargar a otras partes*'.[105]

Conclusions

In the late fifteenth century, the strategic position within international commerce occupied by the Andalusian Atlantic littoral drove various public authorities – and private individuals, as we have described in the case of the Jerez carters – to invest in the improvement of port and road infrastructures. This was stimulated by the voyage of Christopher Columbus to America in 1492. It was a process parallel to that taking place all over Europe, as we have mentioned. Stone wharves gradually replaced the precarious timber structures which, with the constant onslaught of harsh weather and the incessant arrival of ships, barely permitted the work of cargo handlers. This also occurred in the case of the shipyards. Except for the *Reales Atarazanas* for galleys in Seville, until the end of the Middle Ages these ports did not have the necessary conditions to satisfy the demand for ships in response to the increase in maritime traffic. Gradually, ports were populated with warehouses, tolls, taverns and inns to receive merchants and mariners from all points of origin.

Although artificial installations began to appear in Andalusian ports, beaches and riverbanks persisted as the main landing sites of the towns. At these sites, the main actors were the smaller boats moving cargo to and from the ships, given the technical and natural obstacles for larger ships that crossed the Atlantic and the Mediterranean. We can clearly observe this scenario in the engravings of Cádiz of 1513 or in Flemish paintings from the second half of the sixteenth century. The need to protect commercial activities justified the implementation of regulations to prevent the saturation of waterways as occurred in the case of El Portal de Jerez or in the natural estuary harbour where the latest archaeological interventions have rediscovered the port of Palos de la Frontera.

103 Enrique Pérez Fernández, 'Las intervenciones antrópicas en el Curso Bajo del Guadalete y en San Pedro durante la Edad Moderna', *Riparia*, 4 (2018), 146–190.

104 Richard Hoffmann, 'Economic Development and Aquatic Ecosystems in Medieval Europe', *The American Historical Review*, 101.3 (1996), 631–669.

105 'many vessels would land in other places'. Antonio Domínguez Ortiz, 'La Baja Andalucía', in *Historia de Andalucía*, ed. Manuel González Jiménez and José Enrique López de Coca (Madrid, 1980), vol. IV, pp. 335–336.

7

Ports and Port Labour in Tenerife during the Transition from the Middle Ages to the Modern Age

ROBERTO J. GONZÁLEZ ZALACAIN

IEMYR – University of La Laguna

ABSTRACT. This chapter focuses on the analysis of the ports of the island of Tenerife following the conquest of the island by the Crown of Castile. The different port enclaves and their trajectory throughout the first half of the fifteenth century are examined, with particular attention to two key aspects of port operation: infrastructures and the different tasks performed in them.

The culmination of the conquest of the island of Tenerife in 1496 concluded the process of European territorial dominion of the Canary Islands, with the incorporation of this island under the royal jurisdiction of the Crown of Castile.[1] At the time, before the impact of Christopher Columbus's arrival in the Americas was fully felt, the archipelago already held an essential strategic position in the maritime traffic of the south Atlantic, the 'Atlantic Mediterranean', as described in maritime historiography.[2] In this context of the inception of colonisation, the insular port system developed from very early on to become a space offering essential connections to the exterior, both in import and export processes; it was also crucial for the military provision of fleets frequenting the African coastline, and to the consolidation of the American route. In the following decades, with the exponential and rapid growth of maritime traffic between Europe, Africa and America, the islands further consolidated their

1 This chapter is a result of the project 'El mar como frontera. Transgresiones legales en el Atlántico bajomedieval' (PGC2018-095719-B-I00), Government of Spain.

2 Archibald R. Lewis and Timothy J. Runyan, *European Naval and Maritime History, 300–1500* (Bloomington, IN, 1985), p. 145.

geostrategic significance, to become an essential enclave within this tricontinental navigation.[3]

Being an island territory, all connections, those of Tenerife in particular, and of the other islands in general, were done by sea. In this sense, it is important to underline that during those initial stages, port infrastructures were part of a much wider set of infrastructures of all sorts; these had to be put in place if the islands were to be inhabited and exploited to European socio-economic standards. This makes the Canarian case an exceptional model for analysis, where, rather than witnessing a gradual process of *maritimisation*,[4] the crucial importance of maritime communications for the whole territory suggests privileged investments and interventions in those spaces. However, as we shall see in the following pages, throughout the sixteenth century, inter-island, intra-island and exterior maritime traffic developed under deficient material conditions.

The following pages analyse the essential role of port labour in the formation of the islands' economy, where ports became the gateways for communication between Canarian productive systems and the exterior. The case of Tenerife was chosen as a model since it provides the largest amount of documentation of the all the islands. To a great extent, the description of this port system is also applicable to the remaining islands, in particular those under the royal jurisdiction, Gran Canaria and La Palma. In these three islands we find the largest presence of the sugarcane industry, which from the onset underpinned the trade balance of the Canarian economy, was the foundation for the society that developed throughout the sixteenth century, and, in particular, contributed to the development of local oligarchies.

This investigation provides an opportunity for analysis of the implementation of diverse port spaces, allowing us to understand the most significant variables in the formation of infrastructures constituting these enclaves, the relations between the different ports of the area, and their links with the hinterland.[5] All this at a time of great significance for the historical transformation of ports, which witnessed, in this transition from the fifteenth to the sixteenth

3 Manuel Lobo Cabrera, *El comercio canario europeo bajo Felipe II* (Santa Cruz de Tenerife and Las Palmas de Gran Canaria, 2008).

4 GIS d'Histoire Maritime, *La Maritimisation du monde de la préhistoire à nos jours* (Paris, 2016). Recently Solórzano Telechea has described the northern ports of the Crown of Castile between the thirteenth and fifteenth centuries. See Jesús Ángel Solórzano Telechea, 'Integración económica, competencia y jerarquización de los puertos atlánticos del Norte de España (siglos XIII–XV)', *Anuario de Estudios Medievales*, 48.1 (2018), 213–242, in particular pp. 225–236.

5 Amélia Polónia, 'European Seaports in the Early Modern Age: Concepts, Methodology and Models of Analysis', *Cahiers de la Méditerranée*, 80 (2010), 17–39.

centuries, an intense process of change that would impact their configuration on all levels.[6]

Precedents and Early Stages: Port Spaces prior to the Conquest and during the Early Colonisation

As mentioned above, in the final years of the fifteenth century, the infrastructures of the island of Tenerife were inadequate for the operative necessities of European societies. Thus, in the first instance, operators had to make do with natural harbours and anchorages in use prior to the conquest. It is important to highlight that the indigenous societies of the Canary Islands did not engage in navigation, so the newcomers had no prior knowledge to draw upon for these activities. Thus, all prior experience was always derived from the attempts Europeans, namely Castilians, had made throughout the second half of the fifteenth century to permanently occupy the island.

For this, they took advantage of natural sites providing landing spots for navigators, and the first testimony we have thereof relates these sites with military endeavours, which were to continue throughout the process of exploration, conquest and colonisation of the archipelago. Hence, the first chronicle recounting these initial phases of the process, *Le Canarien*, explicitly states that the island of Gran Canaria had 'good access sites', while others (El Hierro, La Gomera, La Palma and northern Lanzarote) were 'very strong', in terms of the detection or not, during the inspections carried out by the navigators, of spots providing accessible landing places.[7] From the description included in the *Crónica de Guinea* of Gomes Eanes de Zurara we are informed that Portuguese navigators, commanded by Álvaro de Ornelas, anchored in an inlet on the island of La Palma and disembarked to continue reconnaissance on foot.[8]

There are scarce references to the specific case of the island of Tenerife on this. There is evidence that island inlets were employed for these missions, but we have very few documented testimonies. One of the most ancient, which does explicitly mention the term 'port', is the narrative known as 'Acta del Bufadero', a document recording the oath of submission sworn by the *menceyes* – indigenous chiefs – before Diego de Herrera, Lord of the Canary Islands.[9] The

6 Cátia Antunes and Louis Sicking, 'Ports on the Border of the State, 1200–1800: An Introduction', *International Journal of Maritime History*, 19 (2007), 273–286.

7 Eduardo Aznar Vallejo *et al.*, *Le Canarien, retrato de dos mundos. I, Textos* (San Cristóbal de La Laguna, 2006), p. 39.

8 Gomes Eanes de Zurara, *La Crónica de Guinea*, ed. Eduardo Aznar Vallejo, Dolores Corbella Díaz and Antonio Tejera Gaspar (Barcelona, 2012), p. 271.

9 Antonio Rumeu de Armas, *La conquista de Tenerife 1494–1496* (San Cristóbal de La Laguna, 2006), Lámina 1.

exact location cannot be determined, though it seems to be the same site as the one chosen by Castilian troops to establish military camps for their final campaign in the conquest of the island, in the vicinity of the present-day city of Santa Cruz de Tenerife.

This was all the prior knowledge available to Castilian colonisers when establishing port communications on the island of Tenerife once the conquest was over. From that moment on, the network of insular connections was to be articulated according to the emerging social organisation derived from the new forms of economic exploitation of the island.[10] Hence, we must first consider the productive configuration developing during the first decades following the conquest. It is a relatively well-known process[11] and has been the object of recent studies, such as the work of Francisco Báez Hernández[12] where he describes, in great detail, the gradual configuration of land property distribution and agricultural exploitation, from information provided by the land grants conferred by local authorities, in this case the governor of the island, Alonso Fernández de Lugo.

This configuration of the productive space led to several economic activity axes based on agricultural produce. Sugarcane plantations were established on the island, as had occurred previously on other islands in the royal domain.[13] These estates were located both in the northern lands and in the Güímar valley to the south. To these quasi-industrial holdings, we must add the increasingly profitable economic activity based on other crops. So, from the mid-fifteenth century onward, the northern area of the island witnessed the development of significant vinicultural activity, setting the foundation for the flourishing wine trade with Europe that was to develop throughout the seventeenth century.[14]

10 For an introduction to the study of the development of basic infrastructure on the island of Tenerife after the conquest see Juan Manuel Bello León, 'Primeras obras públicas en Canarias: caminos, puertos y abastecimiento de agua en el siglo XVI', *Estudios Canarios. Anuario del Instituto de Estudios Canarios*, 50–51 (2006–2007), 595–618.

11 For everything related to this process, see the seminal work of Eduardo Aznar Vallejo, *La integración de las islas Canarias en la Corona de Castilla (1478–1526). Aspectos administrativos, sociales y económicos*, 3rd edn (Santa Cruz de Tenerife, 2009).

12 Francisco Báez Hernández, *El repartimiento de Tenerife (1493–1569)* (San Cristóbal de La Laguna, 2016).

13 On the development of the sugar industry in Tenerife, see the essays in Ana Viña Brito (ed.) *Azúcar y Mecenazgo en Gran Canaria. El oro de las islas, siglos XV y XVI* (Las Palmas de Gran Canaria, 2014); and Ana Viña Brito and Dolores Corbella Díaz (eds.), *La ruta azucarera atlántica: Historia y documentación* (Funchal, 2012); Benedicta Rivero Suárez, *El azúcar en Tenerife: 1496–1550* (San Cristóbal de La Laguna, 1991); and Miguel Ángel Gómez Gómez, *Análisis histórico de una hacienda azucarera del siglo XVI: el heredamiento de Güímar [Tenerife]* (Santa Cruz de Tenerife, 2018).

14 Antonio Macías Hernández, 'Expansión ultramarina y economía vitivinícola: el ejemplo de Canarias (1500–1550)', *Investigaciones de Historia Económica*, 3–8 (2007), 13–44.

The southern lands of the island remained sparsely populated, although some economic activities did develop, in particular under the auspices of the main landholders such as the Duke of Medina Sidonia, whose channels of communication with the rest of the island and the exterior were to be crucial in the development of maritime routes.

Parallel to these developments, we must consider the increasingly significant American commerce within the Atlantic framework of the time. As mentioned above, in the early years of the period analysed in this chapter, the impact of Columbus's arrival to America was scarcely felt; however, from 1520 onwards, commerce with the Americas acquired a value in itself and the Canarian archipelago played a fundamental role in this commercial route, becoming the essential port of call for ocean crossings to the newly discovered continent.[15]

As occurred in the ports of the European continent, this process of economic development in the insular hinterland culminated with the formation of a port environment where the city of Santa Cruz de Tenerife became the principal export outlet for the all the activities generated in the capital, San Cristóbal de La Laguna. Meanwhile, the port of Garachico became the outlet for the increasingly dynamic activity in the north of the island. In both the southern part of the island and the less active settlements, a dense secondary network of maritime connections developed through the exploitation of shallow inlets and harbours found along the littoral. However, as we shall see below, it is only in the main ports of the island, those of Santa Cruz and Garachico, that we can identify, and even then with some difficulty, some of the elements proper to port installations in use at the time.

The result of the process was described with great precision by Leonardo Torriani in the depiction of the Canary Islands included in the project for the building of fortifications commissioned by Felipe II in the late sixteenth century.[16] The images reveal that the island of Tenerife at that time had a considerable number of havens and anchorages, the most important of which are mentioned above. Torriani made specific depictions of these with clear descriptions of port infrastructures. These, as will be described below, developed later, following the initial period analysed in this chapter.

15 In this regard see the seminal work of Francisco Morales Padrón, *El comercio canario-americano (siglos XVI, XVII y XVIII)* (Seville, 1955).

16 Leonardo Torriani, *Descripción e historia del reino de las Islas Canarias, antes Afortunadas, con el parecer de sus fortificaciones*, trans. Alejandro Cioranescu (Santa Cruz de Tenerife, 1999).

The Configuration of the Tenerife Port Model in the First Quarter of the Sixteenth Century: Infrastructures and Port Labour

To provide a detailed analysis of the configuration process of the port network of the island of Tenerife following the conquest, we have an abundance of documentary sources which, however, do not allow us to approach all facets of port reality. We have the council acts from 1497, practically from the beginning of the colonisation, as well as other local documentation offering information, to a greater or lesser extent, on how the legal and administrative development of the ports were initiated. Notarial documentation offers abundant accounts of commercial traffic in these ports. The archive holding notarial documents of the island includes numerous examples of freight contracts. These record not only the ports of destination of the ships departing from the various parts of the island, but also, with notable precision in many cases, the internal maritime communication routes these ships had to follow to embark their cargo before setting sail for their final destination. However, there are scant references to the specific details of the social and work life in the ports, hindering a precise account of the different infrastructures these ports acquired over time.

Before discussing the details of the configuration of the port network of the island, it is convenient to highlight the administrative structure ruling the island during this period. After the military occupation, the administrative framework established by the Crown deemed the island to be a *concejo de villa y tierra* [town and territorial council], with its capital San Cristóbal de La Laguna, at 600 metres of altitude and several kilometres from the coast, holding jurisdiction over the whole island.[17] This circumstance is relevant, since, throughout the period studied, the central authority and justice of the island resided in the capital, but the gradual economic development we will describe generated a complex urban geography, with its corresponding port development at an insular level, and with consequent implications in economic, administrative or defensive orders (figure 7.1).

In the following section we will describe the progression of the three port axes evolving on the island in the wake of the economic growth described above. First, we will describe the port of Santa Cruz, the natural outlet and port of the island capital, San Cristóbal de La Laguna. Next, we will analyse the development of the ports on the island's northern façade, which channelled a significant volume of agricultural produce for exterior markets. Last, we will focus on the ports on the southern façade, much poorer in terms of their nearest hinterland but essential insofar as they represented the sole means of communication between the area and the capital. And we must not forget

17 Eduardo Aznar Vallejo, 'La época fundacional y su influjo en el patrimonio histórico de San Cristóbal de La Laguna', *Anuario de Estudios Atlánticos*, 54.1 (2008), 169–205.

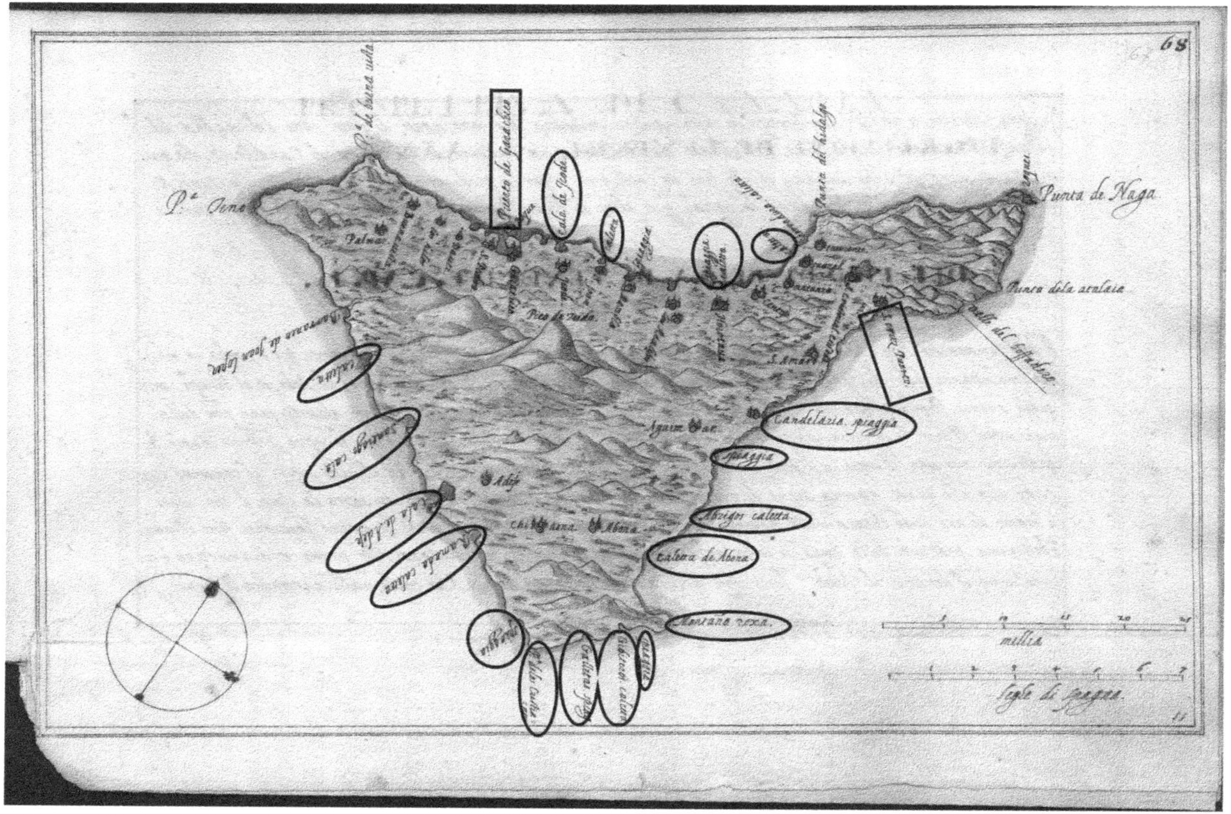

Figure 7.1. Ports and inlets of the island of Tenerife. Based on Leonardo Torriani, *Descrittione et historia del regno de l'isole Canarie* (1590)

that the different pre-existing infrastructures in the indigenous settlements were inadequate for the demands for overland transport derived from the new economic scenario. Therefore, in addition to the creation of new roads to connect the growing agricultural areas on the island, the largest volumes of local production were transported by sea, transforming the main ports of the island into hub and trans-shipment ports.[18] These not only concentrated the dispatch of goods from the hinterland, but also channelled both the dispatch of products brought from smaller ports and inlets on the coast and the redistribution of products arriving to these same inlets and smaller ports.

The Port of Santa Cruz

The port of Santa Cruz de Tenerife (figure 7.2) was to become an essential centre in the island's maritime communication. Prior to its development as a population nucleus, the area hosted the conquering armies, chosen as a base camp for the troops on account of its favourable conditions as a landing spot for ships connecting Castilian troops with the exterior.[19] Relatively easy connection with the capital made Santa Cruz one of the main port nodes from the start of occupation in the late fifteenth century. Traditional historiography has highlighted its unquestionable role as base of operations from very early on,[20] despite not being the best shelter for ships.[21] Notarial documentation supports this impression, and from the earliest surviving notarial protocols we have evidence of the port's being used for a variety of purposes. It remained an essential site for military provisioning. The crews recruited for incursions on the African coast had the port of Santa Cruz as their main point of supply.[22]

But the main reason Santa Cruz became the principal port of the island during those first decades was its central position in terms of the commercial businesses of the different areas of the island. Being the port of the capital, a very significant proportion of the ships berthed there to carry out different businesses in San Cristóbal de La Laguna. Documents recording these contracts confirm how the ships departing from Santa Cruz would stop at different ports of call on the island to load goods prior to sailing to other areas. This is proven in the lease between Rodrigo Dorantes and Antón Ruiz of a boat berthed in Santa Cruz, to transport a certain amount of sugar to the Bay of Cádiz, which

18 Báez Hernández, *El repartimiento de Tenerife*, p. 82.

19 Rumeu de Armas, *La conquista de Tenerife*.

20 Alejandro Cioranescu, *Historia de Santa Cruz de Tenerife. I. 1494–1803* (Santa Cruz de Tenerife, 1977).

21 Emilio Hardisson Pizarroso, 'Santa Cruz de Tenerife y su puerto', *Revista de Historia*, 76 (1946), 370–390.

22 Juan Manuel Bello León, *Los protocolos notariales de los escribanos de Tenerife Sebastián Páez y Antón de Vallejo (años 1505–1506)* (San Cristóbal de La Laguna, 2015), no. 652. 28 August 1506.

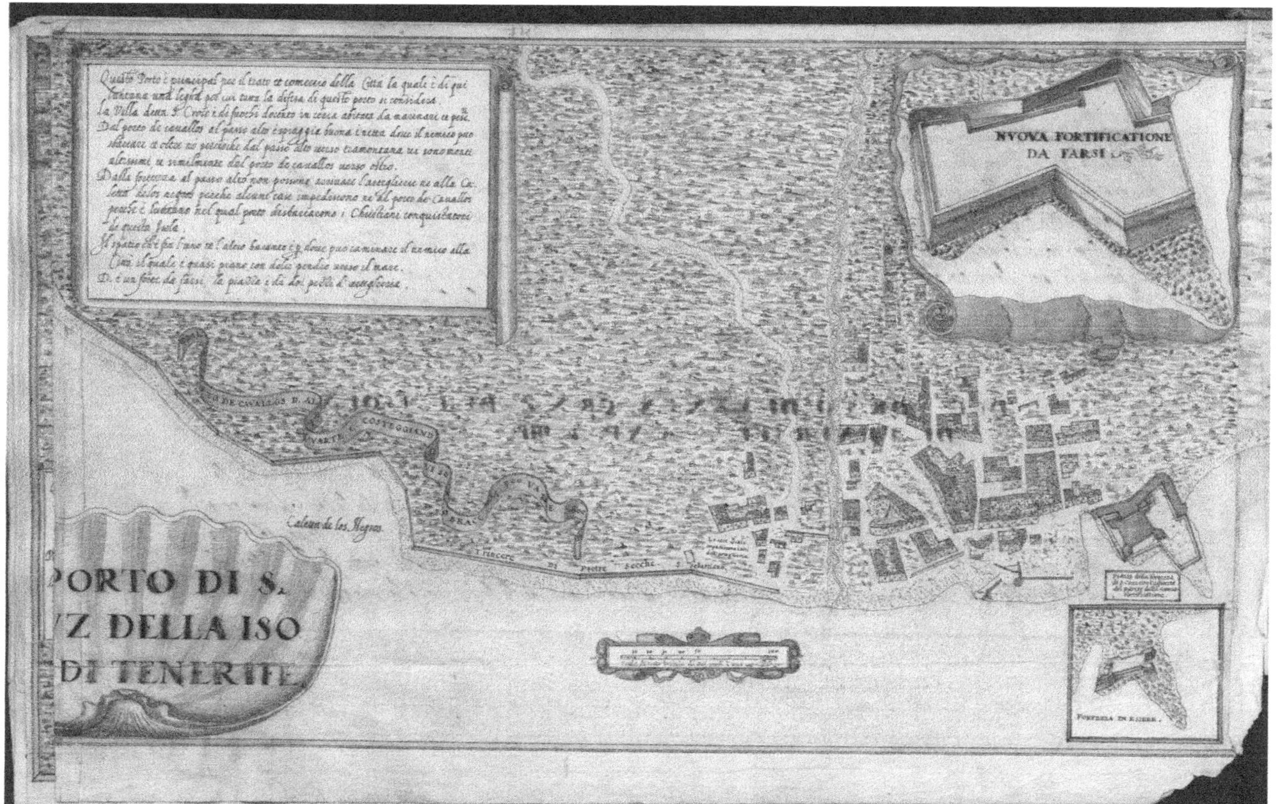

Figure 7.2. The port of Santa Cruz de Tenerife, as depicted in Leonardo Torriani, *Descrittione et historia del regno de l'isole Canarie* (1590)

was to be embarked in the port of Garachico.[23] This practice the must have been relatively frequent, since we have other similar examples.[24]

In addition to the sugarcane business, we find comparable practices for other types of products. In this manner, a similar strategy was employed in the transport of barley and other cereal collected in the various ports of the island before sailing to the African coast[25] or Portugal.[26] Other examples of commercial agreements signed in La Laguna involve ships sailing from the port of Santa Cruz whose final destination, after calling at other ports of the island to load merchandise, was another island of the archipelago.[27]

To this we must also add the impact of the Americas Route on the development of the port network, both in its commercial and its military aspects. The port of Santa Cruz was a habitual berth for the Americas fleet, as seen in the episode involving Diego de Ordaz's expedition to the river Marañón in 1530. The difficulties they encountered in victualling their ships were caused by the refusal of the island authorities to release the wine the sailors required, the authorities claiming the wine was required for internal consumption. However, beyond this, it was clearly a habitual practice for the vessels sailing to the Americans to berth in Canarian ports, and more specifically in that of Santa Cruz, to obtain the necessary victuals for the ocean crossing, denoting thus a function as sourcing ports. We must not forget that the islands held a royal licence for direct trade with the Americas,[28] and, in this sense, the episode we have just mentioned was a determining factor in the Crown's

23 Emilio Alfaro Hardisson, 'Documentos para el estudio de los puertos y de la navegación marítima en Tenerife en el siglo XVI', *Fuentes Canarias en Red*, 4 (2017), no. 9. 15 November 1507.

24 *Ibid.*, no. 2, 5 May 1507.

25 This is the case of the Portuguese shipmaster Diego Fernández, whose ship was victualled in the port of Santa Cruz, and the freight contract with Ruy González to load in it as much barley it could carry in the ports of Garachico and La Orotava, with destination to the city of Safi, without making any other stopovers. *Ibid.*, no. 21, 30 April 1520. This is another example of the role of the Canary Islands as a supplier of the Portuguese territories in the African Atlantic façade. Emilio Alfaro Hardisson, 'Canarias y el mar', in *Navíos y gentes del mar. Siglos XVI–XVIII* (Santa Cruz de Tenerife, 2003), pp. 14–18.

26 We have the example of another Portuguese shipmaster, Juan Pérez, who chartered the Portuguese merchant Diego Ribero, also from Santa Cruz, to fill the ship with all the barley he could from bow to stern at the port of Buenavista, with the mandate sail directly to Lisbon or Setubal. *Ibid.*, no. 23, 5 May 1520.

27 This is the case of the lease contract between the shipmaster Pedro de Amores, from the port of Santa Cruz, who chartered it to Diego Sánchez to load a series of wooden instruments, to be loaded in the port of Taganana, from where the ship was to sail to the port of Santa Cruz to embark a passenger, and from this port sail to Isleta of Gran Canaria. *Ibid.*, no. 67, 15 June 1522.

28 As one of the few exceptions, together with Cádiz, the port of Seville through which the American trade was centralised. José Peraza de Ayala Vallabriga, 'El régimen comercial

decision to renew, in 1533, the authorisation to victual ships en route to the Americas on the island of Tenerife, sidestepping the monopoly of the *Casa de Contratación*.[29] This is, undoubtedly, a critical element in understanding the role of the islands in general, and that of Tenerife in particular, within the sixteenth-century Atlantic.

From early on, this intense commercial activity drove the development of an institutional framework to guarantee the authorities' control of the capital's port. Hence, from 1507, as a result of the arrival on the island of a vessel hailing from Sanlúcar de Barrameda and Gran Canaria, whose crew suffered an outbreak of the plague, we have evidence of the existence of a guard of the port of Santa Cruz. The guard lived in the port with his family and was appointed to guarantee the proper running of all activities carried out in the port, monitoring both the salubrity of incoming vessels and the loading and unloading of cargo.[30] This position was complemented by another of a military character, that of the tower warden of Santa Cruz, extant from 1511 onward, when Juan de Benavente received a lifetime appointment to this role.[31]

Among extant documentation we find numerous references to the appointment of the various holders of these positions, mentioned repeatedly with references to their twofold function of controlling the loading and unloading of merchandise and ensuring the salubrity of incoming ships. These mentions occur namely in claims for the payment of their salaries.[32] Additionally, we also find indirect references to the presence of fiscal agents,[33] thus suggesting the fiscal weight of port activities, although the islands were exempt of some of the main Castilian taxes in the sixteenth century.[34]

As we can confirm, the port of Santa Cruz de Tenerife came into being during the early stages of colonisation and manifested a gradual economic and administrative development, making it one of the main, if not the main, ports of the island. However, this status did not entail the development of adequate infrastructures. Available records are fragmented but do present a scenario with

de Canarias con las Indias en los siglos XVI, XVII, y XVIII (I)', *Revista de Historia*, 92 (1950), 339–383.

29 Pedro Martínez Galindo, *La vid y el vino en Tenerife en la primera mitad del siglo XVI* (San Cristóbal de La Laguna, 1998), p. 715.

30 Elías Serra Ráfols, *Acuerdos del Cabildo de Tenerife I (1497–1507)*, 2nd edn (San Cristóbal de La Laguna, 1996), no. 711, 19 February 1507.

31 Báez Hernández, *El repartimiento de Tenerife*, p. 36.

32 As was the case with Luis de Lugo, who in 1525 claimed the payment of his salary as mayor of the port. Leopoldo de la Rosa Olivera and Manuela Marrero Rodríguez, *Acuerdos del Cabildo de Tenerife V (1525–1533)* (San Cristóbal de La Laguna, 1986), no. 9. 19 June 1525.

33 Alfaro Hardisson, 'Documentos para el estudio de los puertos', no. 87. 28 November 1522.

34 Aznar Vallejo, *La integración de las islas Canarias en la Corona de Castilla*.

scant human intervention to improve the port, in contrast to the interventions carried out in the Peninsular and other European ports at that time. The first references correspond to what we could define as minor interventions. There are early references, from 1509, to the building of waterwheels and the excavation of wells to provision the ships arriving at port.[35] We lack, however, further information allowing us to visualise more significant transformations.

Several years later, in 1526, the council of Tenerife debated the need to build a quay in the port of Santa Cruz and the possible cost of this. The building was approved, signalling the importance of the area on account of the number of vessels arriving from diverse places, including those en route to the Americas. Clear mention is made of the argument that transit was frequently impeded by the fierceness of the coast, and that this could be solved by building a dock. A financial petition was presented to the court, with the argument that a dock would result in more contracts for the port and thus increase royal revenue.[36]

The arguments put forward by the island authorities clearly indicate the deficient infrastructures in the port of Santa Cruz de Tenerife. It is not, however, the sole instance of such initiatives in the archipelago, since we know that, around the same time, the building of a dock in the port of Santa Cruz de la Palma was well underway.[37] In addition, from a regional perspective, documents inform us of the first constructions undertaken in the port of Angra, in Azores.[38]

This initiative, however, appears to have been unsuccessful, since council accounts twenty years later again mention the need to build a dock. This was put forth by the governor of the island, the *licenciado* Bautista de Ayora, who expressly noted that no construction had been carried out since the island was conquered.[39] Even if we consider the possible propagandistic intentions of the governor's words, his reasoning indicates a lack of vigour in the development of infrastructures in the port of Santa Cruz de Tenerife.

This reference to the construction of a dock in Santa Cruz de Tenerife brings us to the mid-sixteenth century, over half a century after Castilian occupation. During this time, the port consolidated its position as the preferred export outlet for business ventures in the capital and become the habitual port of call for the Americas fleets. We even find some documentary references to the

35 Leopoldo de la Rosa Olivera and Elías Serra Ràfols, *El adelantado don Alonso de Lugo y su residencia por Lope de Sosa* (San Cristóbal de La Laguna, 1949), p. 46.

36 Rosa Olivera & Marrero Rodríguez, *Acuerdos del Cabildo de Tenerife V*, no. 135. 15 October 1526.

37 Eduardo Aznar Vallejo *et al.*, *Documentos Canarios en el Registro General del Sello (1518–1525)* (San Cristóbal de La Laguna, 1991), no. 212. 1 September 1520.

38 Ana Catarina Abrantes Garcia, 'Angra e Funchal, dois portos atlânticos no contexto do império marítimo português. Análise comparativa sobre espaços, estruturas e dinámicas', *Nuevo Mundo Mundos Nuevos* (2016), online [accessed 14 August 2019].

39 Manuela Marrero Rodríguez *et al.*, *Acuerdos del Cabildo de Tenerife VII (1545–1549)* (San Cristóbal de La Laguna, 2000), no. 243. 31 May 1549.

royal port of Santa Cruz,[40] granting it pre-eminence within the insular port hierarchy. It is clear, however, that the port's importance and the volume of commercial activity did not coincide with the development of adequate infrastructures for the necessities of oceanic navigation. A significant part of the merchandise arriving at the port was transported by land to the capital, and the rapid dispatch through secondary transport routes to other parts of the islands – which, as verified by the documentation, was very frequent – meant that demand for port infrastructures, such as warehouses or docks, was not as significant as in other locations.[41]

Other essential aspects of port infrastructures are those related to the building and maintenance of ships. We know this activity was carried out from early on from documentary references where shipbuilding is mentioned.[42] However, in spite of these references and the confirmation of the presence of shipwrights, as we shall see in the corresponding section, there are no mentions

40 We find references to that denomination from early on. In 1506 he appears cited as such in the testimony derived from the inquiry promoted by the crown to supervise the work of Alonso Fernández de Lugo as governor of the island. Reform of the Department of Tenerife in 1506 and collection of documents on the *avanzado* and his governance, San Cristóbal de La Laguna, Instituto de Estudios Canarios, 1949, p. 46. For its part, in 1510, this is recorded for the first time in the minutes of the municipal council. Elías Serra Ràfols and Leopoldo de la Rosa Olivera, *Acuerdos del Cabildo de Tenerife II (1508–1513)* (San Cristóbal de La Laguna, 1952), no. 108. 30 August 1510. It is repeated, from that moment on, with relative frequency in chapter proceedings.

Although the denomination per se as a royal port did not necessarily imply such circumstance, the truth is that the formulation with which it appears on some occasions does seem to prove it. Thus, in a council session of 1517 in which the situation of the port guards was discussed, it is expressly stated that 'in the guard of Santa Cruz, the royal port of the island [...]', which allows us to infer that the aldermen had internalised this was the only port thus qualified. Elías Serra Ráfols and Leopoldo de la Rosa Olivera, *Acuerdos del Cabildo de Tenerife III (1514–1518)* (San Cristóbal de La Laguna, 1965), no. 199. 14 August 1517. In addition, there is no mention of other royal ports in the documentation throughout the island.

41 An example is the case of Portugal or the Netherlands, where in the late Middle Ages numerous constructions are undertaken employing stone in the building work, for commercial and defensive purposes. Amândio Barros, 'A construção de um centro portuário atlántico O Porto nos séculos XV e XVI', in *La gobernanza de los puertos atlánticos, siglos XIV–XX: políticas y estructuras portuarias*, ed. Amélia Polónia and Ana María Rivera Medina (Madrid, 2016), pp. 193–218; Louis Sicking, 'Portas para o mar: infraestruturas portuárias nos Païxes Baixos na Idade Média', in *European Seaport Systems in the Early Modern Age – A Comparative Approach*, ed. Amélia Polonia and Elena Osswald (Porto, 2007), pp. 96–106.

42 In the residence trial of governor Fernández de Lugo in 1506, a ship of his property is mentioned, which is usually piloted by Rodrigo San Telmo, and which was built on the island. Rosa Olivera & Serra Ràfols, *El adelantado don Alonso de Lugo*, p. 85.

of specific port precincts devoted to this activity until much later, and even in these, it is difficult to place these within the port of Santa Cruz.[43]

There are significant references manifesting concerns about the protection of the island, namely of the royal port. The insular territory was, by definition, extremely vulnerable to attacks from the exterior. From very early on, we find information regarding this concern in the town council proceedings and there were attempts to establish military outposts in the port of Santa Cruz.[44] Additionally, documents record frequent debates regarding both the building of a tower[45] and the installation of artillery to defend the port.[46]

Finally, the pre-eminent position of the port of Santa Cruz is also demonstrated through another series of administrative resolutions. This occurs with the salubrity controls of the island. We have seen how, from the first days of colonisation, port authorities of Santa Cruz de Tenerife appointed a port guard with the mandate, among others, to control this aspect. At times of epidemic crisis, guards were placed along the coastline to alert the island in case of danger. They would serve to warn of the arrival of ships suspected of bringing the dreaded plague from foreign ports. Once these possible occurrences were detected, the island authorities would frequently attempt to centralise the arrival of all ships to the island through the port of Santa Cruz, in order to control this risk more effectively.[47]

In 1523, during a council session where some of these aspects regarding the salubrity of the ports were discussed, the issue of centralising all commercial activity around the port of Santa Cruz was raised. This was not so much a matter of favouring the port itself as an attempt to guarantee that imported merchandise was traded within the capital, thus preventing possible trade fraud through secondary ports of the island.[48] Presumably, this was a relatively frequent practice, as reflected in the first measures implemented by the *licenciado* Bautista de Ayora when he was made governor of Tenerife in the mid-sixteenth century, banning residents of port towns from being appointed for port surveillance.[49] Indeed, beyond fraud control, it is clear that this type of decision further strengthened the role and significance granted by insular

43 In 1563 we have evidence of an agreement between the shipwright Bartolomé Hernández, resident of Santa Cruz, and Salvador Álvarez, who had commissioned the former to build a ship whose delivery was delayed and was to be delivered finished at the shipyard. It was to be delivered in January, but the shipwright was unable to fulfil the commission in the shipyard. Alfaro Hardisson, 'Documentos para el estudio de los puertos', no. 243. 7 March 1563.

44 Serra Ràfols and Rosa Olivera, *Acuerdos del Cabildo de Tenerife II*, no. 251. 8 April 1513.

45 *Ibid.*, no. 378. 13 March 1523.

46 *Ibid.*, no. 259. 8 April 1513.

47 *Ibid.*, no. 370. 30 January 1523.

48 *Ibid.*

49 Martínez Galindo, *La vid y el vino en Tenerife*, p. 770.

authorities to the royal port of the island, although the reiteration in these injunctions suggest they were not very successful.

The Northern Ports of the Island (La Orotava, Garachico and San Pedro de Daute)

The second port axis articulating the connection between the insular hinterland and external markets is found scattered throughout several towns on the northern façade of the island. Here we find fertile land and good conditions for agriculture, which made this, with the region surrounding the island capital, the area with greatest population growth from the early years following the conquest. Hence, it is not surprising to find explicit mentions of long-distance port activity on these coasts. Some of the documentary references mentioned earlier describe the productive sugarcane industries in this area. This produced the first crop for export to contribute to the insular balance of payments in a period of great demand for resources to establish a new society. It is therefore not surprising to also find in this area, during early times, further freight contracts negotiating the hiring of transport for a specific vessel loaded with sugar from these ports to the exterior. An interesting aspect of some of these examples is the demonstration that the ports of Garachico (figure 7.3) and San Pedro de Daute, a short distance from each other, also functioned as operative centres as we have seen in the case of Santa Cruz de Tenerife.[50]

Notwithstanding, insular authorities attempted a gradual centralisation of loading and unloading operations of the area exclusively through the port of Garachico.[51] This was agreed during a council session of 1539, banning the dispatch of merchandise from the port of San Pedro de Daute, and limiting this activity to that of Garachico.[52] This decision was made within the context of the development of viniculture and wine production in the northern region of the island, which would gradually replace sugarcane production as the main

50 As in the charter between the Portuguese shipping master Gonzalo Fernández, whose ship was berthed in the port of San Pedro de Daute, and the Genoese merchant Silvestre Pinelo, to carry orchil and sugar to Flanders, without layovers. What is interesting about this agreement is the spatial triangulation, since it was agreed that Pinelo would pay the freight in the port of San Pedro de Daute, and that the cargo would be loaded in Garachico and Santa Cruz. Alfaro Hardisson, 'Documentos para el estudio de los puertos', no. 39. 2 July 1521.

51 This was is not a radical replacement. For a long time the exports of sugar and wine coexisted, along with other produce, as confirmed by the activities of the Flemish merchant Juan de Vite, who operated on the island from 1542. His commercial activities were based on the export of cane juice and sugar in exchange for which he received clothing and money from Flanders. We know several freights were negotiated where the port of embarkation was the La Orotava inlet, present-day Puerto de la Cruz. Martínez Galindo, *La vid y el vino en Tenerife*, pp. 174–175.

52 Manuela Marrero Rodríguez *et al.*, *Acuerdos del Cabildo de Tenerife VI (1538–1544)* (San Cristóbal de La Laguna, 1997), no. 96. 16 June 1539.

Figure 7.3. The port of Garachico, as depicted in Leonardo Torriani, *Descrittione et historia del regno de l'isole Canarie* (1590)

export produce. Wine permitted a more decentralised production and was less dependent on large investments in productive infrastructures, and became from the central decades of the sixteenth century a highly demanded product in European and American markets.[53] This circumstance reflected on the island's port network. As a port for the distribution of exports, we can verify how the port of Garachico became, with the port of Santa Cruz de Tenerife and other minor ports in the north of the island, one of the main outlets of these products,[54] functioning on some occasions as the primary port in the network, but on others as an autonomous entity.[55]

The value of a port is not to be measured solely by its importance as an export outlet but must also include its value as a site for incoming goods. The island of Tenerife, which did not have sufficient timber for the mass production of wine barrels, had to import large quantities of wood from the Iberian Peninsula to cover production needs.[56] This meant that ports for wine export also became ports of reception for the wood necessary to produce these barrels, which was then distributed, as occurred with wine produce, throughout the network of inlets and minor ports both on the northern and the southern coasts of the island.[57]

In terms of infrastructure, the port of Garachico enjoyed very favourable natural conditions for the loading and unloading of merchandise and the protection of the vessels anchored there, unlike the port of Santa Cruz de Tenerife where, as we have seen, the documents of the period describe the difficulties of sailing in rough seas. These favourable natural conditions were not present in all situations, however, and in some inlets and minor ports on the northern façade of the island authorities undertook the building of docks to mitigate the difficulties that could arise during storms. Hence, barely five years after the conquest of the island, we find references to the authorisation

53 Although there were moments of decline in trade. See Martínez Galindo, *La vid y el vino en Tenerife*, pp. 711–738.

54 Note the legend of the Leonardo Torriani Garachico port map. The port is named *Garachico. Porto principale della Isola de di Tenerife*, proving its importance at the end of the sixteenth century.

55 In the manner of the small ports described by Gérard Le Bouëdec in the case of French Atlantic ports. Gérard Le Bouëdec, 'Small Ports from the Sixteenth to the Early Twentieth Century and the Local Economy of the French Atlantic Coast', *International Journal of Maritime History*, 21.2 (2009), 103–126.

56 Documents include explicit references to the import of wood, mainly from Galicia. Martínez Galindo, *La vid y el vino en Tenerife*.

57 As an example, such as the detail of Gonzalo García's freight in 1548: after loading wine and other goods in La Rambla, the ship stopped in Santa Cruz to load additional cargo and, from there, set sail to La Española (*Ibid.*, p. 811). Also, the freight contract of 1549 in which Doménigo Rizo leased a vessel to carry wines from La Rambla to Santa Cruz, and from there set sail to New Spain (*Ibid.*, p. 810).

to build a dock in La Rambla de Castro, another important anchorage of the area.[58] Likewise, from 1506, insular authorities undertook the building of another dock in the port of La Orotava.[59] In both cases we lack more explicit references about the nature and endowment of these port facilities, but these references do indicate the intention of the authorities to protect these ports.

The port of Garachico also developed naval construction activities, although, as with the port of Santa Cruz, explicit references to shipyards appear later in the period analysed. These references, contrary to the case of the island's royal port, do provide specific information on its location.[60]

As occurs with infrastructures, we also have abundant evidence, in extant documents throughout the period, of the increased control exercised by insular authorities of all these ports and harbours through the appointment of different officials responsible for controlling salubrity issues and overseeing all matters relating to loading and unloading tasks or taxation.

The South of the Island and Maritime Communications

The southern port axis of the island clearly held a lower status in terms of traffic and infrastructure complexity. It did, however, cover the most extensive area of the island, that of the southern coast, towards both the southeast and the southwest. As mentioned above, the area was thinly populated, on account of its less favourable conditions for agriculture and its arid coastline.[61]

Thus, in the central area of the southern region, at an altitude of 500 metres above sea level but at a considerable distance from the coast, small farm holdings were scattered during the modern age, and the coastline was occupied by small fishing settlements that channelled port traffic.

Documentary references are fragmented but, in general, allow us to identify information related to ports in practically all southern districts. We find very early references to the port of Los Abrigos,[62] in the Abona district; the port of

58 In 1502 Francisco de Medina received the authorisation of the governor. Elías Serra Ràfols, *Las datas de Tenerife (Libros I al IV de datas originales)* (San Cristóbal de La Laguna, 1978), no. 277-4. 3 March 1502.

59 Serrá Ràfols, *Acuerdos del Cabildo de Tenerife I*, no. 672. 7 December 1506.

60 In a notarial mandate, addressed to the shipwright Juan Blas, resident of Garachico, demanding he finish a boat he had left unfinished in Garachico shipyard, these facilities are located 'in the site of the ancient municipal *corral*, by the house of Pedro González Gavado'. Alfaro Hardisson, 'Documentos para el estudio de los puertos', no. 194. 10 August 1556.

61 Báez Hernández, *El Repartimiento de Tenerife*, pp. 126ff.

62 In the ownership title of a fountain granted to Pedro Madalena. Serra Ráfols, *Las datas de Tenerife*, no. 749.30. 14 October 1504. There are some references in notarial documents to the port of Abona at equally early dates, but it is unclear if they involve the same site. Emma González Yanes and Manuela Marrero Rodríguez, *Protocolos de Hernán Guerra (1508–1510)* (San Cristóbal de La Laguna, 1958), no. 586. 13 April 1509.

Güímar[63] and the port of 'La Cera' (present-day Las Heras),[64] in the Güímar valley district; the outlet from the port of Los Cristianos[65] or the inlet of Adeje.[66] Throughout this period, these sites were the outlets for the main exports of the area: wine, tar and later sugar. They served simultaneously as reception centres for incoming merchandise for the main ports of the island.[67]

However, despite the scant archival evidence of its existence, undoubtedly the most famous port of southern Tenerife is that of Montaña Roja, signalled in the diary of Antonio Pigafetta[68] as a port of call for Magellan's expedition, six days after sailing from the port of Sanlúcar de Barrameda en route to the Maluku Islands.[69] The purpose of this call was to provision the ships with water and wood. The travel log conveys barely any further details about the port, but it was clearly adequate to accommodate large ships.

Port Labour

Having established the different port spaces and the relations between them in the first half of the sixteenth century, we will now analyse the human element of these ports. Their definition is determined by a twofold conditioning. First, in the period soon after colonisation the degree of economic specialisation of the inhabitants was scant.[70] This would, however, gradually diversify due to the increase in population, and eventually give rise to a more complex economy with more effective political and administrative controls. The second determinant is the direct link of the islands with the Andalusian maritime tradition. In southern Andalusia, counter to what occurred in ports of the northern Peninsula, seamen did not form homogeneous social groups, and their bonds were reliant on other relational variables.[71] Something similar occurred in the case of the Canarian archipelago, and more specifically on the island

63 Rosa Olivera & Marrero Rodríguez, *Acuerdos del Cabildo de Tenerife V*, no. 359. 19 May 1531.

64 Báez Hernández, *El Repartimiento de Tenerife*, p. 159.

65 Delfina Galván Alonso, *Protocolos de Bernardino Justiniano (1526–1527)*, vol. II (San Cristóbal de La Laguna, 1990), no. 1660. 6 August 1527.

66 Martínez Galindo, *La vid y el vino en Tenerife*, p. 204.

67 *Ibid.*

68 Italian explorer, author of *Relazione del primo viaggio intorno al mondo* (1524), the principal source of information on the Magellan Elcano expedition resulting in the first circumnavigation of the planet.

69 Antonio Pigafetta, *Primer viaje alrededor del globo*, ed. Benito Caetano (Seville, 2012), pp. 12–13.

70 Aznar Vallejo, *La integración de las islas Canarias en la Corona de Castilla*.

71 Roberto J. González Zalacain, 'Apuntes para una ¿prosopografía? de las gentes del mar en Andalucía durante la baja Edad Media', in *Gentes del mar en la ciudad atlántica*

of Tenerife. There were no confraternities of seamen or fishermen, nor any structure that would suggest the maritime structure of the Castilian north[72] or other contexts of Atlantic Europe. References to the people of the sea are to be gleaned from general documents which do not identify relational patterns or provide details of operational aspects of port labour.[73]

Regarding port labour, the only certainty we can derive from documentary evidence is, at best, the establishment the different contracts carried out in the scriveners' offices of the island. According to these sources the different goods were loaded *a la lengua del mar* [at the sea tongue], which must be interpreted as 'the seashore'. There is hardly any further information about the loading process; on occasions when maritime transport was contracted, it was specified that this was to be *cargada debajo de verga* [loaded beneath the yard], that is, already stowed on board.[74] On occasions, more information was provided, by stating that this must be done *con su saca y acarreto* [with its withdrawal and haul], thus including all stevedoring tasks. There are, however, no explicit descriptions of how this merchandise was brought to the ships, which indirectly informs us that stevedoring tasks were in the hands of unskilled temporary workers.

We must suppose, from the indirect references, that merchandise was loaded and unloaded on boats that generally accompanied the ships themselves.[75] For this reason, we could identify that one of the professions involved in the loading and unloading of merchandise was that of boatmen, a common occupation in port environments.

Various residents of the island are identified as boatmen from early on,[76] though it is impossible to confirm that loading and unloading of ships was their sole occupation, since these same boats could be employed for other

medieval, ed. Jesús Ángel Solórzano Telechea, Michel Bochaca and Amélia Aguiar Andrade (Logroño, 2012), pp. 123–146.

72 See the references analysed in the chapter by María Álvarez Fernández in this volume.

73 This was also quite common in the Andalusian ports that were closely connected with the Canary Islands, such as Jerez de la Frontera, where references to the different crafts of the sea are practically non-existent. Roberto J. González Zalacain and Víctor Muñoz Gómez, 'Jerez y el Mar en la Baja Edad Media', *Actas del Congreso 750 aniversario de la incorporación de Jerez de la Frontera a la Corona de Castilla: 1264–2014*, ed. José Sánchez Herrero and Manuel González Jiménez (Jerez de la Frontera, 2014), pp. 307–327.

74 The bibliographical references corresponding to notarial protocols for this chapter contain numerous examples of this type.

75 For example, that of the caravel *Santa María la Bella*, owned by the Flemish merchant Jácome Casteleyn, which was to be employed to embark the cargo onto the vessel. González Yanes and Marrero Rodríguez, *Protocolos de Hernán Guerra*, no. 1103. 5 January 1509.

76 Already in 1505, the first year of extant notarial records, we find the boatman Ginés Bernal acting before a notary. Bello León, *Los protocolos notariales*, no. 1033. 6 November 1505.

tasks, such as transport between islands or inshore fishing. There is however, an isolated reference, namely a contract signed by a mother for her son to enter into apprenticeship with two boatmen to serve 'in his employment as a carter'.[77] This document certifies that, at least in some cases, transport and haulage of merchandise was a significant part of the people's livelihood, within the framework of a specialised trade.

Beyond this inference, it is reasonable not to presume any high degree of professionalisation or exclusive dedication in the majority of these boatmen. What is more, in almost all their appearances in notarial documents, they appear in the context of transactions that are unrelated to the loading and unloading of merchandise or any other maritime business, but rather are related to trade or agriculture. This fact is a clear evidence of professional multiactivity in these contexts.

Within this socio-professional context, we can also surmise a more or less significant participation of fishermen in loading and unloading vessels. This is an occupation that was already present among the population of the first colonisation[78] in the early sixteenth century. Many of these fishermen settled in the principal ports we have analysed above, and they probably combined their main activity of catching and selling fish with other complementary tasks in the port.

Both boatmen and fishermen must have been preferential customers of the shipwrights developing their activity in the precarious shipyards we have mentioned in the section on port infrastructure. We also have early references to their presence island,[79] as mentioned above, with evidence of shipbuilding activities from the early years of colonisation. From then on, as occurred with boatmen and fishermen, we encounter persons identified as shipwrights throughout extant notarial documentation, though their appearance is not in all cases related to their professional practice. Archival sources hold abundant examples of apprenticeship or indenture contracts, and we find some contracts for shipbuilding activities and equally frequent documentary references mentioning persons of this profession, albeit in business ventures unrelated to maritime activity.[80]

77 Galván Alonso, *Protocolos de Bernardino Justiniano*, vol. I, no. 843. 6 January 1527.

78 Some fishermen are listed as beneficiaries of land distribution in the first years of the colonisation of the island. Serra Ràfols, *Las datas de Tenerife*. For an analysis of the fishing sector in Andalusia and the Canary Islands see Juan Manuel Bello León, *La pesca en Andalucía y Canarias en el tránsito de la Edad Media a la Moderna* (Santa Cruz de Tenerife, 2008).

79 Although, unlike fishermen, no beneficiary of land distribution is identified as a shipwright.

80 Alfaro Hardisson, 'Documentos para el estudio de los puertos.'

This set of references to the persons who, in one way or another, were professionally related to the maritime world are our fundamental source of knowledge about port labour on the island of Tenerife at the time. Beyond these mentions we lack any documentary evidence to allow us further insight into the subject. In any case, we can at least infer from what we have posited above, a multifaceted professional sphere linked to the maritime world, where the people of the sea coexisted with other professional sectors that, at specific times, intersected to perform the diverse activities generated within the ports. We have not analysed other professions present in the ports, for instance those of merchants trading there or scribes who attested to the validity of transactions.[81] Broaching the mercantile sphere would deviate us notably from the aim of this chapter, though commercial networks and the volume of transactions were significant in these ports. And, of course, we must not forget shipmasters and mariners in general, who appear in documents almost exclusively when freights were transacted to transport merchandise to other ports,[82] and who seem to have been responsible for many of the stevedoring tasks carried out at the time in auxiliary boats of the main vessels, employed for disembarkation at the ports.

Conclusions

Analysis of the configuration of the port network of the island of Tenerife after its conquest and incorporation into the Castilian Crown provides a series of elements of interest for the study of ports and port systems during the transition from the Middle Ages to the modern age. In these very early periods of one of the focal points of European expansion, first in the Atlantic and later within a global context, the islands became a fundamental port of call for the vessels traversing these seas. They thus became centres of first commercial order, both for their strategic position and for the value of their agricultural and industrial produce, first sugar and later wine. This led to the formation of an economic reality requiring adequate port infrastructures. We have confirmed

81 We must consider that in the recent works on people of the sea, it is very common that their study is limited to the role of merchants in the urban sphere. See in this regard some of the works included in the volume edited by Éric Guerber and Gérard Le Bouëdec, *Gens de mer. Ports et cités aux époques ancienne, médiévale et moderne* (Rennes, 2013).

82 We have, of course, some other interesting documentary reference about the life of the sailors in the port, such as the accusation in 1523 of the Portuguese shipmaster Gaspar Rodríguez Cachera, who was in Tenerife for business, for the sin of sodomy. Despite being an isolated reference, it leads to a port life in the style of that of other places and times, which have generated the archetype of a sailor on land that still exists today. Roberto J. González Zalacain, *Familia y sociedad en Tenerife a raíz de la conquista* (San Cristóbal de La Laguna, 2005), pp. 140–141.

with the analysis of port development how the material and social foundations were relatively precarious. No large construction projects were undertaken to promote and facilitate port activities despite the appeals before the Crown of local authorities for investments in such facilities. Quite the contrary, the port network of the island of Tenerife developed basically under the pull of two complementary factors. On the one hand, the natural conditions of the different sites provided havens and landing spots for ships, connected with the period prior to the conquest and occupation of the territory; and on the other, the uneven economic development taking place on the island as sugar and wine production grew. All this formed a porous network of ports through which many goods were imported and exported, in spite of the efforts of authorities to control such activity and centralise commerce through the port of Santa Cruz de Tenerife.

Therefore, the study of port development offers the possibility of getting to know the construction of the port system *ex novo*, without any prior inheritance in the indigenous reality of the island, by virtue of the construction of a new society within an Atlantic context which undoubtedly conditioned its development. This allows us to establish the central role of economic activity in the dynamisation of some of the port enclaves of the island, particularly on the northern façade. In this case, the configuration of the port network was driven not by the political impulse of the authorities, be they local or the Crown itself, but rather by the economic activities developed in the different regions of the island.

Hence, we can define the port network of the island of Tenerife in particular, and of the Canary Islands in general, as a differential example with regard to other port contexts. The insular particularity, with the fundamental characteristic of the porosity of its coastline, where practically every inlet was a potential landing spot, rendered the centralising efforts of the Crown futile and forced a dispersion of the necessary resources for the development of port infrastructures, with an obvious impact on the varying degrees of development of the ports. This process was initiated later than in other Atlantic ports, on account of the overarching context of the creation of a new socio-economic system which demanded important economic and human investments to establish a new society.

Conclusions: The Port Phenomenon of Medieval Atlantic Europe

JESÚS ÁNGEL SOLÓRZANO TELECHEA

University of Cantabria (UNICAN) (Santander, Spain)

Littus ama, altum alii teneant
Virgil

Nearly fifty years ago, Herman Van Der Wee and Theo Peeters presented the concentration of much of the economic activity in a small number of ports as one of the explanations for the crisis of the late Middle Ages. Since then, historiography has not paid due attention to the efforts of port societies to build strong port infrastructures and improve port services, these efforts being some of the most important factors for the revitalisation of the European economy from the mid-fifteenth century onwards. This volume offers such material: transport and port infrastructures, cargo handling, labour groups and port services help us understand the reasons for their success.

From Antiquity, cities have emerged along the littoral, with few regions in the world ever being totally self-sufficient.[1] As the Latin name *portus* reveals, these are gateways from the sea to land allowing for the flow of merchandise, people, knowledge and, also, disease and violence. The benefits – and drawbacks – derived thereof were numerous. With seaborne traffic being much faster and more direct than overland transport, the main benefit was the supply of commodities to the population. During Antiquity, the proximity of the sea to a city did have adverse consequences. As Plato describes in his *Laws* dialogue, cities should be located at a distance of 80 stadia from the sea to counteract the

1 This chapter is part of the research carried out in the project: 'Politics, Institutions and Governance of the European Atlantic Ports in the Late Middle Ages: A Transnational Comparative Analysis' (HAR2017-83801-P), funded by FEDER / Spanish Ministry of Science and Innovation / National Research Agency.

inherent dangers of maritime cities, namely the influence of foreign customs, the drive for gain and profit, corruption and the inclination for travelling and venturing overseas:

> although there is sweetness in its proximity for the uses of daily life; for by filling the markets of the city with foreign merchandise and retail trading, and breeding in men's souls knavish and tricky ways, it renders the city faithless and loveless, not to itself only, but to the rest of the world as well. (*Laws* 705a)

In his *Politics*, Aristotle does not hold such a negative view of port cities. In his view, ports of transit are necessary for subsistence, commercial and military purposes; he does, however, oppose the development of a city into an *emporium*.

The negative view of maritime cities during Antiquity changed radically during the Middle Ages. Definitions during the medieval period of the concept of 'port' made distinctions between two main functions. On the one hand, cities were characterised by infrastructures that could accommodate vessels, persons and merchandise. On the other, some ports acted as nodal points in commercial traffic networks between internal and foreign regions. Hence, the port was a gateway between sea and land, and an entryway that facilitated the circulation of people and commodities, and guaranteed the communication between maritime, fluvial and land transport. As an example, the *Partidas* describe ports as follows:

> Puerto es dicho lugar encerrado de montañas, o en la ribera del mar, donde se cargan o descargan las naos o los otros navíos. Otro tal sería todo lugar do la nave pudiese invernar estando sobre ancoras, mas los otros lugares do pueden ancorar, e non se podrían defender de gran tormenta son dichos playa o piélago. (*Partida* VII, title 33, law 8)[2]

According to the historian Rodrigo Sánchez de Arévalo in his *Suma de la Política*:

> Ser muy cumplidero que la cibdad fuesse muy junta al mar, ca terná más abundancia de las cosas necessarias a la vida umana, y aun será más fuerte, porque podrá aver socorro por mar y por tierra contra sus enemigos.[3]

2 'Port is the place locked between mountains or on the seashore, where ships and other vessels are loaded or unloaded. Such would also be any place where a ship may anchor during winter, but the other places where the ship may anchor but not be defended against great storms are known as beach or sea.'

3 'It is very convenient that the city be very near the sea, as it will have more abundance of the necessary things for human life, and will even be stronger, because it may obtain aid from sea and from land against its enemies.' Rodrigo Sánchez de Arévalo, *Suma de la Política* (Madrid, 1959), p. 265.

Yet, a port is not solely defined by its proximity to the sea. The concept of a port city involves a closely knit interplay between the port and the urban centre from a topographic, socio-economic and political viewpoint. Indeed, port activities exerted a quadruple impact on the urban centre, in terms of urban planning, labour, commerce and fiscality. The intertwining between the port and the city generated a highly particular urban landscape, characteristic of both Mediterranean and Atlantic ports.

The study of ports has privileged the commercial function of these urban centres, possibly due to the influence of the Belgian historian Henri Pirenne, thus producing a limited version of their role in society. Ports are more than their docks and infrastructures. At times they were havens for ships in times of danger, although they mostly served as loading and unloading spots for merchandise, and they were intimately connected with their urban centres, hosting seafarers, merchants and travellers. This required lodgings, facilities for the storage of merchandise, toll houses, trading halls, markets and shipyards, among others. Furthermore, these facilities required proper planning and, therefore, an authority to organise it. In fact, most of the medieval port towns were the product of a political intention. The foremost *emporia* in the North Sea during the eighth century, or the port towns of the Iberian Peninsula during the twelfth and thirteenth centuries, were created as a result of a regal or seigneurial impulse, even in cases with extant settlements. The kings and, to a lesser extent, the lords, transformed these small maritime enclaves into port towns and cities. Precisely the interest of kings and lords in the ports informs us of another function of ports, their role as fiscal generators, since the circulation of commodities generated local, royal and seigneurial taxes, to feed local, royal and seigneurial coffers. Another frequently underestimated function is that ports provided sustenance to the local populations, through fishing, commerce, naval war and piratical activities whose profits contributed to defray the building of ships.

The requisite all port cities had to meet was to possess port infrastructures, defensive measures for the port and ships, a commercial activity, a population well instructed in the matters of the sea, relations with other port centres and the interior, an administrative autonomy, and a culture differentiated from the rural inland. In this manner, a port was not only a material reality – its infrastructures – but also a venue for the transaction of commodities and the exchange of persons and ideas, a population nucleus where specific crafts were practised, and a place where economic and political privileges were granted to secure these transactions and their protagonists. This involved the development of an urban morphology, and specific socio-professional and legal structures that defined medieval port cities.

Given their multifunctional nature, it is a complex task to analyse and classify port cities. Both in Europe and in other parts of the world, ports have played a significant role in the urbanisation of countries and regions, but the analyses of these entities have been highly fragmented, given the predominance in the historical research of navigation, maritime history and the history of commerce over studies of port history. This places Port History as a recent specialty of Urban History which did not exist thirty years ago. Navigation historians were not concerned with the urban context whence ships departed or to which they arrived. Economic historians centred their efforts on commerce and the interplay between ports and their hinterlands, while archaeologists and geographers busied themselves with the study of port infrastructures. Though themes such as social conflict, social groups, slave labour, immigration, diplomacy or governance were studied by social and cultural historians, this was done without integrating their relationship with maritime activities. Consequently, there remains much to study with regard to port societies, including, for example, minorities and marginal groups. In this respect, I wish to signal the chapter by Amândio J. M. Barros, where he analyses the logistics of slave trade in the ports of northern Portugal, as well as the presence of slave labour in these ports. This is a valuable and pioneering work bringing to light the significance of slaves in loading and unloading tasks.

On the Atlantic coast, the ports that emerged during the twelfth-century commercial revolution were mostly driven by a well-defined growth pattern. We must make a distinction between ports located on the coastline and those located on the banks of navigable fluvial courses found near the coast. A substantial number of the large ports in Atlantic Europe belong to the latter category: Seville, Lisbon, Bilbao, London, Chester, Bordeaux, Caen, Nantes, Rouen, Bruges, Bremen, Hamburg, etc. These ports often had outer ports, as was the case of Bruges, with first Damme and later Sluys, Cork with Dobh, Bilbao with Portugalete, Seville with Sanlúcar de Barrameda, Hamburg with Cuxhaven, and Nantes with Saint-Nazaire, among many others. As an example, Enrique José Ruiz Pilares offers a detailed analysis of the transformation of the Atlantic littoral in Andalusia in the late fifteenth century, when public and private powers invested in the building of port and road infrastructures to improve the work of cargo handlers and to cope with the growth in maritime commerce. Still, transport with river barges remained the main mode of shipping on the Guadalquivir, given the impossibility of deep-draft vessels navigating this watercourse. The aggradation of the Guadalquivir's riverbed represented a serious problem for navigation, forcing local authorities to promulgate various norms to address it.

In general, medieval ports located along the actual coastline experienced smaller growth. These include Gijón, Portugalete, San Sebastián, Laredo, Santander, La Coruña, Cádiz, Hull, Plymouth, Dover, La Rochelle, Calais, Dieppe and others. Into the fifteenth century, these were enclaves on the coast, with small wooden piers and later more specialised piers for cargo handling. A solid study of the infrastructures in smaller ports is offered by María Álvarez Fernández in her article on the ports of Asturias. These were modest in comparison with the commercial activity developed in the neighbouring Cantabrian and Basque ports. The ambition of these ports was to achieve a greater exterior projection, which required the transformation of wooden piers into masonry structures, much safer and more appropriate for the loading and unloading of cargo and commercial progress. Along these lines, the chapter by Sara Pinto analyses maritime transport logistics in the port of Caminha, on the border with the kingdom of Castile, on the mouth of the river Minho. The originality of this study lies in the observation of the behaviour of a border port.

We must equally make a distinction between enclaves with port infrastructures and those without them. In fact, until the fifteenth century, the majority of Atlantic ports lacked solid port infrastructures. Among the factors leading to the construction of these infrastructures we find, first, natural factors such as changes in sea levels, climate change, coastal erosion and the silting-up of ports; second, artificial factors such as dams, canals or bridges; third, economic factors such as market dynamics, production specialisation and the transformation of ports from a local to an international scope; fourth, navigational factors such as increased size or greater specialisation of the vessels. All these factors must be borne in mind when building port infrastructures. The underlying aim of these infrastructures was to ensure the transfer of commodities and persons between the port and the ships. In his remarkable chapter, Mathias Tranchant analyses the different modalities of loading and unloading processes, and services implemented in over 620 ports between the eleventh and fifteenth centuries.

The ports of the European Atlantic façade, developing in the Middle Ages, were successful because they were underpinned by a series of determinants such as geographic conditions, their extremely dynamic infrastructures, and societies. This success of Atlantic port centres – mostly located in peripheral sites – was also due to the adoption by urban governance of traits that were both common and different from those of cities in the continental interior. Further, a port had to guarantee legal safety for cargo handling tasks, as has been studied by Ana María Rivera, who provides a meticulous comparative analysis between Basque ports and other Atlantic ports. In her chapter she studies the organisation of port spaces, technical and logistic transferences and the regulation of cargo handling labour through confraternities, although cargo handlers never actually constituted guilds, contrary to what occurred in the ports of the North Sea. Further, the intimacy of maritime ties between the ports entailed the exchange of ideas and information and the transfer of technology and knowledge to bolster the competitive capacity of these centres.

We must thus make distinctions between the different types of ports, considering whether they participate in a large-scale trade or a local and regional commerce. Equally, the study of port cities must have due regard for factors other than economic determinants, such as the geographic features, their role as urban markets, the ability to establish trust networks within the merchant community, their relations with the hinterland, and their political connections. In terms of this, Roberto J. González Zalacain analyses port infrastructures of the island of Tenerife. This island differs from other continental Atlantic ports, given its insular characteristics. Almost all beaches and inlets of the islands were exploited for loading and unloading cargo in transit to the interconnected ports. This was fundamentally an export traffic which countered the centralising efforts of the Crown in its attempt to concentrate activity in the port of Santa Cruz de Tenerife.

The study of medieval Atlantic ports compels us to formulate an analysis with a transnational and comparative approach. Port towns and cities have played an essential role in the economic integration of Europe and the process of globalisation. In this manner, this volume offers answers to several questions that arise regarding the importance of the port phenomenon along the Atlantic coast, without which it would not be possible to understand the Atlantic expansion of Spain and Portugal during the modern period, or the specific contribution of Europeans to economic globalisation.

Sources and Bibliography

Manuscript and Unpublished Sources

Archives Départementales de Charente-Maritime, La Rochelle
Archives Départementales de Seine-Maritime, Rouen
Archives Municipales de Bayonne
Archives Nationales de France
Archivo de la Diputación Foral de Bizkaia
Archivo General de Indias
Archivo General de Simancas
Archivo Histórico Provincial de Vizcaya
Archivo Municipal de Jerez de la Frontera
Arquivo Distrital do Porto
Arquivo Histórico Municipal do Porto
Arquivo Nacional da Torre do Tombo
Biblioteca Nacional de Portugal
Biblioteca Pública Municipal do Porto
Bibliothèque Nationale de France

Printed Primary Sources

Álvarez Arias, C., *Documentos orixinales del monasteriu de San Vicente d'Uvieu (1231–1238)* (Oviedo, 2008)

Álvarez Fernández, María, 'De alcabalas y arrendadores. La contribución de concejos y parroquias asturianas a la hacienda regia en 1494', *Cuadernos de Estudios Gallegos*, 129 (2016), 205–242

Ayerbe Iribar, M. A., 'Las ordenanzas de San Sebastián de 1489', *Boletín de estudios históricos sobre San Sebastián*, 40 (2006), 11–91

Aznar Vallejo, Eduardo, *et al.*, *Documentos Canarios en el Registro General del Sello (1518–1525)* (San Cristóbal de La Laguna, 1991)

Bello León, Juan Manuel, *Los protocolos notariales de los escribanos de Tenerife Sebastián Páez y Antón de Vallejo (años 1505–1506)* (San Cristóbal de La Laguna, 2015)

Capmany Surís y de Montpalau, Antonio, *Codigo de las costumbres marítimas de Barcelona, hasta aqui vulgarmente llamado Libro del Consulado. Nuevamente traducido al castellano con el texto lemosin restituido á su original integridad y pureza; é ilustrado con varios apéndices, glosarios, y observaciones históricas* (Madrid, 1791)

Cartulaire de l'ancienne estaple de Bruges. Recueil de documents concernant le commerce intérieur et maritime, les relations internationales et l'histoire économique de cette ville, ed. Louis Gilliodts van Severen, 6 vols (Bruges, 1904–1909)

Cartulaire des sires de Ray, 1160–1449, t. XXX, ed. René Blanchard, 2 vols (Poitiers, 1898–1899)

Censo de Pecheros: Carlos I, 1528 (Madrid, 2008), t. II

Cleirac, Estienne, *Us et coustumes de la mer, divisées en trois parties. I. De la navigation. II. Du commerce naval, & contracts maritimes. III. De la juridiction de la marine. Avec un traicté des termes de Marine, & reglemens de la navigation des fleuves & rivieres* (Bordeaux, 1671)

Comptes et enquêtes d'Alfonse comte de Poitou, 1253–1269, ed. Abel Bardonnet (Poitiers, 1879)

Foedera, conventions, literae, and cujuscunque generis acta publica, inter reges Angliae, and alios quosvis imperatores, reges, pontifices, principles, vel communitates, ab ineunte saeculo duodecimo, viz. ab anno 1101, ad nostra usque tempora, habita aut tractata, ex autographis, infra secretiores archivorum regiorum thesaurarias, per multa saecula reconditis, fideliter exscripta, ed. Thomas Rymer, t. I (The Hague, 1740)

García Larragueta, Santos, *Colección de documentos de la Catedral de Oviedo* (Oviedo, 1962)

Gautier Dalché, Patrick, *Du Yorkshire a l'Inde. Une géographie urbaine et maritime de la fin du XIIe siècle (Roger de Howden)* (Geneva, 2005)

La Rochelle au fil des ans avec Nicolas Baudouin, t. II: *XVe siècle*, ed. Mathias Tranchant (Saintes, 2008)

Le vieux coustumier de Poictou, ed. René Filhol (Bourges, 1956)

Les édicts et ordonnances des Roys de France depuis Louys VI dit le Gros, jusques à présent, ed. Antoine Fontanon, t. III (Paris, 1611)

Livre des Bouillons, Archives Municipales de Bordeaux, t. 1 (Bordeaux, 1867)

Livre des coutumes, publié avec des variantes et des notes, Archives Municipales de Bordeaux, t. 5 (Bordeaux, 1890)

Miguel Vigil, Ciriaco, *Asturias monumental, epigráfica y diplomática* (Oviedo, 1887)

Miranda Duque, Andrea, and Celia Álvarez Arias, *Documentos orixinales del monasteriu de San Vicente d'Uvieu (1239–1250)* (Oviedo, 2012)

Ordonnances des rois de France de la troisième race, vol. 2, ed. Eusèbe-Jacob de Laurière (Paris, 1729); vol. 8, ed. Denis François Secousse (Paris, 1750); vol. 21, ed. Jean-Marie Pardessus (Paris, 1849)

Pereda, Felipe, and Fernando Marías (eds), *El Atlas del Rey Planeta. La 'descripción de España y de las costas y puertos de sus reinos' de Pedro Texeira (1634)* (Hondarribia, 2002)

Pigafetta, Antonio, *Primer viaje alrededor del globo*, ed. Benito Caetano (Seville, 2012)

Recueil des actes de Philippe-Auguste, roi de France, ed. Henri-François Delaborde, t. I (Paris, 1916)

Recueil général des anciennes lois françaises depuis l'an 420 jusqu'à la Révolution de 1789, ed. François-André Isambert, Athanase-Jean-Léger Jourdan and Decrusy, t. X: *1461–1483* (Paris, 1825)

Rosa Olivera, Leopoldo de la, and Manuela Marrero Rodríguez, *Acuerdos del Cabildo de Tenerife V (1525–1533)* (San Cristóbal de La Laguna, 1986)

Rosa Olivera, Leopoldo de la, and Elías Serra Ràfols, *El adelantado don Alonso de Lugo y su residencia por Lope de Sosa* (San Cristóbal de La Laguna, 1949)

Ruiz de la Peña Solar, Juan Ignacio, *Las polas asturianas en la Edad Media. Estudio y diplomatario* (Oviedo, 1981)

Sampedro Redondo, Laura, *Sobre el cay. Libro 2º. Libro de Actas del Ayuntamiento de Gijón (1560–1577)* (Gijón, 2005)

Sanz Fuentes, María Josefa, Miguel Calleja Puerta and José Antonio Álvarez Castrillón (eds), *Colección diplomática del concejo de Avilés* (Avilés, 2011)

Sanz Fuentes, María Josefa, and Juan Ignacio Ruiz de la Peña Solar, *Colección diplomática del Monasterio de San Vicente de Oviedo (1201–1230)* (Oviedo, 1991)

Serra Ráfols, Elías, *Acuerdos del Cabildo de Tenerife I (1497–1507)*, 2nd edn (San Cristóbal de La Laguna, 1996)

———, *Las datas de Tenerife (Libros I al IV de datas originales)* (San Cristóbal de La Laguna, 1978)

Serra Ráfols, Elías, and Leopoldo de la Rosa Olivera, *Acuerdos del Cabildo de Tenerife II (1508–1513)* (San Cristóbal de La Laguna, 1952)

———, *Acuerdos del Cabildo de Tenerife III (1514–1518)* (San Cristóbal de La Laguna, 1965)

The Black Book of the Admiralty, ed. Travers Twiss (London, 1871–1876)

Tieullier, Guillaume, *Le coustumier de la vicomté de Dieppe*, ed. Emmanuel Coppinger (Dieppe, 1884)

Torriani, Leonardo, *Descripción e historia del reino de las Islas Canarias, antes Afortunadas, con el parecer de sus fortificaciones*, trans. Alejandro Cioranescu (Santa Cruz de Tenerife, 1999)

Vigil Montes, Néstor, *La villa de Avilés en 1602. Estudio del protocolo notarial de Julián de Valdés León* (Oviedo, 2011)

Secondary Sources

Abrantes Garcia, Ana Catarina, 'Angra e Funchal, dois portos atlânticos no contexto do império marítimo português. Análise comparativa sobre espaços, estruturas e dinámicas', *Nuevo Mundo Mundos Nuevos* (2016), online

Adaro Ruiz, Luis, *El puerto de Gijón y otros puertos asturianos* (Gijón, 1976)

Aguiar Andrade, Amélia, 'A importancia da linha costeira na estruturaçao do Reino medieval portugués. Algumas reflexões', *Historia Instituciones, Documentos*, 35 (2008), 9–24

———, 'Vilas, poder régio e fronteira: o exemplo do Entre Lima e Minho medieval' (PhD diss., Universidade Nova de Lisboa, 1994)

Alfaro Hardisson, Emilio, 'Canarias y el mar', in *Navíos y gentes del mar. Siglos XVI–XVIII* (Santa Cruz de Tenerife, 2003), pp. 14–18

———, 'Documentos para el estudio de los puertos y de la navegación marítima en Tenerife en el siglo *XVI*', *Fuentes Canarias en Red*, 4 (2017), 9–242

Álvarez Carballo, Marta, 'Arquitectura y ciudad. Urbanismo medieval en Asturias: Llanes' (PhD diss., Universidad de Oviedo, 2012) <http://digibuo.uniovi.es/dspace/handle/10651/13006>

Álvarez Castrillón, José Antonio, 'Aproximación histórica a la cuenca del Eo: desde los primeros testimonios a la época medieval', in *En torno al bimilenario del Eo* (Oviedo, 2002), pp. 405–438

Álvarez Fernández, María, 'Abastecimiento y consumo de pescado en Oviedo a finales de la Edad Media', in *La pesca en la Edad Media* (Santiago de Compostela, 2009), pp. 71–86

———, 'Alfonso X el Sabio, promotor del desarrollo urbano de la Asturias Medieval', in *El mundo urbano en la Castilla del siglo XIII*, ed. M. González Jiménez, vol. 2 (Seville, 2006), pp. 21–32

———, *Oviedo a fines de la Edad Media. Morfología urbana y política concejil* (Oviedo, 2009)

Álvarez Fernández, María (ed.), *Quinientos años después. Villaviciosa: 1517–2017. La época en que D. Carlos vino a Asturias* (Oviedo, 2019)

Alves, António Maria Caetano, 'Causas e processos da dinâmica sedimentar na evolução actual do litoral do Alto Minho' (PhD diss., Universidade do Minho, 1996)

Amorim, Inês, *Porto de Aveiro: entre a terra e o mar* (Aveiro, 2008)

Anes Álvarez de Castrillón, Gonzalo, *Economía y sociedad en la Asturias del Antiguo Régimen* (Barcelona, 1988)

Antunes, Cátia, and Louis Sicking, 'Ports on the Border of the State, 1200–1800: An Introduction', *International Journal of Maritime History*, 19 (2007), 273–286

Aramburu Zabala, Miguel Ángel, and Begoña Alonso Ruiz, *Santander: un puerto para el Renacimiento* (Santander, 1994)

Araújo, Assunção, 'A evolução do litoral em tempos históricos: a contribuição da Geografia física', in *Actas 'O Litoral em Perspectiva Histórica (séc. XVI a XVIII)* (Porto, 2002), pp. 73–91

Araújo, Francisco, and Sandra Alves, 'Escravos e libertos em Leça da Palmeira (1560–1836)', *Africana Studia*, 7 (2004), 53–72

Arízaga Bolumburu, Beatriz, 'Bayona y el control del curso inferior del Adour del siglo XV al principio del siglo XVI', in *Musulmanes y Cristianos frente al agua en las ciudades medievales*, ed. María Isabel del Val Valdivieso and Olatz Villanueva Zubizarreta (Santander, 2008), pp. 215–229

Arízaga Bolumburu, Beatriz, and Michel Bochaca, 'Caractères généraux des villes portuaires du littoral castillan nord-peninsulaire au Moyen Âge', in *Ports maritimes et ports fluviaux au Moyen Âge* (Paris, 2005), pp. 63–78

Arízaga Bolumburu, Beatriz, and Sergio Martínez Martínez, *Atlas de villas medievales de Vasconia. Bizcaya* (San Sebastián, 2006)

Arízaga Bolumburu, Beatriz, and Jesús Ángel Solórzano Telechea, 'La construction d'infrastructures portuaires dans les villes du nord de la Péninsule Ibérique à la fin du Moyen Âge', in *Ports et littoraux de l'Europe Atlantique. Transformations naturelles aménagements humains (XIVe–XVIe siècles)*, ed. Michel Bochaca and Jean-Luc Sarrazin (Rennes, 2007), pp. 121–140

———, (eds), *Ciudades y villas portuarias del Atlántico en la Edad Media* (Logroño, 2005)

Armas, Duarte de, *Livro das Fortalezas, Facsimile do Ms. 159 da Casa Forte do Arquivo Nacional da Torre do Tombo* (Lisbon, 1997)

Armas Castro, José, 'Mercaderes portugueses en Pontevedra en el siglo XV', in *Actas do Congresso Internacional Bartolomeu Dias e a sua época*, vol. III (Porto, 1989), pp. 217–230

———, *Pontevedra en los siglos XII a XV. Configuración y desarrollo de una villa marinera en la Galicia medieval* (Pontevedra, 1992)

Aznar Vallejo, Eduardo, 'Andalucía y el Atlántico Andalucía y el Atlántico Norte a fines de la Edad Media', *Historia. Instituciones. Documentos*, 30 (2003), 103–120

———, 'Barcos y barqueros en Sevilla', *Historia. Instituciones. Documentos*, 21 (1994), 1–12

———, 'El mar fuente de conflictos y exigencia de paz', *Edad Media. Revista de Historia*, 11 (2010), 63–89

———, 'La conexión marítimo-terrestre en la baja Andalucía. El ejemplo de Sevilla', in *De mar a mar. Los puertos castellanos en la Baja Edad Media*, ed. Eduardo Aznar Vallejo and Roberto J. González Zalacain (San Cristóbal de La Laguna, 2015), pp. 125–146

———, 'La época fundacional y su influjo en el patrimonio histórico de San Cristóbal de La Laguna', *Anuario de Estudios Atlánticos*, 54.1 (2008), 169–205

———, *La integración de las islas Canarias en la Corona de Castilla (1478–1526). Aspectos administrativos, sociales y económicos*, 3rd edn (Santa Cruz de Tenerife, 2009)

———, 'La regulación de los oficios del mar en Andalucía', in *Gentes de mar en la ciudad atlántica medieval*, ed. Jesús Ángel Solórzano Telechea, Michel Bochaca and Amélia Aguiar Andrade (Logroño, 2012), pp. 95–122

———, 'Marinos vascos en la guerra naval de Andalucía durante el siglo XV', *Itsas Memoria. Revista de Estudios Marítimos del País Vasco*, 5 (2006), 41–52

———, 'Marinos y pescadores', *Medievalismo: Boletín de la Sociedad Española de Estudios Medievales*, 13/14 (2004), 234–235

Aznar Vallejo, Eduardo, *et al.*, *Le Canarien, retrato de dos mundos. I, Textos* (San Cristóbal de La Laguna, 2006)

Azpiazu Elorza, José Antonio, 'Las mujeres vascas y el mar', *Itsas Memoria. Revista de Estudios Marítimos del País Vasco*, 8 (2016), 811–829

Báez Hernández, Francisco, *El repartimiento de Tenerife (1493–1569)* (San Cristóbal de La Laguna, 2016)

Balard, Michel, and Christian Buchet (eds), *The Sea in History / La mer dans la histoire: The Medieval World* (Woodbridge, 2017)

Balasque, Jules and Ernest Dulaurens, *Études historiques sur la ville de Bayonne* (Bayonne, 1862), t. III

Baquero Moreno, Humberto, 'Relações entre Portugal e a Galiza nos séculos XIV e XV', *Revista da Faculdade de Letras. Historia*, 7 (1990), 34–46

Barbot, Amos, *Histoire de La Rochelle* (Paris, 1886)

Barral Rivadulla, María Dolores, *La Coruña en los siglos XIII al XV: historia y configuración urbana de una villa de realengo en la Galicia medieval* (La Coruña, 1998)

Barré, Éric, 'Le droit d'épave une aubaine', *Chronique d'histoire maritime*, 67 (December 2009), 109–126

———, 'Notes sur l'amirauté de France en Normandie au Moyen Âge', 'Les Amirautés en France et outre-mer du Moyen Âge au début du XIXe siècle', special issue, *Revue d'Histoire Maritime*, 19 (2014), 1–31

Barros, Amândio, 'A construçao de um centro portuário atlântico: O Porto nos séculos XVI e XVII', in *La gobernanza de los puertos atlánticos, siglos XIV–XX: Políticas y estructuras portuarias*, ed. Amélia Polónia and Ana María Rivera Medina (Madrid, 2016), pp. 193–218

———, 'Trato de escravos e economia atlântica. O contrato do navio Conceição', in *Trabalho Forçado Africano. Articulações com o poder político* (Porto, 2007), pp. 15–46

———, *Porto. A construção de um espaço marítimo no início dos tempos modernos* (Lisbon, 2016)

———, *Porto: a construção de um espaço marítimo nos alvores dos tempos modernos*, vol. I (Porto, 2004)

Bello León, Juan Manuel, 'Almadrabas andaluzas a finales de la Edad Media', *Historia. Instituciones. Documentos*, 32 (2005), 81–114

———, 'El marco jurídico y fiscal en los puertos andaluces a finales de la Edad Media', in *De mar a mar. Los puertos castellanos en la Baja Edad Media*, ed. Eduardo Aznar Vallejo and Roberto J. González Zalacain (San Cristóbal de La Laguna, 2015), pp. 17–58

———, 'El Reino de Sevilla en el comercio exterior castellano (siglos XIV y XV)', in *Castilla y Europa. Comercio y Mercaderes en los siglos XIV, XV y XVI*, ed. Hilario Casado Alonso (Burgos, 1995), pp. 57–80

———, *Extranjeros en Castilla (1474–1501): notas y documentos para el estudio de su presencia en el reino a fines del siglo XV* (Tenerife, 1994)

———, *La pesca en Andalucía y Canarias en el tránsito de la Edad Media a la Moderna* (Santa Cruz de Tenerife, 2008)

———, 'Mercaderes del siglo XV de Jerez de la Frontera', *Historia. Instituciones. Documentos*, 41 (2014), 11–44

———, 'Mercaderes extranjeros en Sevilla en tiempos de los Reyes Católicos', *Historia. Instituciones. Documentos*, 20 (1993), 47–84

———, 'Primeras obras públicas en Canarias: caminos, puertos y abastecimiento de agua en el siglo XVI', *Estudios Canarios. Anuario del Instituto de Estudios Canarios*, 50–51 (2006–2007), 595–618

———, '¿Quiénes eran los mercaderes de Sevilla a finales de la Edad Media?', in *Gentes de mar en la ciudad atlántica medieval*, ed. Jesús Ángel Solórzano Telechea, Michel Bochaca and Amélia Aguiar Andrade (Logroño, 2012), pp. 249–274

Bello León, Juan Manuel, and Alejandro Martín Perera, *Las atarazanas de Sevilla a finales de la Edad Media* (Madrid, 2012)

Beltrán Suárez, María Soledad, *Marineros de Luarca a la caza de la ballena. El primer contrato conocido, 1477* (Luarca, 2019)

Bennett, Judith M., and Ruth M. Karras (eds.), *The Oxford Handbook of Women and Gender in Medieval Europe* (Oxford, 2013)

Bermejo Meléndez, Alberto, and Javier Bermejo Meléndez, 'Las instalaciones del puerto de época colombina de Palos de la Frontera (Huelva): la alota y el campo de hornos', in *Actas de las Jornadas Historia sobre el Descubrimiento de América*, t. IV (Seville, 2019), pp. 513–541

Bernal Rodríguez, Antonio Miguel, and Antonio Collantes de Terán Sánchez, 'El puerto de Sevilla, de puerto fluvial medieval a centro portuario mundial (siglos XIV–XVII)', in *I porti come impresa economica*, ed. Simonetta Cavaciocchi (Florence, 1988), pp. 779–824

Bernard, Jacques, *Navires et gens de mer à Bordeaux (vers 1400–vers 1550)* (Paris, 1968)

Bochaca, Michel, 'El control del puerto de Burdeos y de su tráfico mercantil del siglo XIII al XV: jurisdicciones y estructuración del espacio', in *Ciudades y villas portuarias del Atlántico en la Edad Media*, ed. Beatriz Arízaga Bolumburu and Jesús Ángel Solórzano Telechea (Logroño, 2005), pp. 91–113

———, *La Banlieue de Bordeaux. Formation d'une juridiction municipale suburbaine (vers 1250–vers 1550)* (Paris, 1997)

———, 'Typologie et fonctions des ports du Bordelais (fin XVe–début XVIe siècle)', *Historia, Instituciones, Documentos*, 35 (2008), 63–83

———, 'Un témoignage des relations maritimes et commerciales entre Bordeaux et la Bretagne le plus ancien contrat d'affrètement conservé dans le fonds de la Garde-Note de Bordeaux (27 décembre 1445)', *Anales de historia medieval de la Europa atlántica: AMEA*, 2 (2015), 65–79

Bochaca, Michel, and Beatriz Arízaga Bolumburu, 'Ports, havres et mouillages de Bayonne (Gascongne) à Bayona (Galice) d'après les routiers de la fin du Moyen Âge', in *Fronteras de agua: las ciudades portuarias y su universo cultural (siglos XIV–XXI)*, ed. Manuel-Reyes García-Hurtado and Ofelia Rey Castelao (Santiago de Compostela and La Coruña, 2016), pp. 47–58

Borrero Fernández, Mercedes, *La organización del trabajo. De la explotación de la tierra a las relaciones laborales en el campo andaluz (siglos XIII–XVI)* (Seville, 2003)

Braga, Isabel Maria Ribeiro Mendes Drumond, *Península Ibérica: um espaço, dois reinos: interrelações na época de Carlos V* (Lisbon, 1996)

Brito, Luís Felipe Aviz de, *Desembocadura do Rio Minho nos Tempos Antigos* (Caminha, 1987)

Bronseval, Claude de, *Peregrinatio Hispanica 1531–1533*, t. 1 (Paris, 1970)

Cabantous, Alain, *Dix mille marins face á l'océan. Les populations maritimes de Dunkerque ao Havre aux XVIIe et XVIIIe siècles (vers 1660–1794): Etude sociale* (Paris, 1991)

Caldeira, Arlindo Manuel, 'Angola and the Seventeenth-Century South Atlantic Slave Trade', in *Networks and Trans-Cultural Exchange: Slave Trading in the South Atlantic, 1590–1867*, ed. David Richardson and Filipa Ribeiro da Silva (Leiden and Boston, 2015), pp. 101–142

Campos Carrasco, Juan Manuel, 'El descubrimiento arqueológico del Puerto Colombino de Palos de la Frontera', in *Actas de las Jornadas Historia sobre el Descubrimiento de América*, t. IV (Seville, 2019), pp. 443–462

Carriazo Rubio, Juan Luis, 'Pesca, frontera y señorío: Ayamonte de la Edad Media a la Edad Moderna', *Huelva en su Historia*, 8 (2001), 41–66

Carvalho da Costa, Antonio, 'Da Villa de Caminha', in *Corografia portugueza, e descriçam topografica do famoso reyno de Portugal* (Braga, 1868–1869)

Casado Alonso, Hilario, 'Los agentes castellanos en los puertos Atlánticos: Los ejemplos de Burdeos y los Países Bajos (Siglos XV y XVI)', in *Navegación y puertos en la época Medieval y Moderna*, ed. Adela Fábregas García (Granada, 2012), pp. 163–194

Casariego, José Evaristo, *Historia del Derecho y de las instituciones marítimas del mundo hispano* (Madrid, 1947)

Castañón, Luciano, 'El gremio de mareantes de Gijón', *Boletín del Instituto de Estudios Asturianos*, 107 (1992), 835–858

Caunedo del Potro, Betsabé, 'El desarrollo del comercio medieval y su repercusión en las técnicas mercantiles. Ejemplos castellanos', *Pecvnia*, 15 (2012), 201–220

Caunedo del Potro, Betsabé, and Margarita Sánchez Martín, 'Exportación de lana: Diferentes manipulaciones en su transporte marítimo', in *Actas de las I Jornadas sobre minería y tecnología en la Edad Media peninsular* (Madrid, 1995), pp. 704–716

Cavaciocchi, Simonetta (ed.), *I porti come impresa economica. Atti della XIX settimana di studi dell'Istituto Internazionale per gli Studi Economici 'F. Datini'* (Florence, 1988)

Cavaco, Carminda, *A região de fronteira do rio Minho. Projecto de Estudos de Geografia Humana e Regional: Relatório no. 1* (Lisbon, 1973)

Cioranescu, Alejandro, *Historia de Santa Cruz de Tenerife, I. 1494–1803* (Santa Cruz de Tenerife, 1977)

Ciriquiáin Gaiztarro, Mariano, *Los puertos marítimos vascongados* (San Sebastián, 1951)

Collantes de Terán Sánchez, Antonio, and Antonio García-Baquero González (eds), *Andalucía 1492: razones de un protagonismo* (Seville, 1992)

Colón, Hernando, *Descripción y cosmografía de España por Fernando Colón* (Madrid, 1910)

Contamine, Philippe, 'Équipements et installations portuaires en France, de la fin du Moyen Âge aux Temps modernes', in *I porti come impresa economica*, ed. Simonetta Cavaciocchi (Florence, 1988), pp. 7–20

Córdoba de la Llave, Ricardo, 'Los instrumentos de la relación comercial: Medios, técnicas y útiles de transporte en la España bajomedieval', in *El comercio en la Edad Media: XVI Semana de Estudios Medievales* (Logroño, 2006), pp. 237–249

Córdoba de la Llave, Ricardo, and Pilar Hernández Iñigo, 'El utillaje de los transportes en la Andalucía del descubrimiento', *Historia. Instituciones. Documentos*, 30 (2003), 159–180

Coronas González, Santos M., 'La jurisdicción mercantil de los Consulados del Mar en el Antiguo Régimen', in *Actas del V Centenario del Consulado de Burgos* (Burgos, 1995), pp. 251–279

Corte-Real, Manuel, *Feitoria de Andalucía. A feitoria portuguesa na Andaluzia (1500–1532)* (Lisbon, 1967)

Cuartas Rivero, Margarita, *Oviedo y el Principado de Asturias a fines de la Edad Media* (Oviedo, 1983)

Curtin, Philip D., *The Atlantic Slave Trade* (Madison, WI, 1969)

Darsel, Joachim, 'L'Amirauté en Normandie. III. – Amirauté de Fécamp', *Annales de Normandie*, 20.2 (1970), 85–117

———, 'Seigneuries maritimes de Bretagne', *Bulletin philologique et historique, année 1966* (1968), 35–59

Daveau, Suzanne, 'Caminhos e fronteira na Serra da Peneda: Alguns exemplos nos séculos XV e XVI e na actualidade', *Geografia*, 1st ser. 19 (2003), 81–96

Davy, Gilduin, '*Consuetudines maris* et *maritimas consuetudines*: les coutumes maritimes en Normandie à la lumière des chartes ducales (fin Xe–milieu XIIe siècle)', *Les annales de droit*, 1 (2007), 91–110

Derville, Alain, 'Le marais de Saint-Omer', in *Le paysage rural: réalités et représentations*, actes du 10e congrès de la Société des historiens médiévistes de l'enseignement supérieur public (Lille, 1979), *Revue du Nord*, 62 (1980), 73–93

———, 'Les origines de Gravelines et de calais', *Revue du Nord*, LXVI (October–December 1984), 1051–1096

——— (ed.), *Histoire de Saint-Omer* (Lille, 1981)

———, *Saint-Omer: des origines au début du XIVe siècle* (Lille, 1995)

Doehaerd, Renée, 'Les Galères génoises dans la Manche et la Mer du Nord à la fin du XIII et au début du XIV', *Bulletin de l'Institut Historique Belge de Rome*, 19 (1938), 5–76

Domínguez Ortiz, Antonio, 'La Baja Andalucía', in *Historia de Andalucía*, ed. Manuel González Jiménez and José Enrique López de Coca (Madrid, 1980), vol. IV

———, 'La población del Reino de Sevilla en 1534', *Cuadernos de Historia. Anexos Hispania*, 7 (1977), 337–355

Doop, Thomas, 'People, Ships, Harbours and Towns: Exploring the Impact of Maritime Commerce on Urban Topography in 12th to 14th Century Northern Europe', in *Sea Lines of Communication Conference Proceeding*, ed. Brenna Gibson, Minke Jonk and Joel Found (Southampton, 2014), pp. 109–127

Du Tillet, Jean, *Recueil des Roys de France, leurs couronne et maison* (Paris, 1580)

Echegaray Corta, Bonifacio de, *La vida civil y mercantil de los vascos a través de sus instituciones jurídicas* (San Sebastián, 1923)

Eltis, David, *The Rise of African Slavery in the Americas* (Cambridge, 2000)

Engerman, Stanley L., and Eugene D. Genovese (eds), *Race and Slavery in the Western Hemisphere: Quantitative Studies* (Princeton, 1975)

Erkoreka Gervasio, Josu Iñaki, *Análisis político institucional de las Cofradías de Mareantes del País Vasco* (Vitoria, 1991)

Espinosa, Fernanda, *Escritos históricos* (Porto, 1972)

Fagel, Raymond, 'Los hombres de la lana y del hierro: mercaderes vascos en los Países Bajos siglo XVI', in *El licenciado Poza en Flandes, dos conferencias* (Bilbao, 1996), pp. 55–66

Fangueiro, Oscar, 'Relações pesqueiras e comerciais luso-galegas', in *Colóquio de etnografia marítima* (Santiago de Compostela, 1984), pp. 251–276

Favreau, Robert, 'La côte du Bas-Poitou aux XIVe et XVe siècles', in *Les Vendéens et la mer, de la grande pêche au Vendée Globe*, Proceedings of the Conference held at Les Sables d'Olonne, 20–22 September 2007 (La Roche-sur-Yon, 2008), pp. 89–113

———, 'Les ports de la côte poitevine au XVe siècle', *Bulletin philologique et historique, année 1962* (1965), 13–61

Fernández Cuesta, Gaspar (ed.), *Vrbe II. La construcción histórica de la ciudad de Gijón* (Oviedo, 2015)

Fernández Suárez, Jesús, *'Entrambasauguas'. La marina occidental asturiana en la Plena Edad Media* (Oviedo, 2017)

Ferreira Priegue, Elisa, *Galicia en el comercio marítimo medieval* (La Coruña, 1988)

———, 'Galicia en la Marisma de Castilla. La dinámica de los intercambios mercantiles', in *Ciudades y villas portuarias del Atlántico en la Edad Media*, ed. Beatriz Arízaga Bolumburu and Jesús Ángel Solórzano Telechea (Logroño, 2004), pp. 165–186

Flores Varela, Carlos, 'La evolución de la población urbana de Andalucía en los siglos XV y XVI', *En La España Medieval*, 28 (2005), 97–125

Fonseca, Jorge, *Escravos e senhores na Lisboa quinhentista* (Lisbon, 2010)

Franco Silva, Alfonso, *Estudios sobre ordenanzas municipales (siglos XIV–XVI)* (Cádiz, 1999)

———, *Rota en la Edad Media* (Rota, 1983)

Freire Costa, Leonor, *Naus e Galeões na Ribeira de Lisboa. A construção naval no século XVI para a Rota do Cabo* (Cascais, 1997)

———, 'O transporte no Atlântico: as frotas do açúcar (1580–1663)' (PhD diss. Universidade Técnica de Lisboa, 2000)

Fréville, Ernest de, *Mémoire sur le commerce maritime de Rouen depuis les temps les plus reculés jusqu'à la fin du XVIe siècle*, 2 vols (Rouen, 1857)

Gallicé, Alain, and Laurence Moal, 'Les brefs de Bretagne: un exemple de réglementation publique en réponse aux risques maritimes dans le duché de Bretagne (XIIe–XVe siècles)', *Annales de Bretagne et des pays de l'Ouest*, 119.2 (2012), 81–108

Galván Alonso, Delfina, *Protocolos de Bernardino Justiniano (1526–1527)*, 2 vols (San Cristóbal de La Laguna, 1990)

García Cuetos, Pilar, *Arquitectura en Asturias (1500–1580). La dinastía de los Cerecedo* (Oviedo, 1996)

García Fernández, Ernesto, 'Finanzas municipales y fiscalidad real en el País Vasco en el tránsito del Medievo a la Modernidad', in *Fiscalidad de Estado y fiscalidad municipal en los reinos hispánicos medievales* (Madrid, 2006), pp. 171–196

———, 'Las cofradías de mercaderes, mareantes y pescadores vascas en la Edad Media', in *Ciudades y villas portuarias del Atlántico en la Edad Media*, ed.

Beatriz Arízaga Bolumburu and Jesús Ángel Solórzano Telechea (Logroño, 2004), pp. 257–294

García-Arreciado Batanero, María Auxiliadora, 'La villa de Huelva en la Baja Edad Media', *Huelva en su historia*, 2 (1988), 175–230

Giles Pacheco, Francisco, Francisca Piñatel Veram, María Isabel Gómez Arroquia and Clive Finlayson, 'Las atarazanas medievales de Gibraltar', *Almoraima*, 25 (2001), 221–238

Giry, Arthur, *Les établissements de Rouen: études sur l'histoire des institutions municipales de Rouen, Falaise, Pont-Audemer, Verneuil, La Rochelle, Saintes, Oleron, Bayonne, Tours, Niort, Cognac, Saint-Jean d'Angély, Angoulême, Poitiers, etc.* (Paris, 1883–1885)

GIS d'Histoire Maritime, *La Maritimisation du monde de la préhistoire à nos jours* (Paris, 2016)

Godefroy, Frédéric, *Dictionnaire de l'ancienne langue française et de tous ses dialectes du IXe au XVe siècle* (Paris, 1881–1902)

Godinho, Vitorino Magalhães, *Os Descobrimentos e a economia mundial*, vol. II (Lisbon, 1981)

Gómez Gómez, Miguel Ángel, *Análisis histórico de una hacienda azucarera del siglo XVI: el heredamiento de Güímar [Tenerife]* (Santa Cruz de Tenerife, 2018)

González Arce, José Damián, 'Los flujos comerciales en el puerto de Bilbao con la Europa Atlántica (1481–1501)', *Cuadernos Medievales*, 19 (2015), 82–110

González Arce, José Damián, and Joaquín Gil Sáez, 'El Puerto de San Sebastián y su Cofradía de Mareantes de Santa Catalina (1450–1550)', *Tst: Transportes, Servicios y telecomunicaciones*, 21 (2011), 84–111

González Arévalo, Raúl, 'Comercio exterior del reino de Sevilla a través de los manuales de mercaderías italianos bajomedievales', *Historia. Instituciones. Documentos*, 38 (2001), 219–253

———, 'La integración de los italianos en las sociedades portuarias andaluzas (siglos XIII–XV)', in *Las sociedades portuarias de la Europa Atlántica en la Edad Media*, ed. Beatriz Arízaga Bolumburu and Jesús Ángel Solórzano Telechea (Logroño, 2016), pp. 337–364

———, 'Presencia diferencial italiana en el sur de la Península Ibérica en la Baja Edad Media. Estado de la cuestión y propuesta de investigación', *Medievalismo*, 23 (2013), 175–208

González Cruz, David, and Julio Izquierdo Labrado, 'Astilleros, barcos y construcción naval en tiempos de los descubrimientos: Palos de la Frontera y puertos del litoral onubense (Huelva, Saltes y San Juan del Puerto)', in *Barcos y construcción naval entre el Atlántico y el Mediterráneo en la época de los descubrimientos (siglos XV y XVI)*, ed. David González Cruz (Madrid, 2018), pp. 51–88

González Díaz, Antonio Manuel, 'Barcos y carpintería de ribera en el marquesado de Ayamonte', in *Barcos y construcción naval entre el Atlántico y el Mediterráneo en la época de los descubrimientos (siglos XV y XVI)*, ed. David González Cruz (Madrid, 2018), pp. 153–172

González García, Isabel, and Juan Ignacio Ruiz de la Peña Solar, 'La economía salinera en la Asturias medieval', *Asturiensia medievalia*, 1 (1972), 11–89

González Gómez, Antonio, 'Las Ordenanzas Municipales de Palos de la Frontera (1484–1521)', *Historia. Instituciones. Documentos*, 3 (1976), 249–280

———, *Moguer en la baja edad media (1248–1538)* (Huelva, 1977)

González Yanes, Emma, and Manuela Marrero Rodríguez, *Protocolos de Hernán Guerra (1508–1510)* (San Cristóbal de La Laguna, 1958)

González Zalacain, Roberto J., 'Apuntes para una ¿prosopografía? de las gentes del mar en Andalucía durante la baja Edad Media', in *Gentes de mar en la ciudad atlántica medieval*, ed. Jesús Ángel Solórzano Telechea, Michel Bochaca and Amélia Aguiar Andrade (Logroño, 2012), pp. 123–146

———, 'De puerto a puerto. Las relaciones entre los puertos de la Bahía de Cádiz (Siglos XV–XVI)', in *De mar a mar. Los puertos castellanos en la Baja Edad Media*, ed. Eduardo Aznar Vallejo and Roberto J. González Zalacain (San Cristóbal de La Laguna, 2015), pp. 147–177

———, *Familia y sociedad en Tenerife a raíz de la conquista* (San Cristóbal de La Laguna, 2005)

González Zalacain, Roberto J., and Víctor Muñoz Gómez, 'Jerez y el Mar en la Baja Edad Media', in *750 aniversario de la incorporación de Jerez a la Corona de Castilla: 1264–2014*, ed. José Sánchez Herrero and Manuel González Jiménez (Jerez de la Frontera, 2014), pp. 351–372

Gouron, Marcel, *L'Amirauté de Guienne, depuis le premier Amiral anglais en Guienne jusqu'à la Révolution* (Paris, 1938)

Goyheneche, Eugène, *Bayonne et la région bayonnaise du XIIe au XVe siècle. Études d'histoire économique et sociale* (Leioa, 1990)

Green, Toby, *The Rise of the Trans-Atlantic Slave Trade in Western Africa, 1300–1589* (New York, 2012)

Guerber, Éric, and Gérard Le Bouëdec (eds), *Gens de mer. Ports et cités aux époques ancienne, médiévale et moderne* (Rennes, 2013)

Guiard y Larrauri, Teófilo, *Historia del Consulado y Casa de Contratación de Bilbao y del Comercio de la Villa* (Bilbao, 1972)

Guillemet, Dominique, *Les îles de l'Ouest, de Bréhat à Oléron, du Moyen Âge à la Révolution* (La Crèche, 2000)

Hardisson Pizarroso, Emilio, 'Santa Cruz de Tenerife y su puerto', *Revista de Historia*, 76 (1946), 370–390

Heers, Jacques, *Escravos e servidão doméstica na Idade Média no mundo mediterrânico* (Lisbon, 1983)

Herrero Liceaga, Victoriano José, 'Ordenanzas de la Cofradía de San Pedro de mareantes de la villa de Fuenterrabía (1361–1551)', *Vasconia: Cuadernos de historia – geografía*, 10 (1988), 315–334

Hinojosa Montalvo, José, 'Ciudades portuarias en la Corona de Aragón durante la baja edad media: los ejemplos de Mallorca, Valencia y Alicante', in *Città portuali del Mediterraneo. Storia e archeologia*, ed. Ennio Poleggi (Genoa, 1989), pp. 151–165

Hoffmann, Richard C., 'Economic Development and Aquatic Ecosystems in Medieval Europe', *The American Historical Review*, 101.3 (1996), 631–669

Iglesias Rodríguez, Juan José, *Monarquía y nobleza señorial en Andalucía: estudios sobre el señorío de El Puerto (siglos XIII–XVIII)* (Seville, 2003)

Igual Luis, David, 'Merchant Groups and Urban Oligarchies in Late Medieval Castile: Different Models of Interrelationship?', paper presented to European Social Science History Conference (Belfast, 4–7 April 2018), online version through Researchgate, DOI: 10.13140/RG.2.2.27423.87201

———, 'Non ha porto alcuno, ma solo spiaggia. La actividad marítima valenciana en el siglo XV', *Aragón en la Edad Media*, 25 (2014), 101–134

Izquierdo Labrado, Julio, 'Análisis demoeconómico de la costa de Huelva (1510–1530)', *Huelva en su Historia*, 2 (1988), 347–358

Jean-Marie, Laurence, 'Le prince, la Normandie et la mer (milieu du XIIe–1204)' (thesis for Accreditation to Direct Research, Université de Caen-Normandie, 2016)

Jones, Michael, 'L'amirauté et la défense des côtes de Bretagne à la fin du Moyen Âge', in *Défense des côtes et cartographie historique*, ed. Jean-Pierre Bois (Paris, 2002), pp. 17–32

Kagan, Richard L., *Ciudades del Siglo de Oro: las vistas españolas de Anton van den Wyngaerde* (Madrid, 1986)

Kerhervé, Jean, *L'État breton aux 14e et 15e siècles: les ducs, l'argent et les hommes* (Paris, 1987)

Kowaleski, Maryanne, 'Peasants and the Sea in Medieval England', in *Peasants and Lords in the Medieval English Economy: Essays in Honour of Bruce M. S. Campbell*, ed. Maryanne Kowaleski, John Langdon and Phillipp Schofield (Turnhout, 2015), pp. 353–376

———, 'Port Labor in Medieval England', in *The Sea in History – The Medieval World*, ed. Christian Buchet and Michel Balard (Woodbridge, 2017), pp. 619–628

———, 'The Maritime Trade Networks of Late Medieval London', in *The Routledge Handbook of Maritime Trade around Europe, 1300–1600* (Oxford, 2017), pp. 383–410

L'Amirauté en Bretagne, des origines à la fin du XVIIIe siècle. Présentation de la thèse de Joachim Darsel, ed. Gérard Le Bouëdec (Rennes, 2012)

La Trémoïlle, Louis-Charles de, *Les La Trémoïlle pendant cinq siècles*, t. II: *1431–1525* (Nantes, 1892)

Labayru y Goicochea, Estanislao, *Historia general del Señorío de Bizcaya* (Bilbao, 1968)

Ladero Quesada, Miguel Ángel, *El siglo XV en Castilla. Fuentes de renta y política fiscal* (Barcelona, 1982)

———, 'Los señoríos medievales onubenses. Período de formación', in *Huelva en la Edad Media 20 años después*, ed. Juan Luis Carriazo Rubio and José María Miura Andrade (Huelva, 1998), pp. 203–227

Ladero Quesada, Miguel Ángel, and Manuel González Jiménez, *Diezmo eclesiástico y producción de cereales en el reino de Sevilla (1408–1503)* (Seville, 1979)

Le Bouëdec, Gérard, 'Small Ports from the Sixteenth to the Early Twentieth Century and the Local Economy of the French Atlantic Coast', *International Journal of Maritime History*, 21.2 (2009), 103–126

Lencastre, Francisco Salles, *Estudo sobre as portagens e alfândegas em Portugal (séculos XII a XVI)* (Lisbon, 1891)

Leroux, Nicolas, 'L'anthropisation médiévale des rives de la Seine entre Rouen et le Havre et ses conséquences économiques' (PhD diss., Université de Rouen, 2012)

Lewis, Archibald R., and Timothy J. Runyan, *European Naval and Maritime History, 300–1500* (Bloomington, IN, 1985)

Linebaugh, Peter, and Marcus Rediker, *The Many-Headed Hydra: Sailors, Slaves, Commoners, and the Hidden History of the Revolutionary Atlantic* (Boston, 2000)

Lobo Cabrera, Manuel, *El comercio canario europeo bajo Felipe II* (Santa Cruz de Tenerife and Las Palmas de Gran Canaria, 2008)

López Alsina, Fernando, *Introducción al fenómeno urbano medieval gallego a través de tres ejemplos: Mondoñedo, Vivero y Ribadeo* (Santiago de Compostela, 1976)

López Capont, Francisco, *El desarrollo industrial pesquero en el siglo XVIII* (La Coruña, 1998)

Macías Hernández, Antonio, 'Expansión ultramarina y economía vitivinícola: el ejemplo de Canarias (1500–1550)', *Investigaciones de Historia Económica*, 3–8 (2007), 13–44

Madeira Santos, M. E., *História Geral de Cabo Verde*, vol. II (Lisbon, 1995)

Malvezin Théophile, *Histoire du commerce de Bordeaux depuis les origines jusqu'à nos jours* (Bordeaux, 1892)

Marques, João Martins da Silva (ed.), *Descobrimentos Portugueses. Documentos para a sua história publicados e prefaciados por João Martins da Silva Marques* (Lisbon, 1988)

Marques, José, 'A fronteira do Minho, espaço de convivência galaico-minhota, na Idade Média e Relações económicas do Norte de Portugal com o Reino de Castela, no século XV', in *Estudos em Homenagem a Luís António de Oliveira Ramos*, vol. 2 (Porto, 2004), pp. 697–712

———, *Relações entre Portugal e Castela nos finais da Idade Média* (Braga, 1994)

Marques, Antonio H. Oliveira, 'Portugal nas crises dos sécs. XIV e XV', in *Nova História de Portugal*, vol. 4 (Lisbon, 1987), pp. 115–121

Marrero Rodríguez, Manuela, *et al.*, *Acuerdos del Cabildo de Tenerife VI (1538–1544)* (San Cristóbal de La Laguna, 1997)

———, *Acuerdos del Cabildo de Tenerife VII (1545–1549)* (San Cristóbal de La Laguna, 2000)

Martín Gutiérrez, Emilio, 'Análisis de la toponimia y aplicación al estudio del poblamiento. El alfoz de Jerez de la Frontera durante la Baja Edad Media', *Historia. Instituciones. Documentos*, 30 (2003), 257–300

———, 'El Estrecho de Gibraltar durante el siglo XIV: medio ambiente y redes comerciales en Algeciras', *Revista del Centro de Estudios Históricos de Granada y su Reino*, 30 (2018), 51–69

———, 'El viñedo en la zona de Jerez a finales de la Edad Media', in *Historia de Andalucía. VII Coloquio*, ed. Antonio Malpica Cuello, Rafael G. Peinado Santaella and Adela Fábregas García (Granada, 2009), pp. 287–300

———, *La organización del paisaje rural durante la Baja Edad Media. El ejemplo de Jerez de la Frontera* (Cádiz and Seville, 2004)

———, 'Los paisajes costeros interpretados desde la riparia. Reflexiones sobre el Golfo de Cádiz a finales de la Edad Media', *Riparia, Suplemento* 2 (2019), 47–79

———, *Paisajes, ganadería y medio ambiente en las comarcas gaditanas. Siglos XIII al XVI* (Cádiz, 2015)

Martín Gutiérrez, Emilio, and Enrique J. Ruiz Pilares, *El viñedo en Jerez durante el siglo XV. Un mercado de trabajo en torno al vino* (Jerez de la Frontera, 2019)

Martínez Galindo, Pedro, *La vid y el vino en Tenerife en la primera mitad del siglo XVI* (San Cristóbal de La Laguna, 1998)

Martínez Gijón, José, 'La jurisdicción marítima de Castilla durante la Baja Edad Media', in *X Coloquio Internacional de Historia Marítima. Les grandes escales* (Brussels, 1974), vol. 1, pp. 347–363

———, 'La práctica del fletamento de mercancías con las Indias (siglo XVI)', *Historia. Instituciones. Documentos*, 10 (1983), 119–155

Matthies, Andrea L., 'Medieval Treadwheels: Artists' Views of Building Construction', *Technology and Culture*, 33.3 (1992), 510–547

Meijide Pardo, Antonio, 'Aspectos del comercio gallego de exportacíon a Portugal en el siglo XVIII', in *Actas de las I Jornadas de Metodología Aplicada de las Ciencias Históricas*, vol. 3 (Santiago de Compostela, 1975), pp. 803–824

Meltzer, Milton, *Slavery: A World History* (New York, 1993)

Ménanteau, Loic, 'L'influence des facteurs naturels et anthropiques sur l'evolution des ports de Basse-Andalousie (XIIIe–XVIe siècles): études de cas (Palos de la Frontera, Séville et Sanlúcar de Barrameda)', in *Ports et littoraux de l'Europe Atlantique. Transformations naturelles aménagements humains (XIVe–XVIe siècles)*, ed. Jean-Luc Sarrazin and Michel Bochaca (Rennes, 2007), pp. 167–187

Mingorance Ruiz, José Antonio, 'Los extranjeros en Jerez de la Frontera a fines de la Edad Media' (PhD diss., University Pablo de Olvide, Seville, 2013). http://hdl.handle.net/10433/755

Molenat, Jean Pierre, 'Chemins et ponts du Nord de la Castille au temps des Rois Catholiques', *Melanges de la Casa de Velázquez*, 7 (1971), 115–162

Morales Padrón, Francisco, *El comercio canario-americano (siglos XVI, XVII y XVIII)* (Seville, 1955)

Moreira, Manuel António Fernandes, *A Alfândega de Viana e o comércio de importação de panos no séc. XVI* (Viana do Castelo, 1992)

———, *O porto de Viana do Castelo na época dos descobrimentos* (Viana do Castelo, 1984)

Moreira, Rafael, and Luís de Albuquerque, *Portugal no mundo: Tentativas para uma ocupação efectiva em Africa no século XIX. A Europa e a Africa na segunda metade do século XIX. O colonialismo português na primeira metade do século XX* (Lisbon, 1989)

Moreno, Humberto Baquero, *Relações entre Portugal e a Galiza nos séculos XIV e XV* (Lisbon, 1996)

Moreno Ollero, Antonio, 'Los nombres del Puerto de Sanlúcar en el siglo XVI: Barrameda, Zanfanejos y Bonanza', *Cartare*, 8 (2018), 1–11

———, *Sanlúcar de Barrameda a fines de la Edad Media* (Cádiz, 1983)

Moreno Ollero, Antonio, and Alfonso Franco Silva, 'Datos sobre el comercio del puerto de Sanlúcar de Barrameda en el primer tercio del siglo XVI', in *Hacienda y comercio: actas del II coloquio de Historia Medieval Andaluza* (Seville, 1982), pp. 283–296

Mourain de Sourdeval, Charles, 'L'amirauté patrimoniale de Talmont', *Annuaire départemental de la Société d'émulation de la Vendée*, 2nd ser. 4 (1874), 49–69

Mugartegui, Juan José de, 'Cómo se reclutaba en el siglo XVI, en nuestras costas, una tripulación para la pesca del bacalao en Terra-Nova', *Revista Internacional de los Estudios Vascos, RIEV*, 19.4 (1928), 632–636

Muñoz Gómez, Víctor, 'Para el conocimiento de la costa de Andalucía atlántica (siglos XIV–XVI), descripciones, relaciones y documentación náutica', *Historia. Instituciones. Documentos*, 40 (2013), 179–205

———, 'Puertos, abras, cabos e islas: la topografía medieval de la costa atlántica de Andalucía a través de las cartas portulanas', in *De mar a mar. Los puertos castellanos en la Baja Edad Media*, ed. Eduardo Aznar Vallejo and Roberto J. González Zalacain (San Cristóbal de La Laguna, 2015), pp. 179–221

Musset, Georges, 'Les ports francs, étude historique', *Recueil de la commission des arts et monuments historiques de la Charente-Inférieure*, XVI (1902), 179–225, 235–275, 283–315

Musset, Lucien, 'Les ports en Normandie du XIe au XIIIe siècle: esquisse d'histoire institutionnelle', in *Autour du pouvoir ducal normand, Xe–XIIe siècles*, ed. Lucien Musset, Jean-Michel Bouvrin and Jean-Marie Maillefer, Cahier des Annales de Normandie, XVII (Caen, 1985), pp. 113–128

Newson, Linda A., and Susie Minchin, *From Capture to Sale: The Portuguese Slave Trade to Spanish South America in the Early Seventeenth Century* (Leiden and Boston, 2007); Herbert S. Klein, *The Atlantic Slave Trade* (Cambridge, 2010)

Núñez Fernández, Eduardo, 'El gremio de mareantes de Luarca. Estado actual de la investigación en torno a esta institución valdesana', *Boletín de la Asociación Asturiana de Bibliotecarios, Archiveros, Documentalistas y Museólogos*, 16.2 (2005), 37–47

Ocampo Suárez-Valdés, Joaquín, Patricia Suárez Cano and Esteban García Canal, *El caso Astilleros Gondán* (Gijón, 2018)

Ortega Villoslada, Antonio, 'El trabajo femenino en Mallorca: la labor de la mujer en la actividad marítima de la primera mitad del siglo XIV', *Espacio, tiempo y forma. Serie III, Historia medieval*, 17 (2004), 461–470

———, 'Las relaciones marítimo-comerciales entre el Mediterráneo y el Atlántico. El papel de Mallorca en el comercio entre Oriente y Occidente Siglos XIV y XV', *Memòries de l'Acadèmia Mallorquina d'Estudis Genealògics*, 20 (2010), 61–80

Osório, Inês Marinho, 'O transporte de escravos no Atlântico: a arqueação dos navios negreiros' (Masters diss., Universidade Nova de Lisboa, 2016). https://run.unl.pt/handle/10362/19616

Otte Sander, Enrique, *Sevilla y sus mercaderes a fines de la Edad Media* (Seville, 1996)

Palenzuela Domínguez, Natalia, *Los mercaderes burgaleses en Sevilla a fines de la Edad Media* (Seville, 2003)

Paviot, Jacques, *La politique navale des ducs de Bourgogne, 1384/1482* (Lille, 1995)

Peraza de Ayala Vallabriga, José, 'El régimen comercial de Canarias con las Indias en los siglos XVI, XVII, y XVIII (I)', *Revista de Historia*, 92 (1950), 339–383

Pereira, João Cordeiro, 'Para a história das alfândegas em Portugal no início do século XVI (Vila do Conde – organização e movimento)' (PhD diss., Universidade Nova de Lisboa, 1983)

Pérez de Castro, José Luis, 'El concejo de Castropol según el catastro de Ensenada', *Archivum: Revista de la Facultad de Filología*, 26 (1976), 261–281

Pérez Fernández, Enrique, 'Las intervenciones antrópicas en el Curso Bajo del Guadalete y en San Pedro durante la Edad Moderna', *Riparia*, 4 (2018), 146–190

Pérez-Mallaína Bueno, Pablo Emilio, *Las atarazanas de Sevilla* (Seville, 2019)

Périsse, Sébastien, 'Les campagnes littorales saintongeaises à la fin du Moyen Âge (XIe–milieu XVIe siècle)' (PhD diss., Université de La Rochelle, 2011)

Pinto, Sara, 'Caminha no século XVI: estudo sócio-económico dos que ganhão suas vidas sobre as agoas do mar' (MA diss., Universidade do Porto, 2008)

———, 'Os homens do mar de Caminha no século XVI. A pluriactividade nas comunidades marítimas', *Revista Estudos Regionais*, 8 (2014), 13–22

Polónia, Amélia, *A expansão ultramarina numa perspectiva local: o porto de Vila do Conde no século XVI* (Lisbon, 2007)

———, 'European Seaports in the Early Modern Age: Concepts, Methodology and Models of Analysis', *Cahiers de la Méditerranée*, 80 (2010), 17–39

———, 'HISPORTOS – A Research Project on Portuguese Seaports in the Early Modern Age', in *European Seaports in the Early Modern Age – A Comparative Approach: Proceedings/International Workshop European Seaport Systems*, ed. Amélia Polónia and Helena Osswald (Porto, 2007), pp. 28–41

———, 'L'historiographie portugaise sur les gens de mer et les communautés littorales: une approche de synthèse', *Revue d'Histoire Maritime – Numéro thématique: La Recherche Internationale en Histoire Maritime*, 11–12 (2010), 175–194

———, *Vila do Conde: um porto nortenho na expansão ultramarina quinhentista*, vol. I (Porto, 1999)

Polónia, Amélia, and Sara Pinto, 'Harbour Construction Policies and Funding Agency in Early Modern Portugal (1400–1800)', in *La gobernanza de los puertos atlánticos, siglos XIV–XX*, ed. A. Polónia and Ana María Rivera Medina (Madrid, 2016), pp. 9–24

Quintanilla Raso, María Concepción, 'La reglamentación de una villa de señorío en el tránsito de la Edad Media a la Moderna. Ordenanzas de Cartaya (Huelva) (Fines s. XV–primera mitad s. XVI)', *Historia. Instituciones. Documentos*, 13 (1986), 189–259

Rabot, Brice, *Les structures seigneuriales rurales. Bretagne méridionale (XIVe–XVIe)* (Rennes, 2017)

Rawley, James A., *London, Metropolis of the Slave Trade* (Columbia & London, 2003)

Rawley, James A. (with Stephen D. Behrendt), *The Transatlantic Slave Trade: A History*, revised edition (Lincoln and London, 2005)

Renouard, Yves, 'La capacité du tonneau bordelais au Moyen Âge', *Annales du Midi*, 65 (1953), 395–403

Ríos Toledano, Daniel, 'Cádiz y el comercio marítimo genovés en el siglo XIV', *Medievalismo*, 28 (2018), 271–293

———, 'La bahía de Cádiz a fines de la Edad Media: paisaje, navegación y comercio, trabajo de fin de máster inédito' (MA diss., University of Cádiz, 2018)

Rivera Medina, Ana María, 'Construire des ports, ouvrir des routes: les villes biscayennes en bord de mer au Moyen Age', in *Ports nouveaux, Ports pionniers, XIVe–XXIe siècle*, ed. Martine Acerra and Bernard Michon (Rennes, 2019), pp. 377–394

———, 'Del mar a la taberna: el vino en Bilbao (Ss. XV–XVII)', *Itsas Memoria. Revista de Estudios Marítimos del País Vasco*, 6 (2009), 615–662

———, '"E tobimos por bien echar sisa". Los impuestos al consumo como medio de financiación concejil. Bilbao, 1300–1550', in *La gobernanza de la ciudad europea en la Edad Media* (Logroño, 2011), pp. 429–449

———, 'Espacios urbano y portuario: las dinámicas de gestión del Canal y Ría de Bilbao, siglos XIV–XVI)', in *De mar a mar. Los puertos castellanos en la Baja Edad Media*, ed. Eduardo Aznar Vallejo and Roberto J. González Zalacain (San Cristóbal de La Laguna, 2015), pp. 93–122

———, *Estudio Histórico del puerto de Bermeo* (Vitoria, 1997)

———, *Estudio Histórico del puerto de Lekeitio* (Vitoria, 2008)

———, *La civilización del viñedo en el primer Bilbao (1300–1650)* (Madrid, 2011)

———, 'La construcción-reconstrucción de un espacio portuario. El canal y ría de Bilbao en los siglos XIV–XVI', in *La gobernanza de los puertos atlánticos, siglos XIV–XX*, ed. Amélia Polónia and Ana María Rivera Medina (Madrid, 2016), pp. 171–191

———, 'Los espacios portuarios vizcaínos: mutaciones y adaptaciones de los puertos vizcaínos, Siglos XIV–XVI', *CEM. Cultura, Espaço & Memória*, 4 (2014), 56–59

———, '"*Mengua y desonestidad*": La polución en la villa y puerto de Bilbao, Siglos XIV–XVI', *Fundación para la Historia de España*, 12 (2015), 438–449

———, '"Por tanto reparo y adereço". Las infraestructuras portuarias y la red de intereses de las villas vizcaínas medievales en la ejecución de las obras', in *Gentes de mar en la ciudad atlántica medieval*, ed. Jesús Ángel Solórzano Telechea, Michel Bochaca and Amélia Aguiar Andrade (Logroño, 2012), pp. 345–357

———, 'Superando fronteras. Mujer y cultura laboral en los puertos del Norte Peninsular, siglos XIV–XVI', in *Fronteras de agua: las ciudades portuarias y su universo cultural (siglos XIV–XXI)*, ed. Manuel-Reyes García-Hurtado and Ofelia Rey Castelao (Santiago de Compostela-La Coruña, 2016), pp. 17–42

———, 'Tavernes, vin et péchés publics dans le Bilbao du Moyen Âge (XIVe–XVIe siécles)', *Bulletin du Musée Basque*, 174 (2009), 5–22

Rivero Suárez, Benedicta, *El azúcar en Tenerife: 1496–1550* (San Cristóbal de La Laguna, 1991)

Rodrigues, Ana M. (ed.), *Os negros em Portugal: sécs. XV a XIX* (Lisbon, 1999)

Rodríguez Estévez, Juan Clemente, *Los canteros de la catedral de Sevilla. Del gótico al renacimiento* (Seville, 1998)

Romero Medina, Raúl, 'Documentos inéditos para el estudio de la temprana Edad Moderna en El Puerto de Santa María (1515–1525)', in *El legado de Jano*, ed. Antonio Aguayo Cobo (El Puerto de Santa María, 2016), pp. 155–175

Romero Medina, Raúl, and Manuel Romero Bejarano, 'Un lugar llamado Jerez. El Maestro Alonso Rodríguez y sus vínculos familiares y profesionales en el contexto de la arquitectura del Tardogótico en Jerez de la Frontera', in *La Catedral de Sevilla después de Carlín*, ed. Alfonso Jiménez Martín (Seville, 2010), pp. 175–280

Romero Portilla, Paz, 'La singular relación Portugal-Galicia y su reflejo en la documentación medieval', *Revista de Ciências Históricas*, 15 (2000), 53–70

———, 'Relaciones entre Portugal y Galicia Siglo XIV–XV', *Revista da Faculdade de Letras. Historia*, 9.1 (2008), 217–270

Ronquillo Rubio, Manuela, *Los vascos en Sevilla y su tierra durante los siglos XIII, XIV y XV. Fundamentos de su éxito y permanencia* (Bilbao, 2004)

Ropero Regidor, Diego, 'Barcos y construcción naval en Moguer en la era de los descubrimientos', in *Barcos y construcción naval entre el Atlántico y el Mediterráneo en la época de los descubrimientos (siglos XV y XVI)*, ed. David González Cruz (Madrid, 2018), pp. 89–118

Rubio Martínez, Amparo, *El reinado de los Reyes Católicos en Galicia: actividad económica y fiscalidad regia* (Santiago de Compostela, 2016)

Ruiz Arzálluz, Íñigo, 'Vasconia en el siglo XII. Roger de Howden, el De viis maris y la extensión del Vizcondado de Bayona', *Anuario del Seminario de Filología vasca 'Julio de Urquijo'*, LII:1–2 (2018), 697–712

Ruiz de la Peña Solar, Juan Ignacio, 'Comercio a escala interregional e internacional: el espacio comercial asturleonés y su proyección atlántica', in *El comercio en la Edad Media, XVI Semana de Estudios Medievales de Nájera* (Logroño, 2006), pp. 39–92

———, 'Conflictos interlocales por el control de los espacios económicos privilegiados: el ejemplo asturgalaico de las pueblas de Ribadeo y Roboredo (1282)', *Boletín del Instituto de Estudios Asturianos*, 138 (1991), 559–588

———, 'El desarrollo urbano de Asturias en la Edad Media', in *El fenómeno urbano medieval entre el Cantábrico y el Duero: revisión historiográfica y propuestas de estudio*, ed. Jesús Ángel Solórzano Telechea and Beatriz Arízaga Bolumburu (Santander, 2002), pp. 349–366

———, 'Funciones y paisajes urbanos de las villas marítimas del norte de España: Avilés (siglos XII–XV)', in *Mercado inmobiliario y paisajes urbanos en el occidente europeo (siglos XI–XV), XXXIII Semana de Estudios Medievales de Estella* (Pamplona, 2007), pp. 691–736

———, 'La atracción del mar: en los orígenes de la apertura de la fachada costera galaico-cantábrica al mundo atlántico (1157–1252)', in *Fernando III y su tiempo (1201–1252), VIII Congreso de Estudios Medievales* (Ávila, 2003), pp. 183–208

———, 'Le ville nuove del nord della Corona di Castiglia (secoli XII–XIV)', in *J. I. Ruiz de la Peña Solar. Estudios de Historia Medieval*, ed. María Soledad Beltrán Suárez and María Álvarez Fernández, vol. II (Oviedo, 2014), pp. 213–252

———, 'Noticia de Tazones y de otros puertos balleneros de la costa asturiana (siglos XIII–XIV)', in *J. I. Ruiz de la Peña Solar. Estudios de Historia Medieval*, ed. María Soledad Beltrán Suárez and María Álvarez Fernández (Oviedo, 2014), pp. 131–144

———, 'Presencia de los puertos cantábricos en las líneas del comercio atlántico bajomedieval: las relaciones entre Asturias y La Rochelle', *Boletín del Real Instituto de Estudios Asturianos*, 141 (1993), 21–48

———, 'Solidaridades profesionales en las ciudades de la Corona de Castilla. Las cofradías de mareantes', in *J. I. Ruiz de la Peña Solar*, ed. Beltrán Suárez and Álvarez Fernández, pp. 363–383

Ruiz de la Peña Solar, Juan Ignacio, María Josefa Sanz Fuentes and Miguel Calleja Puerta (eds), *Los fueros de Avilés y su época* (Oviedo, 2012)

Ruiz Pilares, Enrique J., 'El paisaje portuario en la bahía de Cádiz a finales de la Edad Media: los muelles fluviales', *Riparia, Suplemento* 2 (2019), 173–210

———, 'Jerez de la Frontera: el gran centro productor del complejo portuario de la Bahía de Cádiz a finales de la Edad Media', *Estudios sobre Patrimonio, Cultura y Ciencias Medievales*, 20 (2018), 355–386

———, 'La política viaria municipal a finales de la Edad Media (1430–1530): el caso de Jerez de la Frontera', *Norba. Revista de Historia*, 25–26 (2012–2013), 207–226

———, 'La sociedad jerezana y su implicación en las actividades comerciales. La producción y la comercialización del vino (finales s. XV–inicios s. XVI)', in *Las sociedades portuarias de la Europa Atlántica en la Edad Media*, ed. Beatriz Arízaga Bolumburu and Jesús Ángel Solórzano Telechea (Logroño, 2016), pp. 337–364

Rumeu de Armas, Antonio, *La conquista de Tenerife 1494–1496* (San Cristóbal de La Laguna, 2006)

Ryckaert, Marc, 'La gestion des ports flamands au Moyen Âge, in *I porti come impresa economica*, ed. Simonetta Cavaciocchi (Florence, 1988), pp. 347–368

Sánchez de Arévalo, Rodrigo, *Suma de la Política* (Madrid, 1959)

Sarrazin, Jean-Luc, 'L'État et la seigneurie: le contrôle du littoral poitevin à la fin du Moyen Âge', in *Pouvoirs et littoraux du XVe au XXe siècle, Proceedings of the International Conference of Lorient (September 24, 25, 26, 1998)* (Rennes, 2000), pp. 29–40

———, 'La côte du Bas-Poitou au XIIIe siècle', in *Les Vendéens et la mer, de la grande pêche au Vendée Globe, Proceedings of the Conference Held at Les Sables d'Olonne on September 20, 21, 22, 2007* (La Roche-sur-Yon, 2008), pp. 33–54

———, 'Le littoral poitevin (XIe–XIIIe siècle): conquête et aménagement', *Annales de Bretagne et des Pays de l'Ouest*, 99.2 (1992), 13–31 and 117–130

Saunders, A. C. de C. M., *História social dos escravos e libertos negros em Portugal (1441–1555)* (Lisbon, 1994)

Schreuder, Yda, *Amsterdam's Sephardic Merchants and the Atlantic Sugar Trade in the Seventeenth Century* (New York, 2019)

Serna Vallejo, Margarita, *Los Rôles d'Oleron. El coutumier marítimo del Atlántico y del Báltico de época medieval y moderna* (Santander, 2004)

———, *Textos jurídicos marítimos medievales* (Madrid, 2018)

Sicking, Louis, 'Portas para o mar: infraestuturas portuárias nos Países Baixos na Idade Média', *European Seaport Systems in the Early Modern Age – A Comparative Approach*, ed. Amélia Polónia and Elena Osswald (Porto, 2007), pp. 96–106

Silva, Filipa Ribeiro da, *Dutch and Portuguese in Western Africa: Empires, Merchants and the Atlantic System, 1580–1674* (Leiden and Boston, 2011)

Silva, Francisco Ribeiro da, 'Intercâmbios comerciais entre o norte de Portugal e a Galiza na viragem do século XVII para o século XVIII', *Douro – Estudos & Documentos*, 2.4 (1997), 173–213

Solano Fernández-Sordo, Álvaro, *De Maliayo a Villaviciosa. Un territorio de la marina centro-oriental de Asturias en la Edad Media* (Oviedo, 2016)

———, 'Historia urbana en la Galicia medieval. Balance y perspectivas', *Cuadernos de Estudios Gallegos*, LVII, no. 123 (2010), 55–90

Solórzano Telechea, Jesús Ángel, 'Integración económica, competencia y jerarquización de los puertos atlánticos del Norte de España (siglos XIII–XV)', *Anuario de Estudios Medievales*, 48.11 (2018), 213–242

———, 'La influencia del mar en la conformación de los puertos de "la Marisma e costera de España" en la Baja Edad Media', in *De mar a mar. Los puertos castellanos en la Baja Edad Media*, ed. Eduardo Aznar Vallejo and Roberto J. González Zalacain (San Cristóbal de La Laguna, 2015), pp. 59–92

———, 'Las Nereidas del Norte. Puertos de identidad urbana en la fachada cantábrica entre los siglos XII–XV', *Anales de la Universidad de Alicante: Historia Medieval*, 16 (2009–2010), 39–61

———, 'Los puertos del rey. Síntesis interpretativa del fenómeno urbano en el norte de España durante los siglos XII y XIII', *Temas medievales*, 17 (2009), 207–228

———, 'Protestas del común y cambio político en las villas portuarias de la España atlántica a finales de la Edad Media', in *La comunidad medieval como esfera pública*, ed. Hipólito Rafael Oliva Herrer *et al.* (Seville, 2014), pp. 45–72

———, 'Villas y redes portuarias en la fachada atlántica del Norte peninsular en la Edad Media', in *Castilla y el mundo feudal. Homenaje al profesor Julio Valdeón* (Valladolid, 2009), pp. 485–502

Solórzano Telechea, Jesús Ángel, and Javier Añíbarro Rodríguez, 'Infraestructuras e instalaciones portuarias, fluviales e hídricas en las villas del norte peninsular a finales de la Edad Media: las obras públicas como instrumento de poder', in *Musulmanes y cristianos frente a lagua en las ciudades medievales*, ed. María Isabel Val Valdivieso and Olatz Villanueva Zubizarreta (Santander, 2008), pp. 277–280

Solórzano Telechea, Jesús Ángel, Michel Bochaca and Amélia Aguiar Andrade (eds), *Gentes de mar en la ciudad atlántica medieval* (Logroño, 2012)

Solow, Barbara (ed.), *Slavery and the Rise of the Atlantic System* (Cambridge, 1991)

Suárez Álvarez, María Jesús, 'El nobilísimo gremio de mareantes de Luarca. Ordenanzas del Novilísimo Gremio de mareantes y navegantes fijosdalgos de la villa y puerto de Luarca y Tierra de Valdés, del año 1468', *Asturiensia Medievalia*, 2 (1975), 239–258

Suárez Fernández, Luis, *Navegación y comercio en el Golfo de Vizcaya. Un estudio sobre la política marinera de la Casa de Trastámara* (Madrid, 1959)

Tena García, María Soledad, 'Comercio y transporte marítimo en San Sebastián durante la Edad Media (1180–1474)', *Itsas Memoria. Revista de Historia Marítima del País Vasco*, 4 (2003), 137–138

———, 'Composición social y articulación interna de las cofradías de pescadores y mareantes (Un análisis de la explotación de los recursos marítimos en la Marina de Castilla durante la Baja Edad Media)', *Espacio, Tiempo y Espacio. Serie Historia Medieval*, 8 (1995), 111–134

Tognetti, Sergio, 'The Trade of Black African Slaves in Florence', in *Black Africans in Renaissance Europe*, ed. Thomas F. Earle and Kate J. P. Lowe (Cambridge, 2005), pp. 213–224

Torres Balbás, Leopoldo, 'Atarazanas hispanomusulmanas', *Al-Andalus*, 11 (1946), 175–209

Tranchant, Mathias, 'Au risque de l'étranger: un sujet majeur de gouvernance à La Rochelle à la fin du Moyen Âge', 'Au risque de l'étranger: le protéger et s'en protéger dans les sociétés littorales de l'Europe atlantique au Moyen Âge et à l'époque moderne', special issue ed. Mathias Tranchant, *Annales de Bretagne et des pays de l'Ouest*, 117 (2010), 91–108

———, 'La constitution de la banlieue rochelaise à la fin du Moyen Âge', *Histoire Urbaine*, 8 (2003), 23–40

———, 'La sécurisation du port de La Rochelle et de son accès: actions épisodiques ou véritable politique?', 'Risque, sécurité et sécurisation maritimes depuis le Moyen Âge', special issue ed. Mathias Tranchant and Jean-Pierre Poussou, *Revue d'Histoire Maritime*, 9 (2008), 67–86

———, 'La urbanización del litoral atlántico del reino de Francia en el siglo XII', in *Los fueros de Avilés y su época*, ed. Juan Ignacio Ruiz de la Peña Solar, María Josefa Sanz Fuentes and Miguel Calleja Puerta (Oviedo, 2012), pp. 97–117

———, *Le commerce maritime de La Rochelle à la fin du Moyen Âge* (Rennes, 2003)

———, *Les ports maritimes de la France atlantique (XIe–XVe siècles)*, 2 vols (Rennes, 2017)

———, 'Les ports maritimes en France au Moyen Âge', in *Ports maritimes et ports fluviaux au Moyen Âge* (La Rochelle, 2004), pp. 21–31

Tranchant, Mathias, and Sébastien Hamel, 'Le déploiement de l'Amirauté de France à La Rochelle à la fin du Moyen Âge', 'Les Amirautés en France et outre-mer du Moyen Âge au début du XIXe siècle', special issue, *Revue d'Histoire Maritime*, 19 (2014), 33–49

Tranchant, Mathias, *et al.*, 'Géographie portuaire de la Galice à la Bretagne méridionale à l'aube des Temps Modernes', in *Les ports du golfe de Gascogne de Concarneau à la Corogne (XVe–XXIe siècle)* (Paris, 2013), pp. 19–32

Trillo Santamaría, Juan Manuel, and João Carlos Garcia, 'Galicia-Minho: el cuestionamiento de una frontera. Debates en el discurso geográfico ibérico', *Revista de historiografía*, 23 (2015), 159–189

Txueka Isasti, Fernando, 'El Colegio de Pilotos Vizcaínos de Cádiz. La otra historia marítima de los vascos: del Mare Nostrum al Pacífico', *Itsas Memoria. Revista de Estudios Marítimos del País Vasco*, 8 (2016), 591–645

Uría Ríu, Juan, 'Oviedo y Avilés en el comercio atlántico de la Edad Media (siglos XIII al XVI)', *Boletín del Real Instituto de Estudios Asturianos*, 62 (1967), 199–250

Valin, René-Josué, *Nouveau commentaire sur l'ordonnance de la marine du mois d'août*, 2 vols (La Rochelle, 1760, 1766)

Villada Paredes, Fernando, 'Los puertos del estrecho de Gibraltar en los siglos XIV y XV. Una perspectiva arqueológica', in *De mar a mar. Los puertos castellanos en la Baja Edad Media*, ed. Eduardo Aznar Vallejo and Roberto J. González Zalacain (San Cristóbal de La Laguna, 2015), pp. 213–253

Viña Brito, Ana (ed.), *Azúcar y Mecenazgo en Gran Canaria. El oro de las islas, siglos XV y XVI* (Las Palmas de Gran Canaria, 2014)

Viña Brito, Ana, and Dolores Corbella Díaz (eds), *La ruta azucarera atlántica: Historia y documentación* (Funchal, 2012)

Vissière, Laurent, 'La *Gabrielle*, navire des La Trémoïlle (1489–1496)', *Revue d'Histoire Maritime*, 2–3 (2001), 5–99

Vital, Laurent, *Primer viaje a España de Carlos I con su desembarco en Asturias* (Oviedo, 1992)

Zeller, Heinrich Ludwig, *Die Rechte des Admirals von Frankreich nach der Handschrift Paris, National Library, New French Acquisitions no. 10251* (Heidelberg, 1914)

Zurara, Gomes Eanes de, *La Crónica de Guinea*, ed. Eduardo Aznar Vallejo, Dolores Corbella Díaz and Antonio Tejera Gaspar (Barcelona, 2012)

Dictionaries

Diccionario de la Real Academia de la Lengua Española (RAE), https://www.rae.es/

O'Scanlan, Timoteo, *Diccionario Marítimo Español, que además de las definiciones de las voces con sus equivalentes en francés, inglés e italiano, contiene tres vocabularios de estos idiomas con las correspondencias castellanas, redactado por orden del Rey Nuestro Señor* (Madrid, 1831)

Digital Repositories

Biblioteca Digital Hispánica, www.bne.es/es/Catalogos/BibliotecaDigitalHispanica/Inicio/index.html

E-port, Cartografía Atlántica, siglos XIV–XVIII, http://e-port.linhd.unedes/

Fuentes Documentales Medievales del País Vasco (153 vols), www.eusko-ikaskuntza.eus/es/publicaciones/fuentes-documentales-medievales-del-pais-vasco/bi-127/

GALLICA, https://gallica.bnf.fr

Internet Archive, https://archive.org/

Index

Printed and bound by CPI Group (UK) Ltd, Croydon, CR0 4YY

15/09/2026

14962417-0001